Ayrton Senna

ALL HIS RACES

To Angela, Freya and Olivia, who sacrificed
their summer holiday while I wrote this book.

Published in April 2014

ISBN 978-0-9928209-0-9

Published by Evro Publishing
Westrow House, Holwell, Sherborne, Dorset DT9 5LF
www.evropublishing.com

Printed and bound in the UK by Gomer Press Limited,
Llandysul Enterprise Park, Llandysul, Ceredigion SA44 4JL

Front cover by Getty Images (Rainer Schlegelmilch)

Edited by Mark Hughes
Designed by Richard Parsons

Ayrton Senna

ALL HIS RACES

TONY DODGINS

FOREWORD BY MARTIN BRUNDLE

PHOTOGRAPHS BY SUTTON IMAGES

CONTENTS

FOREWORD
MARTIN BRUNDLE

Ayrton was emotionally driven. He would go out and find those limits. Like at Peraltada, Mexico, when he went upside-down in qualifying, and some of the things at Adelaide in 1989, when he was going crazy.

It was all of those things. Some of his qualifying laps were just... You saw somebody right up hard against the edge of all limits.

As well as being tremendously skilled, he was also highly courageous in a racing car, right up until that Imola afternoon that claimed his life. But again, he was driven by anger that day. He thought he was racing against an illegal car. He was an intelligent man but when push came to shove, his emotions were what drove him. His heart ruled his head.

Obviously we had that fantastic 1983 F3 season that people still talk about in hushed tones in pubs, after which he was very magnanimous and complimentary. Our paths didn't cross too often in F1 but when I got the McLaren drive in 1994, the year after he left, he came down to see me and was genuinely happy for me.

A decade on from our F3 battle, it was ironic that I stepped into his shoes after he went to Williams. I have nothing but total respect for the man and his brilliance. He was a complex character but then aren't all great champions? You don't meet too many Joe Regulars in this business...

← **Martin Brundle with Ayrton at Interlagos in 1994.**

📷 sutton-images.com

MARTIN BRUNDLE
FORMER FORMULA 1 DRIVER

INTRODUCTION
TONY DODGINS

Ayrton Senna was an inspiration to countless millions. Three days of national mourning in Brazil and a huge outpouring of grief during May 1994 were testament to that.

On a personal level, for me as no doubt for many others, what Senna did was what I dreamed of doing – and couldn't. In 1981, all I thought about was motor racing. There was no family fortune and no karting background but I had to have a go. In a gap year before university, a job was taken, a Formula Ford Van Diemen was hired and an engine was bought.

I'd planned a limited programme to secure a national competition licence. Meantime, I followed all professional single-seater categories avidly through the pages of *Autosport*. That's when I first came across Ayrton Senna da Silva. I first saw him in August '81 at Donington, a race he won and in which rival Rick Morris marvelled at the precision of his driving.

Just being around the sport in that '81 season was enough for me to forget all about economics,

accountancy, law and whatever else, and to know that this was what I had to be involved in. When reality dawned about my level of talent and chances, it was an easy decision to retreat behind a typewriter.

Four years later I was working for *Autosport* as a cub reporter covering the national Formula Ford scene that Senna had dominated in '81. I quickly learned the opposite view to the claims that rich, privileged Brazilians had it too good, to the detriment of home-grown talent.

The reality, more often than not, was a young guy, thousands of miles from home, friends and family, shivering in an old set of overalls, Puffa jacket and beanie hat, fingers clasped despairingly round a steaming Styrofoam cup at a foggy, freezing Silverstone in February/March. Usually, they were down-to-earth, friendly and approachable. Men like Roberto Moreno before Senna, Paulo Carcasci in my first year, and then the likes of José Cordova and Gil de Ferran.

Ayrton was the quickest of the lot, so obviously a superstar, that I can still recall the dismay I felt when he made his F1 debut with the fledgling Toleman team. As far as I was concerned, he should have been in a Brabham alongside World Champion Nelson Piquet. Of course, my political awareness growing, it was all too easy to understand why he wasn't. Which is why I was somewhat surprised, although probably shouldn't have been, by his treatment at the hands of the British media over not wanting Derek Warwick as a Lotus team-mate.

For 13 years Ayrton Senna's talent, commitment, passion and complex personality were compelling and fascinating. Long-time engineer Steve Hallam says that he never, ever gave less than 100 per cent in the cockpit. He was a stunning force. They say you shouldn't compare drivers from different eras but in the time that I've been watching motor racing, only Gilles Villeneuve and possibly Michael Schumacher stand any kind of comparison.

I was at Imola on that nightmare weekend in May 1994. Arriving on the Thursday morning, I'd chatted briefly with Roland Ratzenberger, who I hadn't seen since he went to pursue his career in Japan. On the Saturday, a few hours after his fatal accident and knowing I would have to write about its precise circumstances, I headed down to the accident scene.

A fellow journalist joined me and, walking back to the press room, we talked about how it had been 12 years since

⬇ Tony Dodgins is currently the editor of the *Autocourse* grand prix annual, F1 correspondent for *Motorsport News* and works in the BBC commentary box at grands prix.

📷 sutton-images.com

anyone had died at a grand prix – Gilles Villeneuve in Belgium and Riccardo Paletti in Canada during 1982.

"Yeah," I said, "Gilles... that would have been like Ayrton today."

At that point we'd just about got back to Tamburello and, despite years of watching Imola on TV, it was the first time I'd really taken on board that there was so relatively little run-off before the unprotected wall. We talked about that, too.

I can sympathise entirely with McLaren's Martin Whitmarsh who, in this book, describes the events of 24 hours later as slightly surreal, of such enormity that he couldn't quite believe he was in the middle of it, watching on his monitor. To a greater or lesser degree, I think we all felt that.

Shortly after Senna's accident, I went to Brazil to drive in a 24-hour kart race at a place called Itu. It wasn't a big event but, reflecting the passion that Brazilians have for the sport, the likes of Moreno and Cordova were there. Roberto showed me the ropes but he and the others, to a man, only wanted to talk about Senna.

There have been many previous books about Senna. When approached about the concept of a book of 'All His Races', I wasn't sure. A journalist colleague had written another book along a similar theme with Sir Stirling Moss, with the aid of diaries and Stirling's memories. Of course that wasn't possible with Ayrton, but such is his record and his genius that I was happy to compile as detailed a record as I could, provided that I could punctuate it with anecdotal material from those who knew him best.

I hope this book goes some way to doing justice to a brave, complex, entirely dedicated sportsman who was a compelling personality both to me and to millions of others.

↑ **Fellow Brazilian Roberto Moreno, British FF1600 champion the year before Senna, gives Tony some pointers to a lap of the Itu kart circuit, but wasn't around to save him from himself with a hired Van Diemen...**
📷 Tony Dodgins

ACKNOWLEDGEMENTS

I would like to thank many people for their generosity in terms of both knowledge and time – vital to the compilation of this book.

■ Martin Brundle provided an insightful foreword, and was also in the unique position of being able to bring the perspective of a man with a lifetime's respected professional experience in the sport, a significant part of it spent a few inches from Senna's gearbox!
■ My long-time friend and professional colleague Simon Arron agreed to the publication of a revealing, exclusive and previously unpublished interview with Senna from his F3 days.
■ Another regular F1 travelling companion, Mark Hughes, allowed me to reproduce a Senna section from his Tommy Byrne biography, *Crashed and Byrned*, and Maurice Hamilton consented to use of a section of his insightful book, *Williams*.
■ I have relied on the testimony of many of those directly involved and would particularly like to thank Kunihiko Akai, Dick Bennetts, Adam Cooper, Charles Coates, David Coulthard, Ron Dennis, Mike Dixon, Gerry Donaldson, Ralph Firman, Calvin Fish, Terry Fullerton, Steve Hallam, Andy Hallbery, Ian Harrison, Alex Hawkridge, Damon Hill, Matt James, Adam Jones, Eddie Jordan, Josef Leberer, Rick Morris, Jo Ramirez, Nigel Roebuck, Dennis Rushen, Hans Seeberg, Pat Symonds, the late Professor Sid Watkins and Martin Whitmarsh.
■ Steve Rendle, who first commissioned the project, and Mark Hughes, long-time of Haynes Publishing and now part of Evro Publishing, offered editorial wisdom and support.

BIBILIOGRAPHY

For race-by-race factual reference I have relied heavily on the pages of *Autocourse*, *Autosport* and *F1 Racing*. Books that I have consulted are as follows:

Ayrton Senna: Goodbye Champion, Farewell Friend (Karin Sturm)
Ayrton Senna: The Hard Edge of Genius (Christopher Hilton)
Crashed and Byrned (Mark Hughes)
Damon Hill's Grand Prix Year
Eddie Jordan: An Independent Man (with Maurice Hamilton)
Life at the Limit: Triumph and Tragedy in F1 (Prof Sid Watkins)
Prost versus Senna (Malcolm Folley)
The Death of Ayrton Senna (Richard Williams)
The Life of Ayrton Senna (Tom Rubython)
Williams (Maurice Hamilton)

1973–80

THE EARLY YEARS

Ayrton Senna came from a wealthy, privileged Sao Paulo background. Born on 21 March 1960 to Neide Senna and Milton da Silva, he had a sister Viviane, two years older, and a younger brother Leonardo.

A hyperactive child, he initially struggled with co-ordination but rapidly grew out of that from the time when, as a four-year-old, his father – who had a car parts business and extensive cattle farms – built him a small one-horsepower go-kart.

Car-mad, Ayrton entered junior kart races from the age of eight, and most of his rivals were much older. He was also regularly driving a Jeep around the family farms as soon as he was able to reach the pedals.

When Ayrton was just 11 the exploits of Emerson Fittipaldi were being hailed in Brazil. Emerson had had a meteoric rise and won his first world title with Lotus in 1972, repeating the feat two years later with McLaren. Milton da Silva liked racing too and was a fan of Jim Clark, who died just after Senna's eighth birthday. Ayrton would later visit the Jim Clark Room in Duns, Scotland, taken there by F1's medical chief, Sid Watkins.

Although Ayrton practised constantly, it wasn't until he was 13 that he became old enough to officially race pukka 100cc karts. His first race was at Interlagos in July 1973.

← **Ayrton at Kalmar, Sweden, in 1982 – the last of his five attempts to win the World Karting Championship resulted in a dispiriting 14th position.**

📷 sutton-images.com

→ **Ayrton's first wheels, aged four.**
📷 sutton-images.com

⬇ **Aged around seven, the young Senna had an engine behind his shoulders.**
📷 sutton-images.com

Maurizio Sandro Sala was the pacesetter Senna had to aim at, and Ayrton beat him first time out. After that Senna would generally get the better of him. Maurizio would go on to follow the well-trodden path of Formula Ford in England and was a winning F3 driver with Eddie Jordan before funds ran dry.

Although Ayrton was a shy, introverted character who preferred solitary interests, he and Sala did have an arm's-length friendship, and at one stage Ayrton even dated Maurizio's sister Carolina.

The karting guru in Sao Paulo was a Spaniard called Lucio Pascual Gascon, known as 'Tchê', who had looked after Fittipaldi and was regarded as the best engine builder. Tchê quickly appreciated Senna's talents.

Later, at 16, Senna hooked up with another Sao Paulo karting devotee, Mauro de Oliveira Dias, who was simply 'Mauro' to most.

"We had a great time with Ayrton in our karting team," Mauro remembers. "We won two Pan-American championships and a Brazilian championship together.

"When he won his first championship in F1 [1988] I was so happy. The strange thing was that for us in Brazil, Ayrton was already an idol before he'd won

→ Mauro de Oliveira Dias: "We had a great time with Ayrton in our karting team… He was just different – the way he drove, the way he was with people, everything."

LAT

→ Driving a Lotus 72, Emerson Fittipaldi became a Brazilian hero and the sport's youngest World Champion in 1972, when Senna was an impressionable 12-year-old.

sutton-images.com

"At the end of '93 I was with him at the farm and I was getting worried about him. I said, 'Why don't you go and drive for a nice slow team like Ferrari?'

"He said, 'No, I have to be in the Williams, it's the fastest car – don't piss me off Mauro! I'm here to win, lose or die.' Then he signed my blue jacket. Five months later he was dead.

"He once gave me a pair of his driving gloves. A while ago, I went up to this kind of religious sanctuary I know, about 200 miles from Sao Paulo. I took the gloves with me and left them there. It just felt the right thing to do. I have lots of great memories of him. Lots of other drivers will try to be like Ayrton but no one ever will. I think he was born to be great."

Senna dominated Brazilian karting from 1977 to 1981 and won the South American championship in Uruguay in '77. By this time Brazilian Chico Serra, three years older than Senna, was racing cars in the UK. It was Serra who told Ralph Firman, the boss of Formula Ford race car manufacturer Van Diemen, that he needed to get hold of 'fast man'.

the title. We had a three-time World Champion, Nelson Piquet, but for some reason it wasn't the same. The one everybody cared about was Ayrton.

"He was just different – the way he drove, the way he was with people, everything. He always took a lot of risks on the track – it's just how he was. Even when he was in F1 he'd phone me and ask me to bring some karts to a track he had at a family farm near Sao Paulo.

First, though, Senna went to Europe to take on the cream of karting's talent in a bid to win the World Karting Championship. It was a task he never accomplished in five attempts, though twice he finished second.

1978–82
WORLD KARTING CHAMPIONSHIP

13–17 SEPTEMBER 1978

Le Mans • World Karting Championship • 6th

Senna arrived from Brazil with Tchê to drive with the crack DAP squad, for whom Terry Fullerton, world champion five years earlier, was works driver (see 'Recollections of a rival', page 16).

Senna finished seventh in the first part of the three-heat final, collided with Englishman Mickey Allen in the second, and came sixth in the third. His overall result was sixth, which was regarded as a sensational debut at world level.

18–23 SEPTEMBER 1979

Estoril • World Karting Championship • 2nd

In the 1979 World Karting Championship, held in Portugal, Senna had a big accident that he was fortunate to get away with, according to karting legend Martin Hines. It happened in the third semi-final when second place was sufficient for Senna to secure pole for the first final. But the leader's engine seized and Senna, very close behind, hit him and rolled.

Ayrton led the first of the three-race 'final' before dropping back to fifth. In the second, he fought a tough battle with the experienced Peter de Bruyn before coming out on top when the Dutchman's chain snapped, but was passed by another Dutchman, Peter Koene. Senna won the third race.

Senna and Koene had won a race each and had the same number of points. In previous years the result in the other final would have been decisive, giving the title to Senna, but the rules had changed and it was the results in the semi-finals that were significant. Senna's roll had cost him dear. He was hugely disappointed.

17–21 SEPTEMBER 1980

Nivelles • World Karting Championship • 2nd

Once again, Senna had to endure the disappointment of not quite reaching his goal. Although widely recognised as the quickest man on the Belgian track, he again suffered a non-finish and was pipped to the championship by de Bruyn. It was at this point that Senna made the decision to step up into cars and set off for England in search of a seat in FF1600 with Van Diemen.

16–20 SEPTEMBER 1981

Parma • World Karting Championship • 4th

Senna's last two attempts to win the world title were hampered by karting politics and a switch to 135cc machinery. In 1981, Terry Fullerton recalls, Senna's equipment wasn't up to snuff. Komet-engined Birel chassis took the first three places in the hands of Mike Wilson, Lars Forsman and Ruggero Melgrati, with Senna fourth. Ayrton gained little satisfaction from being the only DAP-engined driver among the Komet-engined machinery that otherwise filled the top 17 places!

15–19 SEPTEMBER 1982

Kalmar • World Karting Championship • 14th

Senna's last attempt at the World Karting Championship informed him that he had missed the boat as far as the world title was concerned. The whole karting landscape had changed and was now dominated by the best 135cc engines and superior tyres. At Kalmar in Sweden Senna found that he couldn't compete – a new experience – and he could finish only 14th.

By this time, Senna had cleaned up in FF2000 and was being offered F1 contracts. He abandoned his karting ambition for good. In the period 1981–89, meanwhile, Mike Wilson would win no fewer than six world titles with Birel.

TERRY FULLERTON
RECOLLECTIONS OF A RIVAL

As depicted in the award-winning *Senna* movie documentary, in 1993 in Adelaide, scene of Senna's last grand prix win and arch-rival Alain Prost's last race, Australian journalist Mark Fogarty asked Ayrton who had given him the most satisfaction to race against, past or present.

Senna was silent for a few moments. Most were expecting the answer to be Prost. Some regarded Senna's reply, when it came, as a deliberate knock to Alain. But it wasn't.

"Fullerton," Ayrton said. "Terry Fullerton."

The justification was that Fullerton was a very fast and complete driver and that karting had been 'pure' racing, with no money or politics involved.

It was interesting to hear Senna speak of the 'fight' he had at every level and his belief that nothing came easily. Those without wealthy parents – and hence the opportunity to practise, race and develop their talent – struggled with that observation. But that's not what Senna was speaking of. At any top level of motorsport

⬇ **Terry Fullerton as he is today, talking about his karting exploits.**

📷 sutton-images.com

a driver will encounter rivals with money, talent or both. And to get to the top, you have to beat them.

If you think that karting is basic, think again. Terry Fullerton was a professional driver, even then. He started racing as a 12-year-old in 1965, the same year that brother Alex, a promising motorcycle rider, lost his life in a race at Mallory Park.

"It was very different then. Karts went on car roof racks and karting could be done by people who weren't wealthy. My dad was a maths teacher and I had a brother putting money in. We were just about able to do it to a reasonable level.

"I was good, got noticed and started getting free karts and engines, and eventually won the World Championship in 1973. I turned professional and started getting paid to race.

"I remember getting about a grand a month, which in '73 was pretty decent, but that was to include travel and expenses. When I was driving for Zip Karts, which was when I first met Ayrton in '77–78, it was £100 a week and then they paid all my expenses. It was probably the equivalent of about £40,000 a year now [2014].

"I was able to buy a flat in London, pay the mortgage, have a decent car, go out to eat now and again, that sort of lifestyle. It was great: I was able to do what I loved doing and get paid to do it. It was like all my Christmases had come at once!

"I drove for the Italian teams in 1974–75, then in '76 for an English team called Sprint Karts. That year I had ME, which knocked me properly for six. I got over that by mid-1977 and started driving for Zip Karts. It was at the beginning of '78 when I met Ayrton.

"He'd done a deal to race with DAP and Zip Karts was importing DAP engines from Italy and was using them in European races. I was the Zip driver so I was despatched to Italy. He was racing DAP engines in Brazil and so that was the natural connection. So we both turned up for pre-race testing and bumped into each other in the DAP factory.

"He was quite dodgy about me – a bit edgy and shifty. I guess he'd have heard of me because I was the number one guy at the time and the number one DAP driver definitely, and he was coming along as a paying driver.

"I was 25 and he was 17. I was much more experienced. The impression I got was that he was a bit bamboozled and confused to start with. He really thought that if you could drive fast you were going to win, but it's not quite that simple. There are lots of other things that go with it and, not blowing my own trumpet, I was ahead in all sorts of ways.

"The DAP people didn't really know how to test logically. They'd throw an engine on the best kart, go out, see a time, think, 'Oh jolly good' and go home. But I'd got to the stage where I was testing logically all the time. I'd test engines under controlled conditions with the same set or type of tyre, to make sure you got the right answers. Because, so often, they got the wrong answers when they tested.

"We'd test engines and carburettors early in the week and then chassis. Tyres were the very last thing because that's best done when there's rubber on the track. What's the point of testing tyres at the start of the week when the track's two seconds off? But DAP would test tyres on the first day – they just did illogical things like that.

"Ayrton was involved in that way of thinking. So he was very confused because I'd very often be quicker than him. In fact I was always quicker than him – for those reasons. Not because I could drive around the track quicker than him, but because I was better organised than he was. DAP didn't really get switched on to it for a while.

"What would happen was that his part of the team would be quite smug and pleased with themselves because he'd be doing the fastest times. I wouldn't be concerned about that because I'd just be getting on with my own job, but when it really mattered I'd bolt it all together on the last day and go quicker than him. He'd get very confused and frustrated. A lot of that went on. For three years or so.

"Generally I wouldn't let anyone learn from me. Ayrton did often tag on behind me and, quite often, I wouldn't go for it and just let him stay there. I knew what was going on in that department.

"He had raw speed. Ballistic raw speed. And his determination... He was almost too determined – he pushed so hard that he would actually have a bad accident when he should have backed out of it. He had quite a few nasty ones where he just kept his foot in.

"He'd go up on two wheels and when that happens you've got to steer out of it and lift off the throttle. At Jesolo in Italy I remember him keeping his toe in and the kart just went over and flew into the fence. He must have been doing 70mph and went in head-first with the kart behind him, right in front of where I was standing.

"It was a big one. He knocked the wind out of himself completely and I was the first to get to him. He couldn't breathe, like when you're badly winded, and I undid his helmet and calmed him down. Within about 20 seconds he was breathing again but it was a hell of a whack. He was very lucky to get away with that.

"We did lose people every so often. The karts were direct drive whereas nowadays they've got clutches, bodywork and all sorts of things. In those days all the wheels were open, so you had interlocking wheels and you rolled or got launched. Engines would seize, generally at the most dangerous part of the track, the flat-out corner at the end of the straight. The rear would lock solid and you'd go straight into the fence. I must have rolled a kart 20 times in my career because of that. A seized engine was the most dangerous thing.

"By 1980 Senna was really good and we had a fantastic race at Jesolo in the Champions Cup, which he should really have won that year. I think he won the first and second finals and I beat him in the third one but, because I'd beaten him in qualifying, I ended up winning on points. And I passed him on the last lap and that didn't go down well at all. He was well pissed off!

"I caught him on the very last lap of the last final. It was a long race and we both knew before we started that whoever finished in front would win the championship.

Senna leads a gaggle into the first corner at Wohlen, Switzerland, with Fullerton tucked in right behind him.
📷 Terry Fullerton

"He knocked the wind out of himself completely and I was the first to get to him. He couldn't breathe… Within about 20 seconds he was breathing again but it was a hell of a whack. He was very lucky to get away with that."

He made a different tyre choice; I think he had brand new tyres and I didn't. I had what I considered a very good set but they weren't new.

"At the beginning he shot off into the lead and pulled away on his new rubber. He probably pulled out 100–120 yards. Jesolo has a lot of hairpins and I could see across the other side of them. After about 12 laps he'd stopped pulling away, so I just kept putting in the laps the best I could and realised I was catching him. With about four laps to go I could see that I was definitely going to catch him by the last lap. This was really on!

Senna and Fullerton, in Terry's words, "bracing and holding", almost as a mirror image.
Terry Fullerton

"At Jesolo there's a main straight and at the end of it a flat-out right-hander, but it's only just flat – a real nail-biting corner. Then it's 100 metres into a tight right-hand hairpin. As I came onto the straight I was running quicker than him and would have gone up the inside but he blocked. So I immediately went to the outside as we came up to the flat-out right-hander.

"I knew we were going to cross over and that's what happened, but when he went to block me on the outside I went back inside, and he immediately started driving back to try and block me again into the hairpin. I'd got my front wheels inside by then but he kept coming, he wasn't going to let me go. We touched and he went up on two wheels. I made the corner and won the race.

"He said nothing to me afterwards but he was fuming. They interviewed him and he bad-mouthed me, claiming I'd overtaken him illegally. It wasn't illegal. It was a bloody good move. But he was really upset. It was just an emotional reaction because, basically, I'd robbed him of the race on the very last lap!

"That was probably my best race ever. I knew how good he was, but obviously not how good he would become.

"Being ballistically quick was only part of the deal. I was ballistically quick. You're born with that. Maybe he was a bit quicker than me. I don't know. But there are all sorts of other things you can affect and that's what I worked on. I did feel very much in control, believe it or not, because I thought that ultimately I'd always be able to do a better job than him.

"Technique has something to do with it but, looking back, that kind of evolves. Through the seventies tyres got grippier and grippier and I'd guess that the g-forces in karts almost doubled in that time – the tyres were massively grippy by 1980. Most corners you did on two wheels and if you didn't develop a good technique you couldn't go fast.

"If you just sat there and let the seat hold you in, you couldn't go fast. You had to brace and hold. When the kart went up on two wheels you were bracing and holding. So all the fast drivers developed a technique. And Ayrton did as well. In fact there's one particular photo from the World Championships in 1979 where we're in identical positions in the kart – I'm in front and he's right behind and we're almost a mirror image.

"Of all the people I raced, for speed and ability Senna was in a different league. People talk about François Goldstein [the Belgian multiple World Champion] but he was a different kind of driver, a thinking driver – a bit like me compared to Ayrton I suppose. For raw speed he was good, you have to be good, but he wasn't stunning. He was a very clever all-rounder, good in all conditions, great under pressure, as was Ayrton. He was also well ahead on tyre technology.

"When everyone else was thinking of tyres just as black things that you put on, Goldstein was testing them and machining them so that they were perfectly round. His father imported Continental tyres into Belgium and so there was a bit of inside technical knowledge. He had that kind of advantage for quite a few years before anyone else cottoned on. In fact, when I won the World Karting Championship in 1973 driving for Birel, they built up some wheels and machined the tyres because they'd seen Goldstein doing it the year before. They gave me two or three different sets of tyres built up on wheels. One set of rear tyres returned times about four tenths quicker than the others!

"Alain Prost was at a lot of the earlier world championship and Jesolo races I did, around 1974–76, and he won the junior world championship the year I won the senior championship. I don't remember him as anything formidable. He was quite good, without a doubt, but he didn't leave an impression like Ayrton did. But I do remember him as a very nice bloke. I liked him.

"I also raced against Nigel Mansell, who's the same age as me. He did quite a bit of gearbox karting as well, but I wouldn't put him in the top five people I raced against.

"Maybe it's just a reflection on me, but I felt that Senna was always good at getting people around him.

He didn't set out to do it but he had the kind of charisma, ability and speed that caused people working with him to really, really support him. He did that even in karting. He would also go out of his way to thank each mechanic and be close. But it wasn't false. He meant it. Everyone was involved and he made everyone feel part of the success.

"He had intensity, even in karting. It was just in him but he didn't really know what to do with it. He had this massive determination to succeed and he wanted to focus on something but he wasn't quite sure what. That's the impression I got. Shall we test this? Shall we do that? Is it the engine that really matters? Is it the kart set up? Why is Fullerton two tenths quicker than me? He didn't quite know what to focus on and I'd say there was quite a bit of frustration.

"If there was a problem, he wasn't very good at accepting it. With testing you had to have the mindset that we might not find the problem today, but tomorrow or the day after we will, we'll put it right and we'll move forward. Or, maybe, at this race we're not going to get there. He wasn't very good at accepting those sorts of situations.

Fullerton: "Generally I wouldn't let anyone learn from me. Ayrton did often tag on behind me and, quite often, I wouldn't go for it and just let him stay there."

sutton-images.com

"Senna was always good at getting people around him. He didn't set out to do it but he had the kind of charisma, ability and speed that caused people working with him to really, really support him."

In fact he was very bad at it! It had to all happen today. Right now.

"I don't remember his family being around. He brought a couple of girlfriends now and again. That girl he married, Liliane, he brought her over, but usually he was on his own – a 17-year-old kid on his own. But he was tough. He wasn't a softie. He was mentally strong, he loved what he was doing and he had to make some sacrifices. I'm sure he was lonely and unhappy at times. But I wasn't going to feel too sorry for Ayrton. He had the money to fly home, business class I'm sure!

"He sometimes gave this impression of the world being against him but I don't think it was. No more than it's against anyone trying to be successful and climb ladders. There's always someone trying to knock you off.

"But that side of his character, when channeled in the right direction, had a lot to do with how successful he was. Today, if I'm helping a kid and he doesn't mind about not doing well, you know he isn't going to be any good. It's the ones who cry and desperately want it that have half a chance. And he was certainly one of those. People who hate losing normally end up being quite good at winning.

The two main reasons I didn't have a serious go at cars was that my brother died racing bikes and I always looked at karting as a sport in its own right. I didn't see it as a stepping stone. I was a professional driver and happy with that.

And after my brother, my Mum and Dad would have hated it if I'd gone on to race cars. Plus the fact that I heard Jackie Stewart say that between '68 and '73 you had a one in three chance of dying if you were on the Formula 1 grid. I thought, no thanks, what do I want to do that for? I'm having a good life travelling all over the place and earning money. Stopping and transferring to race in Formula Ford or something like that would have meant spending money or finding money instead of earning it.

"Looking back now I might have become a very wealthy man, or dead… but in reality probably dead. I pushed to the limit too. My wife said to me, 'I'm glad you didn't do it because I know what you're like, and you'd be dead. The same as him.'

"That's what Senna was like. He always pushed to the limit, never lifted, always kept his toe in.

"I did follow Ayrton's career and spoke to him in '83 at Silverstone when he was doing F3. I asked him: 'Anyone you're racing against any good?'

"He said, 'Yeah, Brundle's good. The rest are wankers…'

"At one race, Ayrton had turned up late, done three laps and put it on pole. Calvin Fish couldn't believe that, thought it was impossible. He said to me, 'How can he do that?' I just laughed and said, 'Because he's that bloody good, that's how!'"

DERWENT
TELEVISION
Shell Super Oil
Shell Super Oil
Shell Super Oil
Skid Control
Super Oil
SIMPSON
MINISCER-POWER
DARTFORD 28342
E

1981
THE MOVE TO CARS

The first step on the professional motor racing ladder in the early 1980s was Formula Ford 1600. The cars, relatively simple 'spaceframe' chassis with 125bhp Ford 'Kent' engines and no aerodynamic wings, had much less grip than top-level karts. The idea was that in evenly matched cars the driver made the difference.

The biggest manufacturer of Formula Ford cars was Van Diemen, based in sleepy, rural Norfolk. This was also Lotus country and there was a whole racing cottage industry in the area. Which is why 20-year-old Ayrton Senna made his first foray to Norfolk in November 1980 to meet Ralph Firman, owner and founder of Van Diemen and also Emerson Fittipaldi's former mechanic. Firman's son, Ralph Jr, would go on to drive one of Eddie Jordan's grand prix cars.

Chico Serra, by then an F1 driver with Fittipaldi's own team, was three years older than Senna and formerly a Van Diemen works driver. The Brazilian acted as go-between when Ayrton, whose English was poor at that time, tested a car at Snetterton and then sat down in The Doric restaurant in nearby Attleborough to discuss terms – which, Senna quickly realised, meant how much money you had to pay!

After that first run, Firman had seen enough (see 'Ralph Firman on Senna', page 34). He wanted the Brazilian. It meant that a works seat for the 1981 season would be Ayrton's for £10,000 – about

← **Van Diemen team-mate Alfie Toledano congratulates Senna on his first win.**

📷 sutton-images.com

double a decent annual salary back then. It was a lot of money, but the going rate for 'a works Diemen' was more like £30,000.

Senna would take the place of Roberto Moreno, another young Brazilian who, although penniless by comparison with Senna's family, had just won the major FF1600 championship and the prestigious Formula Ford Festival – important for Ralph's business of selling cars. Firman's other works driver in 1980 had been another well-heeled Brazilian, Raul Boesel.

Alongside Senna, Van Diemen fielded two other South Americans in 1981: 23-year-old Argentine Enrique 'Quique' Mansilla and 22-year-old Mexican Alfonso Toledano, also known as 'Alfie' or 'Poncho'. Toledano thought he was going to be the Main Man in '81 and would become stunned, then even more stunned, by Ayrton's speed as the season progressed.

After three years of karting Alfie had switched to cars, driving his own VW Beetle in saloon races in Mexico. Despite opposition from his widowed mother, he had skipped school and driven to Acapulco for a big annual race, living in the back of the Beetle, roll cage and all. He did odd jobs to raise money for food, begged overalls from a fellow driver and got the car through scrutineering with a fire extinguisher pinched from a local supermarket! Rivals were dismissive of Toledano's old banger but put it on pole and won.

Progressing to begged drives in single-seaters, he came to England in 1979, impressed the PRS (Pro Racing Services) team enough for them to give him a works ride in Formula Ford in 1980 and attracted the backing of the Mexican motorsport federation with his results, and then support from Marlboro Mexico. That led to the works Van Diemen and, in Alfie's head, he was on his way.

Mansilla had impressed an instructor at a Buenos Aires racing school, despite having no karting background, and was encouraged to go to England and complete a course at the Jim Russell Racing Drivers School. Having done that, he entered its World Scholarship and won it. After some promising results in 1980 he bagged the Van Diemen seat for the following season.

Both men had the misfortune to be trying to establish themselves alongside a phenomenon. The young man who began racing as Ayrton Senna da Silva would soon drop the da Silva (in Brazil as prevalent as Smith or Jones) and go on to be recognised the world over as simply 'Ayrton' or 'Senna' – probably the most iconic and instantly recognisable sportsman on the planet at the time of his death.

As Tommy Byrne explains with his 'fast man' anecdote (see 'You've nicked my wheels!', page 32), Senna's arrival on British shores had been anticipated.

1 MARCH 1981

Brands Hatch • Van Diemen RF80
P&O Ferries FF1600 • 5th

Senna's new Van Diemen RF81 – that year's model – wasn't quite ready for his racing debut on the Brands Hatch 'Indy' circuit, so he had to drive a year-old car and play second fiddle to his Van Diemen team-mates, Toledano and Mansilla, as well as veteran Rick Morris in the new Royale car and the talented Dave Coyne.

8 MARCH 1981

Thruxton • Van Diemen RF81
Townsend Thoresen FF1600 • 3rd

There was a mixed grid and those at the front had all set their times in the opening minutes of a wet session before a large quantity of oil was deposited. Senna wasn't among them. The Royales of Morris and David Wheeler dominated the race as Mansilla had a moment in front of the pack. Senna, now in the latest RF81, won an intense battle with his recovering team-mate to finish third.

15 MARCH 1981

Brands Hatch • Van Diemen RF81
Townsend Thoresen FF1600 • 1st

This was Senna's first car victory. He won both a 10-lap heat and the 15-lap final, beating Mansilla and Toledano respectively. It was wet and immediately Ayrton showed freakish natural feel for grip, beating Toledano in the final by 9sec, a huge margin. *Autosport*'s Jeremy Shaw wrote: 'Da Silva's driving was undoubtedly the highlight of the day.'

British fans with long memories, however, love to recall that, in his heat, Senna had to contend with a surprise leader at Paddock Bend on the first lap – club racing stalwart Miki Dee, who was driving his Van Diemen that day only because a hire customer failed to show up! Something for him to tell the grandchildren...

The previous year Moreno had dominated FF1600 and Shaw quoted third-placed Steve Lincoln, a British hopeful, lamenting: 'With Moreno out of the way I was looking forward to a really good year... then this bloke arrives!'

It was a sentiment widely echoed, within Van Diemen particularly – Mansilla swapped championships to avoid Ayrton.

⬇ **Ayrton and wife Liliane celebrate his first single-seater win, at Brands Hatch in March 1981. Alfonso Toledano soon became frustrated by Ayrton's genius.**
📷 sutton-images.com

22 MARCH 1981

Mallory Park • Van Diemen RF81
Townsend Thoresen FF1600 • 2nd

On his first visit to the Leicestershire circuit Senna was in pole position but Mansilla made a better start and took the lead around the outside of Gerard's, leaving Senna to battle with Mexican Ricardo Valerio and Toledano.

Once established in second place, Senna got his head down to catch Mansilla, which he managed on the last lap, but when he attempted to go by Mansilla put him on the grass. Furious, Senna made it to the line just in front of Toledano as the Van Diemen works cars finished 1–2–3.

The atmosphere was frosty in Ralph Firman's office the following morning.

5 APRIL 1981

Mallory Park • Van Diemen RF81
Townsend Thoresen FF1600 • 2nd

Toledano beat Senna to the pole and the pair ran first and second respectively until Senna passed the Mexican four laps into the race. The two Van Diemen works drivers engaged in an entertaining scrap, which the wily Rick Morris watched from close quarters. When Senna and Toledano hit each other with three laps to go, Morris passed the pair to win for Royale. Mr Firman wasn't happy...

3 MAY 1981

Snetterton • Van Diemen RF81
Townsend Thoresen FF1600 • 2nd

Senna took pole at a bleak, windy, wet Snetterton, Van Diemen's home circuit, and won the first of two aggregated races by just over 2sec from Morris's Royale and Toledano. But in the second 10-lapper Morris made the best start and won by a comfortable 7sec, more than enough to overturn his first race deficit and claim the overall win.

What happened to the works Van Diemens? Senna and Toledano tangled at the Esses on the third lap, with Ayrton accepting responsibility. For the second race in succession an internal battle had let in veteran Morris and his Royale. Behind closed doors, Mr Firman was even less happy...

24 MAY 1981

Oulton Park • Van Diemen RF81
RAC British FF1600 • 1st

Senna took pole at the Cheshire track for the first round of the RAC British FF1600 Championship, with Morris and Toledano alongside him on the front row. Toledano made the best start but Senna soon demoted him and won the race with 1.7sec in hand over Morris. As Ayrton mounted the podium to take the victory garland, people were speaking of 'another Piquet'. Despite Nelson being on the way to winning the first of three world titles that year, Ayrton, no doubt, was thinking he was better than that...

25 MAY 1981

Mallory Park • Van Diemen RF81
Townsend Thoresen FF1600 • 1st

After a quick trip down the road to Leicestershire from Cheshire the previous day, Senna took his second victory of the weekend when he led all the way in the sixth round of the Townsend Thoresen series to take a comfortable 6sec win from Morris. The gap was bigger than normal as the wily Morris gave way to Ricardo Valerio, then sat back and watched as Valerio took off fellow Mexican Toledano.

7 JUNE 1981

Snetterton • Van Diemen RF81
Townsend Thoresen FF1600 • 1st

No mistakes by Ayrton this time at his 'home' track as he won in Van Diemen's back yard, taking pole position and fastest lap too. He took the flag less than a second clear of Rick Morris's Royale but it was more comfortable than it appeared because Ayrton backed off on the last lap.

21 JUNE 1981

Silverstone • Van Diemen RF81
RAC British FF1600 • 2nd

The second round of the RAC British FF1600 Championship at Silverstone became one of those races talked about years later. It was Senna's first visit to the Northamptonshire circuit that, in those days, shared the British GP with Brands Hatch in alternating years. Senna didn't win this one. And it irked him. Badly.

A. da Silva

VAN DIEMEN RACING

The race was 10 laps of the GP circuit and the experienced Morris, who judged his Royale a better car than Senna's Van Diemen in Silverstone's quick corners, sat on pole. But Senna made a better start and it took Morris until half distance to work his way on to Ayrton's gearbox.

On the penultimate lap Morris passed Senna on the inside of Stowe but Senna re-passed him at the Woodcote chicane. On the last lap, furious after Senna put him on the grass flat-out down Hangar Straight, Morris flew the chicane, landed on the right side of the penalty line and beat the Van Diemen across the line to score a fabulous win (see 'Recollections of a rival', page 36).

27 JUNE 1981

Oulton Park • Van Diemen RF81
Townsend Thoresen FF1600 • 1st

Senna and Morris were both under the FF1600 lap record as they shared the same qualifying time at Oulton Park six days after their epic Silverstone battle. But this time Morris made an uncharacteristic error on lap 2 at the first corner.

A spin put the Royale out and left Senna to head home Toledano who, by now, had started to accept that it was more sensible to learn from Senna than to try beating him. It took time for the realisation to fully sink in (see 'Ralph Firman on Senna', page 35).

4 JULY 1981

Donington Park • Van Diemen RF81
RAC British FF1600 • 1st

This was Senna's first visit to the track at which, 12 years on, he would drive that unforgettable opening lap in the European GP. He contented himself with his second victory within a week after the reversal at Silverstone that had so annoyed him.

12 JULY 1981

Brands Hatch • Van Diemen RF81
RAC British FF1600 • 4th

This was Ayrton's worst result since the opening day of the season. Set-up problems in qualifying put him back on the third row of the grid, behind Mansilla, Toledano, Robert Gibbs, Andy Ackerley and Morris. But he made a ballistic start, going into Paddock Hill Bend level with his Argentine team-mate, who was forced to cede the lead at Druids hairpin. Ayrton then drove away before

uncharacteristically letting the car get away from him at Clearways, rejoining in fourth place. When Mansilla and Toledano, battling for the lead, hit each other at Paddock Hill Bend, Morris passed both to pick up maximum points.

25 JULY 1981

Oulton Park • Van Diemen RF81
Townsend Thoresen FF1600 • 1st

Senna and Toledano shared the front row with another Brazilian, Fernando Macedo, in a second works Royale. Toledano made the best start but Senna was in control by the end of the first lap and ran out a comfortable winner by 3sec over Morris, who had to fight his way through from the third row of the grid.

26 JULY 1981

Mallory Park • Van Diemen RF81
RAC British FF1600 • 1st

From pole position Senna took his second win in as many days as the schedule served up another back-to-back Oulton/Mallory weekend.

Although just 1.5sec clear of Morris by the end, it was a relatively comfortable win for Ayrton as Rick battled to keep the other two works Van Diemens behind.

2 AUGUST 1981

Brands Hatch • Van Diemen RF81
Townsend Thoresen FF1600 • 1st

Senna jumped ahead at the start and led every inch of the way at the scene of his first victory almost five months earlier. Morris got the better of Toledano to finish second.

9 AUGUST 1981

Snetterton • Van Diemen RF81
RAC British FF1600 • 1st

The Van Diemen works team dominated on home soil, Senna beating Mansilla and Toledano as he opened up a 10-point advantage over Morris to clinch the RAC championship. Morris could only finish fourth.

↑ **Ayrton at Oulton: to modern eyes the Van Diemen RF81 looks a little crude...**
📷 sutton-images.com

← **Liliane, Ayrton and Van Diemen's Malcolm 'Puddy' Pullen wait in the collecting area for Ayrton's first race at Silverstone, where Rick Morris snatched victory on the final lap.**
📷 sutton-images.com

15 AUGUST 1981

Donington • Van Diemen RF81
EFDA Euroseries FF1600 • 1st

This one was a little different. Donington played host to a round of the EFDA Euroseries FF1600 championship, also sponsored by Townsend Thoresen, on the support programme for the track's round of the European F2 championship, won by Geoff Lees. The European Formula Ford drivers, led by Dutchman Cor Euser, must have been a little intimidated to see that Ayrton da Silva was a late entry for their race...

Predictably, the British-based drivers dominated and Senna won another close race with Morris, who was able to make inroads into Ayrton's lead and make interesting observations about his precision while doing so (see 'Recollections of a rival', page 36).

⬇ **On the grid at Brands Hatch for the season finale, where Ayrton finished second and then announced that he was, "going home to Brazil, finished with racing".**

📷 sutton-images.com

31 AUGUST 1981

Thruxton • Van Diemen RF81
Townsend Thoresen FF1600 • 1st

From pole position, half a second quicker than his nearest rival, Senna scored a comfortable win ahead of Toledano and clinched the Townsend Thoresen championship. Rick Morris, the only man who could rob Ayrton of the title, retired early in the 10-lapper.

27 SEPTEMBER 1981

Brands Hatch • Van Diemen RF81
Townsend Thoresen FF1600 • 2nd

There was a rare reversal of fortunes for Senna in the final round when a first-lap incident in soaking conditions saw him rejoin well down the field. While Morris led the race from Toledano, Senna turned in a fabulous recovery drive and finally relieved Toledano of second place.

His championship double accomplished, Senna had shock news when interviewed on the podium. He was, he said, "going home to Brazil, finished with racing".

There were issues. Liliane, his Brazilian wife of less than a year, hated cold Britain and the FF1600 scene, his father wanted him back in Brazil, and Ayrton was disillusioned about the need to pay for drives despite his obvious talent.

To have a competitive car in Formula 3, the natural step for Senna, was going to cost nearly £100,000 for a season, and it wasn't easy to raise sponsorship from Brazil. Anyone close to the British FF1600 scene knew what a talent he was, but despite being the first Brazilian to win both major FF1600 championships in his first season, it proved difficult to generate the interest in his home country that he thought his ability deserved. People were even saying that Formula Ford in 1981 hadn't been a vintage year.

Plenty of Brazilians before Senna had trodden the familiar path. Emerson Fittipaldi's rise to Formula 1 had been meteoric, but that was in a different era. Nelson Piquet had just won his first Formula 1 World Championship for Brabham and Senna's friend, Chico Serra, the 1979 British Formula 3 champion, was now in Formula 1 with Fittipaldi's team.

In Formula 3, both Roberto Moreno and Raul Boesel, works Van Diemen drivers the year before Senna, had won races in 1981, and Moreno had also cleaned up in Formula Ford the previous season in a works Van Diemen. Without money, however, Roberto's Formula 3 graduation had depended on largesse from others – he was forced

to run with an inexperienced team and was unable to do a full season.

Senna had seen that. The team that had won the 1981 British Formula 3 Championship with Jonathan Palmer was West Surrey Racing, run by Dick Bennetts, a Kiwi. Bennetts got Palmer through a 20-race season and 35 test sessions for around £65,000, but a more sensible budget for 1982 was at least £90,000. That was nearly 10 times what Senna's father had given him for his debut season. Milton da Silva doubtless could have afforded it but Ayrton didn't feel he should have to ask – so the conversation hadn't been had.

Keen to get back to his family and the country he knew, Senna left for Brazil straight after the Brands Hatch race, with marriage issues and many other questions in his head. The end-of-season blue riband event, the Brands Hatch Formula Ford Festival and World Cup with almost 200 entrants, was five weeks away and Ayrton would undoubtedly start favourite, and Firman wanted him there in a Van Diemen even though this event hadn't been included in Ayrton's contract. But Senna had problems he needed to resolve.

With the Formula Ford Festival on the calendar for 31 October, Senna got on a plane to Brazil telling Firman that he would let him know by 18 October. He kept his word, on the dot (see 'Ralph Firman on Senna'), but by then it was too late...

⬆ **Despite being clearly 'No 1' – the first Brazilian to win both major FF1600 titles in his debut season – Senna returned home to Brazil with issues to resolve.**

📷 sutton-images.com

YOU'VE NICKED MY WHEELS!

In the cut-and-thrust of junior professional motor racing you need two things: money and talent. Talent is the prerequisite. You might make it without money, or you might not. Nothing illustrates that better than the divergent paths of Ayrton Senna and Tommy Byrne.

Gary Anderson, former Jordan and Jaguar technical director and now a respected F1 technical analyst, says of Byrne: "He is the most naturally talented driver I have ever had the pleasure of working with, and I have worked with many [but not Senna]. The things he could do with a car most drivers – including several Grand Prix winners and world champions – could only dream about."

Byrne and Senna were works drivers for Ralph Firman's Van Diemen outfit at the same time – 1981. Tommy was a year ahead, winning in FF2000 the same year that Ayrton dominated FF1600. Senna was from wealthy Brazilian stock; Byrne was a penniless Irishman from Dundalk.

A short chapter in Mark Hughes' excellent, edgy biography of Byrne, *Crashed and Byrned*, is entitled, simply, 'Ayrton Senna'. It tells how Byrne didn't know what Senna was talking about when, in early 1982, Ayrton returned from Brazil after his 'retirement' and burst into the Van Diemen office calling Tommy "a fucking thief". It goes like this:

"What the fuck yer talking about," says Tommy.

"You stole my fucking wheels, you bastard," says Senna.

"Don't call me a bastard, you bastard! What fuckin' wheels?"

"The wheels off my Alfasud, you bastard."

A scuffle ensued, broken up by Firman's wife, Angie.

Byrne elaborates: "It had started at the end of 1980 when Ralph had promoted me to his works FF2000 car, the next step on the ladder to F1. My sponsor, John McCambridge, was a car dealer and whenever anyone needed cars I'd get them through John. Ralph told me he'd got this Brazilian coming over for '81 and that he needed a car. Could I organise it?

"So I sorted out an Alfasud through John and drove it up to Ralph's. Ralph is already calling this Brazilian 'fast man' before he's even arrived. Here we go again, I thought. One of Ralph's old drivers, Chico Serra, had been telling him about 'fast man' for years, and now he was finally coming over. I was sick of hearing it, to be honest. Fast man... and he's not even in the country yet!

"Ralph replaced me in the FF1600 team with a couple of guys who didn't get the job done [Mansilla and Toledano]. But he also had 'fast man' – the right pain-in-the-arse Senna da Silva, who was even more arrogant than me!

"But he was paying for his drive. He was paying because Ralph knew he had money. That's how it works. If you're very quick but a knacker from Dundalk, you might get a chance if someone like Ralph sees you as a way of enhancing the worth of his business. But if you're very quick from a rich Brazilian family you have to pay for the chance because Ralph knows that someone like Senna will place a value on what Ralph can offer his career prospects. And part of what made that drive so attractive to Senna would have been what I'd done with it the year before.

"Anyway, I wipe up again in Ford 2000 just as Senna is doing in Ford 1600. We both spend time around the Firmans but he doesn't mix socially with the other drivers around Snetterton. It's soon pretty obvious that he resents the fact that he's paying for his ride, whereas I'm getting paid for mine. He talks to Angie and Angie talks to me and I get to hear the gripes.

"So it's coming up to the time, at the end of the season, for the Formula Ford Festival, which is like the world championship of Ford 1600. And suddenly Senna says he's going to retire and move back to Brazil, saying something about being disenchanted with a sport that asks the driver to pay money. Ralph needs his car to win the Festival. His business for the next year pretty much depends on it, but now his hot-shot's gone home in a flounce [Firman himself remembers it slightly differently!].

"'Tommy, will you come back to 1600 and win the Festival for me?' Ralph says. 'Of course I will.'

"So I test Senna's car and it's not that great, I gotta tell you. I'm not convinced. And maybe Ralph's not convinced, either, because the next day he collars me, saying: 'I've got Ayrton waiting at the airport in Brazil ready to come back for the Festival if I really want him to. Are you really sure you can win it?'

"Ayrton at the fuckin' airport – like he can do the job that I can't! Fuck off! 'Hell yes, no problem,' I say."

Despite getting a tougher time than expected from Rick Morris driving for Royale, Byrne does indeed win the Festival for Van Diemen. Just.

But, back to the Alfa Romeo...

"While Senna was in Brazil, 'retired', the Alfasud just stood around in the Van Diemen car park. Ralph had another Brazilian, Mauricio Gugelmin, coming over for '82 and was going to sell the car to him. I had an Alfasud too and was always getting punctures. Instead of getting them fixed, I'd just go and borrow a wheel from the other one. I thought nothing of it."

"Suddenly, Senna 'unretires' and comes back to continue his career in '82 – in Ford 2000, while I move up to F3. I was just happy I'd won the Festival – for Ralph and for myself. And it opened up opportunities for me. I guess Ayrton wasn't as happy about it all as I was..."

To explain Senna's apparently disproportionate anger at Byrne, ostensibly over some missing Alfasud wheels, it's not impossible to picture a scenario in which Ayrton had returned to Brazil with the intention of using his Festival participation as a lever to try and secure a free drive in FF2000 the following year, at the same time as speaking to teams about jumping straight into F3. Was it ever realistic that someone as driven as Senna was really going to retire after coming all the way to the UK and dominating?

But Byrne, by stepping back into Senna's actual car to win the Festival, had stolen Ayrton's thunder. And one of the opportunities it had opened up for Tommy was an F3 drive with Murray Taylor (they went on to win the championship in '82), a man Senna had been talking to. So, in Ayrton's mind, Tommy had stolen his Festival car, a potential F3 seat and now, the final straw, his wheels!

⬇ Tommy Byrne, flanked by runner-up Rick Morris (right) and James Weaver, won the 1981 Formula Ford Festival and World Cup in 'Senna's' Van Diemen.

📷 sutton-images.com

RALPH FIRMAN
ON SENNA

hico Serra, says Ralph Firman, "had told me two years before, 'You've got to get this guy. You must get him!' He was forming his karting career in Italy at the time but eventually he arrived.

"He didn't have a lot of money to spend, to be fair. I wanted him, and that was it. I'd looked at his karting performances. He drove a hard bargain. Chico was the negotiator and said, 'He wants paying.' I replied, 'No, no, no. You pay me. I no pay you.' His English wasn't that good then but I got him to understand that! We agreed on £10,000."

Firman denies that there was much friction with Tommy Byrne, the Van Diemen works driver who was a year ahead of Senna and winning in FF2000, and who, reputedly, wasn't paying.

"No," he says. "Ayrton was the type of man who's hard as nails, but once it's done, that's it. He was a proper man of honour. And he probably didn't admit to anyone that he was paying!

"He was a lovely guy. We stayed in contact during the course of his career and he appreciated the fact that he could come up, say hello and maybe stay, and be on his own without being annoyed by people. He was just Ayrton, a very nice character.

"Years later something he did for me showed that character. I was talking to him when Ralph Jr [Firman's son] got into karting and I told Ayrton that Ralph was going to do a race in Asia. Ayrton was well in with Honda and I asked him about Honda kart engines. He said that Honda didn't make any and I told him that, yes, apparently they did. He said he'd find out. He came straight back and said that it was Honda's son, Hirotoshi, through the Mugen company, and that when Ralph arrived engines would be available to him. When he got there, he had engines, a dedicated engineer, the whole works. Ayrton had just arranged it all himself, which was really nice.

"The true story about him not doing the Formula Ford Festival in '81 was that he wasn't sure whether or not he

⬇ **Ralph Firman (left) and Derek Wild in the Van Diemen workshops in late 1980, working with plans for the RF81 that Senna was to drive.**

📷 Mike Dixon

could come back. He had various issues to overcome. But he said at the end of September, and this was the kind of bloke he was, 'I will let you know by October 18.'

"The days went by and there was nothing, nothing, nothing. And so I started to get cold feet, worried I wasn't going to have somebody quick enough to win the Festival, and so I gave Tommy Byrne the car. I don't know what made me do it, because I could have just built another one and kept it in case.

"On the very day of the 18th Ayrton phoned and said, 'Ralph, I'm at the airport, I'll be in tomorrow.' I said, 'Ayrton, I haven't got a car for you... I'm sorry, but that's it.' It was totally my fault, all down to me. He was absolutely correct. So I must be the only bloke on the planet who ever refused him a drive. He just said, 'OK Ralph, I understand.'

"I know people say he was always going to come back in '82 but I really didn't know. He phoned me out of the blue that February and said he'd like to come back and do FF2000 and could I help him. I said, 'Yeah, get on a plane as quick as you can!' I welcomed him with open arms and we sorted out a deal where Dennis Rushen [who had won FF2000 titles with Byrne in 1981] ran the car.

"I've never compared drivers, year-to-year or decade-to-decade, but it became evident that he had everything, and you started to appreciate that as the season went on. It's often difficult to identify these things though. When a driver cleans up, you don't know whether it's because he's that much better or because it's a poor year for opposition. But I'd started to identify how quick he was straight out of the box and how he found the limit before the others. That, to me, is the sign of a very true driver. That's what makes the difference.

"Toledano was very upset that he wasn't winning. Alfie was a really good driver. His mother came along with a so-called manager one day and she said, 'Look, why is my son not winning races?'

"I said, 'Well, Ayrton is a better driver, it's as simple as that.'

"They said, 'Oh no, the car's not right, the engine's not right, etc, etc.'

"I said, 'Look, I'll tell you what, Alfie. You have to accept it, and the best you can do this year is to learn from Ayrton. And that's the best I can do for you. Because, unfortunately, you're not quite in his class.'

"So at the end of the year they went off, Alfie did his F3 in Germany, did quite well, and two years later he and his mother turned up at my office. They had this beautiful glass Lamborghini. They said, 'Ralph, we've brought you a present. We've come to thank you. We didn't understand at the time but since Ayrton has gone on and done what he's done, we now understand what we were up against... We want to thank you so much for being so kind to us at the time.'

"Lovely people. Don't make any mistake about it, Alfie was a terrific driver but, as I said to him, just really unlucky he picked that year!

"Mansilla was also a fantastic character and he won his BARC championship [which was a weaker series] that year. In the main series he'd said, 'Ah, Ralph, I cannot win!' It was quite important for them to try and win championships to keep their support going. So we pulled him out and went and did another one, and he and his sponsors were happy."

> **"I must be the only bloke on the planet who ever refused him a drive"**

RICK MORRIS
RECOLLECTIONS OF A RIVAL

At 34, Rick Morris was much older than the young FF1600 chargers he was taking on in 1981. He wasn't a professional racing driver, insofar as he had to earn a living elsewhere, but that didn't make him any less competent.

In the year that he gave Ayrton Senna a hard time, he'd also set up his own contract-hire company, which he still operates 30-odd years on, and son Stevie was born. He had a lot going on. But he's that kind of man. When contacted for this book, his response was, 'Make sure you call before next Monday because I'm on a plane to Jo'burg to drive in a round of the South African F1600 series.' Rick Morris is now 66 years old... But he was chuffed that, through cycling, he'd just got his pulse rate below 50!

The racing business keeps you young and, like most, Rick has a tale or two.

"I'd been driving for 10 years by the time Ayrton arrived, but that still wasn't as long as he'd spent in karts. And for all of it bar the previous 1980 season, when Royale's Alan Cornock gave me the works drive, I raced in complete and utter penury.

"My first mechanic was James Weaver and I can remember spending hours at his house. I'd go over there and we'd lap the valves in. In those days you didn't have air filters, so you had to lap the valves in every week because of all the grit that got in between. We had this idea that the valve seat had to be really, really thin, so the biggest expense of the whole season was cylinder head gaskets!

"You simply couldn't afford to go racing if you had to pay someone else because of the hours it took. We were great friends with Jonathan Palmer too and none of us had any social life – we'd spend every night working on the cars. And that lasted from '73 to '80. Every night in the garage, with no money at all.

"In that '81 season my Royale was quicker than Senna's Van Diemen in the fast corners, places like Stowe and Club at Silverstone, but he was so wonderfully quick through the slow corners – that was down to his karting. I just couldn't live with him through somewhere like the right-hander before the bridge at Snetterton, the way it was then. He would hit that apex and get out of it like I couldn't believe. I could then catch him through Coram and Russell but I'd lose out again through Sear, the slow right-hander onto the back straight.

"That was the pattern all year. We'd all be on the first couple of rows and I'd quite often get away fourth and have to get past Toledano and Mansilla and then go after Senna. Quite often I'd get fastest lap catching him, but I couldn't beat him – not often, anyway – because of his metronomic ability to put in quick laps.

"There was one race at Donington [15 August] where it was the same pattern. Again he'd got away on the first lap and I was behind him. He could put the car absolutely where he wanted and coming out of Coppice I watched him take the same amount of dirt just beyond the rumble strips every single lap. It was extraordinary. I would do it once every four or five laps if I pushed too hard, but he was doing it every single lap, by exactly the same amount, quite deliberately. It was absolutely characteristic of him.

⬇ **Rick Morris with Andrew Kitson's painting of his famous moment at Silverstone.**

📷 Tony Dodgins

"I think I had a slight advantage at Donington because only the chicane was really slow. My car was absolutely magic through the Old Hairpin and pretty good elsewhere, because there just weren't the slow second-gear corners – it was always those that caught me out.

"Apart from the car, Senna wasn't as good in fast corners because he still employed the old karting tactic of 'bang it in and let's get to the apex as quick as we can', regardless of what's going to happen coming out. I'd been taught the old-school British way of slowing it down a bit going in and then powering on through, so I could come out of the fast corners slightly quicker than him and getting an ideal tow – which of course made all the difference in the world.

"It pissed him off pretty badly, and we really didn't see eye to eye at all in '81. We had quite a few arguments because, as is well known now, he had that arrogant attitude that anybody who got in the way of him trying to do something was in the wrong. There was no argument for him. So, if I got slightly in his way during a practice session, I'd be told I'd ruined his 'effing' time or whatever. Forget the genteel Christian side of it: it was 'F' this and 'B' that.

"But we were great friends after the season ended, when obviously I wasn't racing him any more. I won the Esso championship in '82 and I was racing against the

likes of Julian Bailey and Mauricio Gugelmin, who was Ayrton's mate. I got on very well with Mauricio. He wasn't at all like Senna but he and his wife Stella were living with Ayrton near Virginia Water, and I visited the house a couple of times.

"But in '81, though, we were almost bitter enemies. If you had the cheek to beat him or get in his way, it wasn't the done thing!

"I beat him at the Brands Hatch race before the Festival. There's a lovely photograph of the podium with me quite joyful with the winner's garland, Senna looking like piss warmed up, second, and a happy Alfie Toledano, third. Alfie and Quique [Mansilla] were always

↑ On his first visit to Silverstone Ayrton is chased by Rick Morris's Royale through Woodcote, where Morris 'mugged' him on the last lap to take the win.

📷 sutton-images.com

"Senna wasn't as good in fast corners because he still employed the old karting tactic of 'bang it in and let's get to the apex as quick as we can', regardless of what's going to happen coming out"

great mates, we all chatted together and were great
friends. Senna was obviously to one side.

"The fact that this was the race before the Festival
may have been one reason why Senna went home to
Brazil, because he didn't think he could win in a Van
Diemen against me in a Royale. There were lots of
other theories going around."

One theory was that Senna wanted a free drive
in FF2000.

"Ralph would always wind Ayrton up, telling him
he couldn't be that good if Morris was beating him!"

With Morris proving to be such a big nuisance to
someone as good as Senna, one wonders why he
wasn't offered a works Van Diemen seat.

"Ralph mainly had pay drivers, but I didn't pay one
penny to Royale's Alan Cornock. Alan paid for my racing
for two years, bless his heart, and he's still a very good
friend. Another of life's real gentlemen."

Gentlemanly bahaviour was certainly not a feature of
Senna's driving on the last lap of their most famous battle,
at Silverstone, which Rick won by flying the Woodcote
chicane, to Senna's intense annoyance.

"Do you know why the bastard had to be beaten?"
Morris laughs. "He nearly bloody killed me in that race.
He had me off down Hangar Straight. Bastard. I mean, you
block the inside and make sure whoever you're fighting
has to take the outside. That's quite normal on the last lap.
But when I flicked back outside he just shoved me on the
grass, flat-out.

"I suppose in an FF1600 car you're not going that fast,
maybe 125mph, but it's fast enough and not pleasant!
That really got my dander up. But I was still close enough
when I got back on and knew I always had a good run
through the following corner, Club [a very fast right-hander
in 1981].

"He did his usual thing, threw it at the corner and
was massively quick going in and relatively slow coming
out. That's fine, but not at a quick place like Silverstone
where you want to be slightly slower in and get earlier on
the power. I came out a couple of car lengths down but
quicker, and got the tow.

"I got away first and thought I had a safe couple of lengths' lead, but Senna just came up the inside, all wheels locked, bashed into my side, pushed me off on the outside and won the race"

"He saw me coming and blocked the inside for the Woodcote chicane. So I got alongside him on the outside going into what was, for me, the best corner in the world – a corner to treasure as a driver. You literally threw the car sideways and had it sliding all the way through. I took it in third gear, something like 80mph, used a little bit of kerb, took off, came down inside the penalty line – and won.

"He was shaking his fist at me – Morris, you bastard – and then he took a Van Diemen guy, Malcolm 'Puddy' Pullen, to investigate a protest. Puddy told me later that he had to calm him down, saying to him, 'Come on Ayrton, get real, you just got beaten.' Which was quite brave..."

Most successful drivers are hard, but was Senna any worse, any more physical than the likes of Toledano and Mansilla, his team-mates?

"Oh crikey, yes! Senna used to be a bit like Dave Coyne – very effectively 'hard'. When my son started racing karts I remembered Ayrton's bright helmet colour scheme and told Stevie, because he was aggressive too, that I wanted people to turn around and immediately know it was him. It makes a difference. If Stevie was on your tail a driver knew about it, knew that he was going to get a nudge or a push or whatever. And it was the same with Senna in '81.

"Early in '81 I was on pole at Oulton Park and can remember why. Pat Symonds, who worked at Royale [and later engineered Senna in his first F1 season at Toleman], and I were trying to work out how to cut down the RP26's understeer. We took a packer out of the rear suspension and I asked Alan Cornock why it was there. He said, 'Well, Rory [Byrne, future Benetton and Ferrari design ace] put it in.' Something like three years earlier...

"So we took out this packer and suddenly found pace. We were on pole by three tenths or something – a massive amount. From the start at Oulton you go up the hill and there's a left-hander followed by a double-apex right, which isn't a normal overtaking place. I got away first and thought I had a safe couple of lengths' lead, but Senna just came up the inside, all wheels locked, bashed into my side, pushed me off on the outside and won the race, while I got caught up in the midfield scrap after I'd sorted myself out.

"That was quite typical. And again that's karting. Watch karters and they all just throw it up the inside and the guy on the outside goes off while the aggressor is stopped from going off by the car he's hit. And that's what he did."

⬇ **The race before Senna's premature 'retirement' and Morris had the victory spoils. And Ayrton, observed Rick, 'had a face like piss warmed up...'**
📷 sutton-images.com

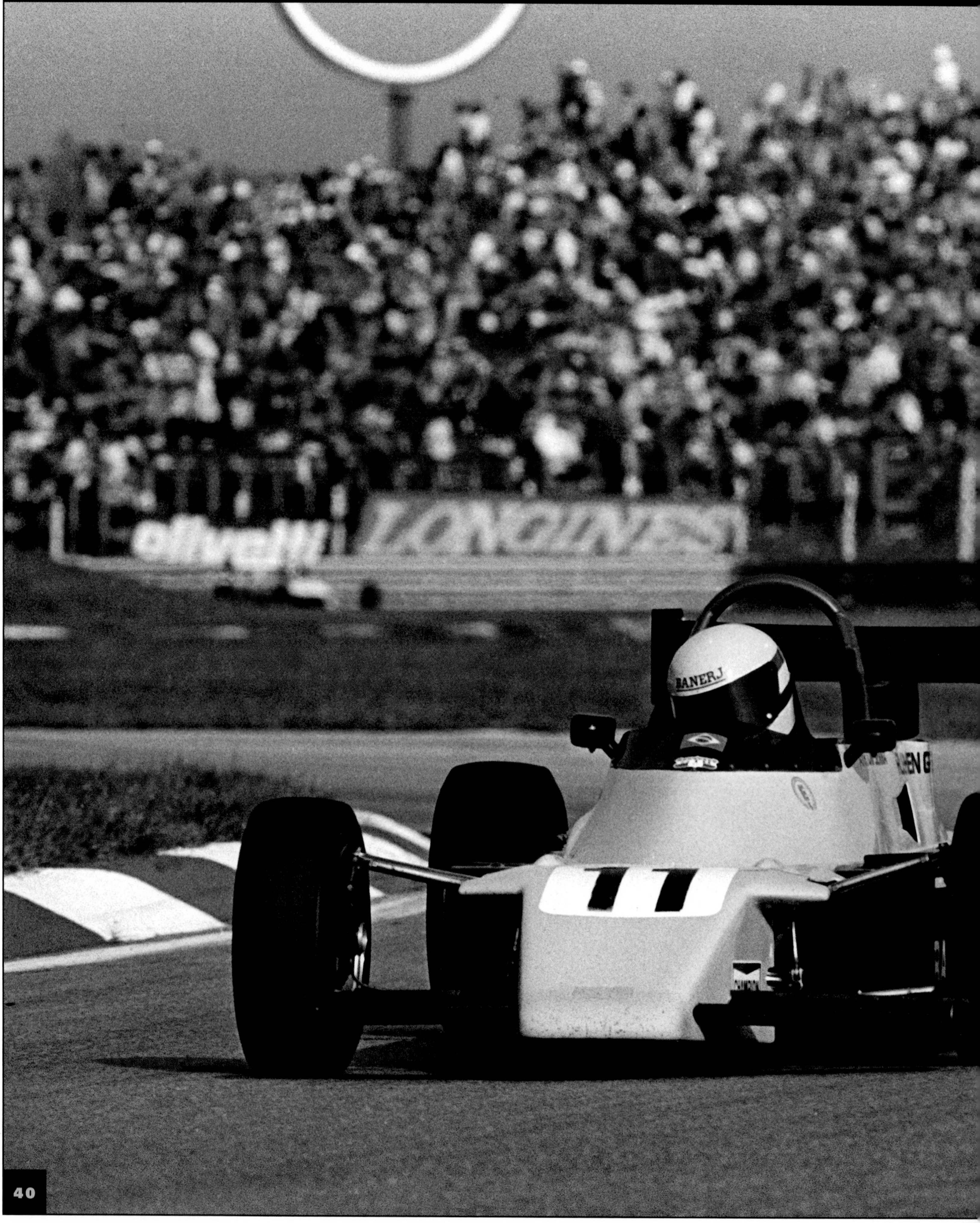
olivetti
LONGINES
BANERJ

1982
MOPPING UP FF2000

Despite a relatively late decision to return to the UK and continue his career in Formula Ford 2000 with Rushen Green's Van Diemen RF82, Ayrton Senna, as he now styled himself ('da Silva' was as common in Brazil as 'Smith' is in Britain), was dominant from the off. He had a record-breaking season in both the UK and Europe, where he took in the EFDA (European Formula Drivers Association) FF2000 series.

With 2-litre rather than 1.6-litre engines, slick tyres and wings, FF2000 cars were about 4sec per lap quicker than FF1600s, closer to 'proper' race cars and nearer to the grip levels of karts. Some thought them better suited to Senna, but Ralph Firman doesn't think it mattered: "He'd have been quick in a wheelbarrow..."

← In front of F1 team bosses, Senna destroyed the opposition in the FF2000 race supporting the Austrian GP.

📷 sutton-images.com

➔ Oulton Park,
27 March, was
the second of
six consecutive
victories for Senna
at the start of his
all-conquering
1982 season in
the Rushen Green
Racing Van
Diemen RF82.

📷 sutton-images.com

7 MARCH 1982

Brands Hatch • Van Diemen RF82
Pace British FF2000 • 1st

Five months out of the cockpit did nothing to dim Senna's competitiveness as he destroyed the field in the opening round of the Pace British FF2000 series. He took pole by 0.6sec, left the field for dead on the opening lap and beat former superkart racer Calvin Fish's Royale by 10sec after 15 laps of the short Brands Indy circuit.

27 MARCH 1982

Oulton Park • Van Diemen RF82
Pace British FF2000 • 1st

It was the same story in Cheshire three weeks later. Senna took pole once again and Fish was his nearest challenger again. Actually, 'nearest' is a misnomer. As in the series opener, Ayrton's winning margin was 10sec.

28 MARCH 1982

Silverstone • Van Diemen RF82
Pace British FF2000 • 1st

⬇ 'Da Silva' was
like 'Smith' in Brazil.
For the 1982 FF2000
season the country's
new rising star had
become plain
Ayrton Senna.

📷 sutton-images.com

Different day, different county, same result. After a Saturday victory at Oulton, Senna and Rushen Green nipped down the road to Silverstone and cleaned up again, this time beating Colin Jack's Reynard by 17sec after 15 laps of the Silverstone Club circuit. Bearing in mind the circuit had only three corners, that margin was quite an achievement!

4 APRIL 1982

Donington • Van Diemen RF82
Pace British FF2000 • 1st

Senna continued his extraordinary dominance with another 17sec victory over Calvin Fish's Royale at Donington, with Russell Spence and Tim Davies third and fourth.

9 APRIL 1982

Snetterton • Van Diemen RF82
Pace British FF2000 • 1st

This one wasn't quite so straightforward for Ayrton but he won it all the same. Having taken pole and led the opening lap, Senna found himself without front brakes and slowed to negotiate wreckage from a first-corner shunt. In a trice he was passed by new Rushen Green team-mate Kenny Andrews and Russell Spence. Quickly adjusting, Ayrton reasserted himself and took the chequered flag by just 12sec this time – with only rear brakes...

"He could have stopped on the line on the slowdown lap," recalls Rushen, "but he stopped halfway to the first corner, just to let everyone know he'd won that race with no brakes."

12 APRIL 1982

Silverstone • Van Diemen RF82
Pace British FF2000 • 1st

After Good Friday success at Van Diemen's home circuit, Ayrton made it six of the best at Silverstone on Easter Monday. Argentine driver Victor Rosso was his nearest challenger this time, but still 14sec behind after 15 laps...

18 APRIL 1982

Zolder • Van Diemen RF82
EFDA Euroseries FF2000 • Retired, 3 laps, engine

A much-anticipated battle with reigning European, Dutch and Benelux FF1600 champion Cor Euser, also unbeaten so far in '82, failed to materialise as Ayrton's Nelson engine expired after just three laps. It didn't appear to be a fair fight prior to that, however, as Senna's Van Diemen outqualified the Dutchman's two-year-old Delta by a full second.

2 MAY 1982

Donington • Van Diemen RF82
EFDA Euroseries FF2000 • 1st

Senna opened his Euroseries account in Leicestershire with a comfortable win from pole despite a misfiring engine. Yorkshireman Russell Spence managed to get a little closer this time, staying within 7sec after 20 laps as Senna lowered his own lap record.

3 MAY 1982

Mallory Park • Van Diemen RF82
Pace British FF2000 • 1st

Amazingly, Senna was beaten to pole position, by Victor Rosso. Ayrton suspected that he had a down-on-power engine, so it was changed in the lunch break – and the race then followed the usual script. Senna shot into the lead and opened up an 8sec margin over Rosso by the end of the 20-lapper.

9 MAY 1982

Zolder • Van Diemen RF82
EFDA Euroseries FF2000 • Retired, 12 laps, accident

This round of the EFDA Euroseries FF2000 championship was totally overshadowed by the death, the day before, of Ferrari driver Gilles Villeneuve in the closing minutes of qualifying for the Belgian GP. It was also to be Senna's second fruitless trip to Belgium in three weeks.

Senna was never in awe of F1 and liked being there. He met Frank Williams for the first time, then went to meet Nelson Piquet but was snubbed – and never forgot it. With that fresh in his head, he took pole by an enormous margin.

Ayrton and Dennis Rushen had one road car between them at the track and Senna wanted to see a girlfriend in Brussels. Rushen told him that if he won, he could take the car and Dennis would find a lift back to the hotel, about 45 minutes away. Senna took pole but, leading by 13sec, he lost concentration and spun into the catch-fencing. Rushen made Ayrton drive him back to the hotel...

"Six years later," recalls Rushen, "I was watching when he was leading the Monaco GP by a country mile and crashed with a few laps to go. I thought, yep, I've seen that before..."

30 MAY 1982

Oulton Park • Talbot Sunbeam Ti
Celebrity race • 1st

The Oulton Park programme opened with a celebrity race in Talbot Sunbeams, with cars going to those who had qualified in the top two for selected events on the afternoon's programme.

It was a seven-lap race and Senna duly disappeared by precisely a second a lap to beat the experienced and slightly bemused John Brindley into second place, while third place went to Jaguar European Touring Car driver Chuck Nicholson.

"That bloke is going to make it..." said Brindley, with foresight.

30 MAY 1982

Oulton Park • Van Diemen RF82
Pace British FF2000 • Retired, 11 laps, puncture

Calvin Fish had jettisoned his Royale and was now in possession of a new Van Diemen RF82, the same as Senna's, and run by respected former Scorpion

Racing and Van Diemen works preparation man Micky Galter. Fish it was who took pole position, with Senna alongside him, once more complaining of a down-on-power engine.

Fish led away and when Senna started slipping back it was clear that he was in trouble. A puncture was the problem and Senna finally retired after 11 laps with his tyre in shreds.

"He definitely had an ego," Rushen says. "He wasn't going to stop until the tyre was in a million pieces and everybody could see he had a puncture..."

31 MAY 1982

Brands Hatch • Van Diemen RF82
Pace British FF2000 • 1st

Races in Cheshire and Kent on successive days was asking a lot of the Pace British FF2000 teams but for the second time in 24 hours Fish managed to beat Senna to pole. It all got a bit tight at the first corner as Fish suffered a damaged nose in a spot of contact. Senna went on to score another win but Fish was again able to offer much more solid resistance and got to the line just 1.6sec adrift.

6 JUNE 1982

Mallory Park • Van Diemen RF82
Pace British FF2000 • 1st

A hat-trick of Pace British non-poles for Senna! This time it was Welshman Tim Davies who beat him to the top spot in variable conditions. It didn't matter to Senna though, Ayrton blasting off into an immediate and decisive lead, coming home 9sec in front of Rushen Green team-mate Kenny Andrews.

20 JUNE 1982

Hockenheim • Van Diemen RF82
EFDA Euroseries FF2000 • Retired, 0 laps, accident

Once more, Europe didn't prove to be a happy hunting ground for Ayrton in the fourth round of the EFDA series. He kept up his 100 per cent record of Euroseries poles but cooked his clutch on the line and then got involved in an incident at the first chicane as everyone took evasive action to miss Cor Euser's rolling Delta.

13 JUNE 1982

Brands Hatch • Van Diemen RF82
Pace British FF2000 • 1st

Senna took pole and a new lap record at Brands Hatch but was pushed every inch of the way by Fish, who continued his new-found form in his Van Diemen RF82 and crossed the finishing line just a second behind.

26 JUNE 1982

Oulton Park • Van Diemen RF82
Pace British FF2000 • 1st

Senna continued his dominance on British soil on a damp but drying track as Van Diemen RF82s took the top six places. It was a more comfortable 4sec victory over Fish this time, Calvin having first to fight his way past Senna's Rushen Green team-mate Kenny Andrews.

⬇ Although Tim Davies was actually on pole at Mallory Park on 6 June, Senna took the lead at the start and won the race comfortably.
📷 sutton-images.com

3 JULY 1982

Zandvoort • Van Diemen RF82
EFDA Euroseries FF2000 • 1st

After missing first practice with clutch problems, in the second half-hour session Senna followed Ron Kluit for a couple of laps to find his way around the seaside track, then went by and promptly took pole position for this Dutch GP supporting race.

Senna missed the change to second gear off the line and had to follow Jaap van Silfhout for a lap before calmly outbraking him into Tarzan to lead. Ayrton didn't do his usual disappearing act because of more clutch trouble, but a 2sec margin over a battling Fish, Cor Euser and Kluit was enough to give him a two-point series lead over Euser.

4 JULY 1982

Snetterton • Van Diemen RF82
Pace British FF2000 • 2nd

This much-remembered round of the British series resulted in a victory for larger-than-life cockles-and-mussels merchant Frank Bradley! The race started on a wet but drying track and Bradley alone gambled on slick tyres. He wallowed at the tail end of the field in the early laps but, as the track dried, rapidly closed in on the leaders.

Senna had initially run behind Fish before passing him and pulling away. Bradley also passed Fish and homed in on Senna. Ayrton, his wets now shredded and almost down to the carcass, hung on grimly. But, at Snetterton's second corner, Sear, Bradley had much more grip and went by to score a massively popular win.

"Ayrton thought it was great!" says Rushen. "He was delighted for Frank, laughing about it and slapping him on the back. Everyone knew it was because of the slicks, so it didn't matter. It was the only time he took being beaten with good grace. He would never have seen it like that if he'd been beaten head-to-head by a rival…"

10 JULY 1982

Castle Combe • Van Diemen RF82
Pace British FF2000 • 1st

Senna lapped almost a second under the circuit FF2000 lap record on the series' lone visit to Wiltshire to beat Calvin Fish to pole by a tenth of a second. He drove his usual ballistic opening lap and was always out of reach, winning by 3sec.

1 AUGUST 1982

Snetterton • Van Diemen RF82
Pace British FF2000 • 1st

Controversy at Van Diemen's home circuit! Senna and Fish qualified on the front row and fought a race-long tussle, with Ayrton in front but Calvin always threatening. It all got physical on the Revett Straight in the closing stages, with Senna putting Fish on the grass and causing him to spin out. Fish protested and Senna was fined but kept his win.

A frosty three-week European trip followed for the two rival camps, who often travelled together and stayed in the same hotels.

8 AUGUST 1982

Hockenheim • Van Diemen RF82
EFDA Euroseries FF2000 • 1st

Supporting the German GP, this is the race where future Lotus race engineer Steve Hallam remembers Senna being so far in front on the opening lap that he thought there must have been a shunt. Ayrton beat Fish by 4sec at the flag but the nearest European runner, Volker Weidler, was 20sec adrift.

15 AUGUST 1982

Osterreichring • Van Diemen RF82
EFDA Euroseries FF2000 • 1st

The Osterreichring, in Austria's Styrian mountains, was a 'proper' circuit and Senna turned in another incredible performance in front of the F1 bosses – if any were watching.

He took pole by a second and a half and beat Fish by 24sec over 12 laps! Kris Nissen, third, was 38sec behind the Rushen Green Van Diemen…

22 AUGUST 1982

Jyllandsring • Van Diemen RF82
EFDA Euroseries FF2000 • 1st

Ayrton clinched the EFDA FF2000 series in Denmark with a more reasonable 2.5sec victory over Fish and then a trio of local drivers – Kris Nissen, Jesper Villumsen and Henrik Larsen.

30 AUGUST 1982

Thruxton • Van Diemen RF82
Pace British FF2000 • 1st

Senna was beaten to pole by Fish on the championship's only visit to the fast Hampshire circuit, Ayrton again feeling that his engine lacked power. That didn't stop Senna hanging on until his oil pressure gauge indicated a problem. He kept going despite a smoky engine and shot through to take the win on lap 13 of the 15 when Fish was tripped up by a backmarker.

3 SEPTEMBER 1982

Silverstone • Van Diemen RF82
Pace British FF2000 • 1st

↓ **Senna with Dick Bennetts before his winning F3 debut in the Thruxton TV race on 13 November. 'Ayrton da Silva' has made a return...**
📷 sutton-images.com

Senna and Fish fought another close battle with identical qualifying times and fastest laps. But in the race Ayrton again got away first and Fish was never close enough to mount a meaningful challenge, finishing half a second adrift.

15 SEPTEMBER 1982

Mondello Park • Van Diemen RF82 • EFDA
Euroseries FF2000 • 1st

Senna was far from amused (see 'Dennis Rushen on Senna' page 54) to lose pole position to local driver Joey Greenan. This was Ireland, timings were a bit random and the Irish happened to bring out the flag for the end of qualifying just after Greenan had done his quick lap and just before Senna was about to embark on his!

In the race, just to make a point, Senna lowered Tommy Byrne's lap record from 58.80s to 57.92s on the way to beating Greenan by almost 20sec over the 20 laps...

26 SEPTEMBER 1982

Brands Hatch • Van Diemen RF82
Pace British FF2000 • 2nd

In a black mood after finishing only 14th in the World Karting Championship (see page 15) at Kalmar, Sweden, Senna suffered his only defeat of 1982 in a race he

finished, other than the Snetterton round when he lost out to the slick-shod Frank Bradley. And, as Dennis Rushen recalls, it was the only occasion where they crossed words, when Senna "spent too much time fiddling around with his front wing" (see 'Dennis Rushen on Senna' page 53).

Senna, Fish and Victor Rosso all recorded the same qualifying time, but Rosso did it first and took pole. Fish bravely went round the outside of Rosso at Paddock Hill Bend and made good his escape while Senna negotiated his way past the Argentine driver. Although the Rushen Green car set fastest lap as it closed in on Fish, Senna was still a second adrift when the flag fell.

13 NOVEMBER 1982

Thruxton • Ralt RT3/82
Non-championship F3 • 1st

This was Senna's first race in a Formula 3 car. This non-championship Thruxton fixture always attracted a decent entry in front of BBC TV outside broadcast cameras but,

for financial reasons, often wasn't on the agenda of the season's F3 regulars.

Tommy Byrne (that year's champion), Quique Mansilla (Senna's FF1600 Van Diemen team-mate), Dave Scott, Martin Brundle and James Weaver were all absentees as Senna drove the West Surrey Racing Ralt RT3/82 in which Mansilla had narrowly lost the title to Byrne. As Senna rated Byrne much more than Mansilla, he was highly impressed that Dick Bennetts' WSR had managed to run the Irishman so close. Senna, incidentally, had also been in contact with Murray Taylor, who ran Byrne. The field also included Calvin Fish and recent Formula Ford Festival winner Julian Bailey.

Bennetts had never seen his car move so fast! Senna took pole with a 1m 13.34s lap that was 0.4sec quicker than Brundle's pole for the Marlboro British F3 championship round three weeks earlier, and nobody else lapped below 1m 14s.

In the race Senna disappeared, beating second-placed Swede Bengt Trägårdh – universally known in motor racing paddocks as 'Bent Track-Rod' – by 13sec. That evening Bennetts and Senna shook hands on an F3 deal for '83 and Senna was back in the UK to ink the contract in January.

↑ On his F3 debut in the West Surrey Racing Ralt RT3/82, Senna took pole at Thruxton and led the race from start to finish. Dick Bennetts: "He just blitzed everyone."

📷 sutton-images.com

DENNIS RUSHEN
ON SENNA

Dennis Rushen of Rushen Green Racing was the man who enjoyed a record-breaking season with Senna in 1982 when Ayrton firmed up his decision to return after 'retirement', continued where he'd left off and cleaned up in the UK and Europe.

Senna's name – Eye-Air-Tonn – was a bit complicated to handle, so to everyone at Rushen Green he became 'Harry', and then simply 'Arry'.

⬇ **Senna returned late from Brazil for 1982 but soon struck up a winning partnership with Dennis Rushen.**

📷 sutton-images.com

"Arry really put himself on the map with a couple of drives in the EFDA series on the F1 support programmes, at Hockenheim and the Osterreichring. Not that he was in awe of F1. It was just something he was going to do. He didn't aspire to it, it was a given. He was going to be an F1 driver because he was Senna. Different mindset.

"Osterreichring was a proper circuit in those days. It had been raining and it was still a bit wet but on slicks he came round five seconds in the lead at the end of the first lap!

"One of my other drivers asked him about Snetterton one time, getting all deep and meaningful about it. He asked him what he was thinking about Riches, the first corner, when he got to the turn-in point. He said, 'I'm not, I'm thinking about Sear [the second corner].' He was dead serious."

Rushen had won FF2000 championships with Tommy Byrne the previous year. Did he think Senna was on another level?

"Oh God, yes. It was only in those early years in the smaller formulae that you really saw how good he was.

↑ Rushen
celebrates Senna's
EFDA Euroseries
FF2000 title with
an impromptu air
guitar session
at Jyllandsring
in Denmark.
📷 sutton-images.com

Once drivers get to F1, it's all disguised, isn't it? Because they've all got different equipment. Apart from when they had the one-lap qualifying tyres. Then you saw how good he was. He'd dance his car. Nobody else could do that. He was the only guy I met who at any one moment knew totally the limit of his tyres at any corner in any conditions. And that's what it's all about, isn't it? That's what makes you faster than anyone else.

"He also used to piss me off though. I remember we were testing early one day at Snetterton, because in those days you could test at 8 o'clock in the morning, with no marshals, no health and safety. He'd come in and say, 'My left rear tyre needs two pounds more pressure. I can see it in my mirror.'

"You'd think, 'Oh bugger off, Arry...' but you'd get Petter, his Swedish mechanic, to check. And Petter would confirm, 'Yes, it's two pounds down.' You just knew the guy was different.

"The one thing that totally, totally, totally got up his nose was that he never won the World Karting Championship. He came back from the last one, when he'd been 14th, and we were at Brands for the last FF2000 race [26 September]. We didn't win that race and it was all because of the karting. He just wasn't interested, he didn't want to be there, and that was it."

"We had a really big argument about the front wing that day. I was saying one thing, he was disagreeing and his head was so much in the wrong place. The

word 'wanker' was used quite a lot, which was my fault because I'd taught it to him! Front wing settings? Normally he wasn't interested. Give him the car and he'd drive it.

"A good example of that was a race at Snetterton. Petter wasn't the most experienced mechanic in the world but he had a great heart and was a good guy. He had the set-up sheet and just before I let Senna out he came up and said, 'Dennis, I made a mistake.'

"I said, 'What do you mean, Petter? What's up, mate?'

"He said, 'Well, all the cambers that are meant to be negative have become positive and for all the toe-ins I've put toe-out.'

"We couldn't do anything about it then, so I bent down and said to Ayrton, 'Arry, we've got a bit of a cock-up

"Osterreichring was a proper circuit in those days. It had been raining and it was still a bit wet but on slicks he came round five seconds in the lead at the end of the first lap!"

going on here, mate. This has become that, and that has become this...' He just looked at me, shrugged and said 'It'll be OK', went out and stuck it on pole. It made no bloody difference to him at all.

"Out of the car he was different. He and I used to drive to all the European races together. Spend that much time with someone and you get to know them. One time, driving to Osterreichring, we were going up a mountain and he asked me to stop a minute. He got out, got his camera and took a picture of a waterfall. He got back in and said, 'I want to send that to my Mum.'

"But if you asked me, did Senna bear a grudge? Yes he did. He never forgot and he never forgave. But if you were his friend, then you were his friend and that never changed.

"Some things though, you could turn around. A classic example was at Mondello Park in Ireland. Joey Greenan was on pole and Ayrton really flew at me. He was telling me, 'He's not on pole! He's not on pole!'

"I said, 'Listen, we're in Ireland... Yes, I know he shouldn't be on pole and I don't know why they want him on pole, maybe to get more people in, I don't know, but don't worry about it, you'll be past him at the first corner.' Joey was pretty good, knew his way around the place and put in a lap with about five minutes to go, so they stopped it and put the flag out. By then Arry had worked out where the circuit went and was just about to go and pulverise Joey's time.

"He goes off on one big-time and is shouting, 'Dennis, Dennis, you've got to go up to the control tower!' So off I go, and I've got a little smile on my face because I know the game and when I get there they're all smiling too and say, 'Relax, we're at Mondello!' Yeah, yeah...

"So I get back and Arry's all, 'What did they say! What did they say!' So I said, 'Oh, they said they're really sorry, they got their timings a bit wrong.' He turned to me and said, 'Don't ever bring me here again.' As if it was my fault! And, of course, he's really angry now, so he goes and completely blows the doors off everyone and smashes the lap record to smithereens. He could almost smile about it afterwards. Almost..."

"Sudden stardom, I think, must be quite hard to cope

with for a basically shy person. And he would very quickly feel that he was being persecuted and picked on. In little ways at first. Like the Mondello thing: why wasn't I on pole? Why didn't I win the World Karting Championship? They're picking on me because I'm Brazilian. A persecution complex maybe.

"He couldn't handle anyone being quicker than him and he couldn't handle anyone having the audacity to pass him. He got very hacked off about Calvin Fish's engine when Calvin suddenly found a heap of pace.

"Arry went on and on and on. He said, 'Dennis, that engine is not legal!' Because there was no way that Calvin could beat Ayrton. That was fairly obvious. Poor Howard Mason, the scrutineer, must have had Calvin's engine apart a million times but never found anything.

"It was a little bit the same the following year in F3 with Martin Brundle – another engine thing. I went down to the last Thruxton race because Dick Bennetts [the West Surrey Racing boss] asked me to. He'd said, 'Dennis, I need you down here. Arry keeps telling me I'm a wanker and it's not going the right way, so would you come down?'

"So I went and saw Senna, went into the back of the truck and just had a chat. I said, 'What are you getting stressed about? Martin ain't gonna beat you, he's not as good as you. So just go out there and do it.' We'd spoken about me running him in F3 after the previous season. but I just said, 'No, go with Dick – he's the best.' Which he was.

"Anyway, back to that Snetterton race… he comes out of Sear onto the back straight and Calvin is on the inside of him, making up ground. He doesn't understand how because he knows he was quicker out of Sear and he's weaved to make sure Calvin can't get a tow. But anyway Calvin's there, so he pushes him onto the grass and keeps him there all the way up to the Bridge. He then has enough sense to let him back on just before they get to the Bridge, but it's close…

"We got called up to the clerk of the course, who said it was a hugely dangerous thing to do and Calvin would have been killed if he'd hit the bridge. We got fined 25 quid or something and Senna was mumbling away saying it's not fair. I said, 'Arry, you kept the poor bloke on the grass the whole length of the back straight! That's not really done...'

"He said, 'They pick on me because I'm Brazilian...'

"He had the engine thing in his head and couldn't handle anyone passing him. Some consider that a weakness but it was also what made him the driver he was. He was quite an introverted character and all the F1 bullshit didn't sit well on his shoulders. He wanted to race, he wanted to beat everyone, but anything else to do with it he found tiresome and irksome. It wasn't his thing. He'd rather be with his family or with a friend."

> "Senna was mumbling away saying it's not fair. I said, 'Arry, you kept the poor bloke on the grass the whole length of the back straight! That's not really done...'"

ARROGANT YOUNG BRAZILIAN SO-AND-SO

McLaren team chief Ron Dennis wouldn't become Senna's boss until 1988 but was aware of him much earlier than that.

"Ayrton was competitive in anything and everything," Dennis says. "The first time I met him he was a young guy, around 22, and he was in Formula Ford [1981], looking to move up into Formula 3.

"I offered to pay for his F3 championship in return for an option on his services. I can't remember the exact words but he was very clear in telling me that he'd pay for his own F3 season. He didn't want anything except a guarantee of a drive rather than an option. And this, remember, was a young guy who'd not yet really proven himself. But he had the self belief that he was going to be a tremendous F1 driver. Definitely, when we parted, I thought, arrogant young Brazilian so-and-so..."

Dennis Rushen elaborates on this.

"One thing hacked off Ayrton and he didn't forget it for a long time. Ron's Project Four team ran Ayrton's mate, Chico Serra, in F3 [in 1979] and he was doing well, but then in F2 [in 1980] Ron brought in Andrea de Cesaris with Marlboro money and suddenly Andrea was beating Chico all the time.

"Ayrton didn't feel it was equal. He felt that the Marlboro money, which Project Four and Ron wanted for F1 [they eventually took over the Marlboro-backed McLaren team], meant that Andrea was being favoured. He really got the hump about that big-time. You couldn't mention Ron Dennis's name in his presence.

"When Ron offered to pay for his F3 drive, that's why he turned him down."

← Senna tested a McLaren in 1983 but initially resented Ron Dennis's perceived treatment of Brazilian buddy Chico Serra and rejected his advances.

📷 sutton-images.com

CALVIN FISH
RECOLLECTIONS OF A RIVAL

Today, Calvin Fish is a motorsport broadcaster in the USA. In 1982 he was a quick 20-year-old superkart racer with an eye on the big time.

He started the year with a Royale, then got some money together and managed to buy a Van Diemen that put him more on the pace. He took two wins, at Oulton Park mid-season and Brands Hatch at the end of the year.

"I look back on the year very fondly, having had some great battles with The Man. He was bloody tough, that's for sure.

"It would get fraught. There was a personality change when you really put him under the gun. He dominated. I finished second to him 15 times in that season. He made me dig deeper and deeper. Deeper than you'd want to, probably, and we ended up pulling ourselves away from the pack.

Formula Ford 2000 rival Calvin Fish is now a motorsport broadcaster in the US.

sutton-images.com

"He was always so bloody good on cold tyres. He had amazing car control. As we saw in future years he just had such an amazing ability to feel the grip. When you look at his F1 career, he was just sensational when they had qualifying tyres. And it was his ability and desire to step over the line and deal with it. Most guys are going to throw it in the fence when they try to do that but he could push the limits and get it back together.

"When I look back at it now, we knew so little about how to go about our business. But Ayrton, for example, was so highly trained from karting days in terms of understanding tyres. We were on a 'spec' Dunlop tyre in FF2000 but it seemed at the time that there was a new batch of tyres every couple of weeks and they took some understanding – which Ayrton was very good at.

"In the first couple of laps of a race he was always dynamite – but, who knows, maybe he was running different pressures or something. Then he always seemed to steady himself and 'plateau', and then I'd be quick at the end. They were such short races, 15 minutes, and it was all over before you knew it. His ability to get it done in the first couple of laps was tough to cope with. In terms of fastest laps we'd be very close but he'd pull a second or so in those first couple of laps.

"He was just such a smart kid and understood the game. Dennis Rushen was running him and we had a little shop next door. We had employed Micky Galter to run the show for a year and I think our car was at times better than Ayrton's. We ran different engine builders too: I ran Neil Browns and he ran Nelsons, and I think we both had the best of the batches, and there wasn't much to choose between them. But I think Micky was the best in terms of setting up the car.

"Ayrton had such tremendous natural ability. My skills were learned but his were just natural. He was the master, had it all, and maturity beyond his years. Out of the car, his ability to deal with the politics and the management around him was light years ahead of anyone else. It's a bit like the way Tiger Woods took on the golf world. He was a man against boys in the junior formulae.

"He arrived very late for the start of that season. Rumour was he'd gone back home to retire and was pretty disenchanted with the sport. I think he felt that his domination should have given him the right to a free deal.

But Ralph Firman was a shrewd businessman and he knew that Ayrton came from money, that if he held out a bit Ayrton would probably stump up and pay. I think we all knew deep down that Ayrton had racing running through his veins and would be back. It was probably a game of poker on Ralph's behalf.

"My win at Brands Hatch was a bit of a shocker. Although I'd beaten him at Oulton when he had his tyre go, this was the first time I'd actually done it with everyone running clean and healthy.

"Rosso had pole and I got round him and realised this was my chance as Ayrton also needed to get by. He started coming back at me and set fastest lap but it was just a question of not making a mistake. I thought that if he got close enough to have a go it certainly wasn't going to be easy. But he'd taught me a few lessons about not letting a win get away and I certainly had the mindset to do the same to him!

"It was a great day. I remember slowing down at the end of the race and going through Paddock Bend. I saw a bunch of friends up in the grandstand cheering like crazy. I think everyone realised what it meant. When you're in the moment and in the middle of your career it's so important, but it's nice now to be able to sit back and reflect. Fun times.

"He was a complex character, so single-minded. I think all along he felt he was destined for greatness and would get to the top, and as long as you were along for the ride he was cool. But when you started to burst his bubble

a bit by sneaking a win or passing him or rubbing tyres with him, there was a different person, almost like a character flaw, that would come out.

"He was certainly one of the most aggressive guys I ever ran against. I recall the race at Snetterton, obviously our home track, and we had the pace on him that day. I had a run on him going down the back straightaway and he just started to block me and then stuck me in the weeds on the left. There was a big appeal and a bunch of nonsense afterwards, and it even went to a tribunal with the RAC. He had that chink in his armour and we saw it at other stages of his career, in the Prost era and times like that.

"Having said that, I met him again when he'd gone on to F1 and my career had gone in a vastly different direction. He was as nice as pie, and certainly a very kind man who did an awful lot for kids and charity. He was a great guy until you threatened him!

"He was definitely a game changer! If my 15 second places had been 15 wins, who knows what might have happened in my career?"

↑ Calvin Fish in his Van Diemen RF82 being passed by Senna at Jyllandsring – one of his 15 second places in 1982.

📷 sutton-images.com

"He was a complex character, so single-minded. I think all along he felt he was destined for greatness and would get to the top"

1983

THAT EPIC F3 YEAR

A fter his return to the UK for FF2000 in 1982 and his dominant British and European seasons, the Senna family had come to accept that motor racing was where Ayrton's future lay. He now had their full support and, after his victory in the 1982 Thruxton TV race with Dick Bennetts' West Surrey Racing, he was red-hot favourite to continue his winning ways in F3.

But, in a season that would go right down to the wire in late October, Senna and Bennetts fought an epic battle with Martin Brundle and Eddie Jordan Racing.

← Senna, leading Brundle, on his way to winning the British GP support race at Silverstone in the West Surrey Racing Ralt RT3/83

📷 sutton-images.com

6 MARCH 1983

Silverstone • Ralt RT3/83
Marlboro British F3 • 1st

With Senna the overwhelming favourite for the new F3
season, a little to the chagrin of Martin Brundle, who was
in his second year in F3, it was a surprise when Scottish
driver David Leslie turned up with the new Magnum 883
and put it on pole, almost a quarter of a second quicker
than Senna's West Surrey Racing Ralt – and Ralts took the
next 14 places on the grid.

It looked like there was finally a challenger to the Ralt
but Leslie, who had set his time in the first session of
practice, was almost a full second slower in the second
session and there were suspicions about the air restrictor
on a car that had done precious little testing. Senna,
meanwhile, said "I think there's a lot more to come"
as he qualified on the front row.

Ayrton drove round the outside of the Magnum at the
first corner, Copse, and was gone. Brundle, meanwhile,
fought his way past American Davy Jones to get through
to second place, having qualified fourth, but could do
nothing to stop Senna, who won by 6.4sec.

13 MARCH 1983

Thruxton • Ralt RT3/83
Marlboro British F3 • 1st

After testing on both Silverstone's GP circuit and
Donington since his win in the opening round, Senna took
a comfortable pole for round two at Thruxton, with 1m
13.46s to Brundle's 1m 13.99s. Nobody else was under
1m 14.50s.

The race wasn't quite so straightforward. Brundle,
despite a stomach bug, was quick in the wet that greeted
the race, Senna having his first experience of an F3 car in
such conditions.

Senna seemed to be quicker in the corners, Brundle on
the straighter sections of the Hampshire circuit. Ayrton,
mindful that Thruxton's abrasive surface was likely to dry
considerably during the 20 laps and possibly destroy the
tyres, said: "I knew that whoever could make their tyres
last longer would win."

Brundle's choice of less rear wing meant that he took
the additional point for fastest lap but had to be content
with second place: "If I'd beaten him off the line then
I don't think he'd have passed me."

20 MARCH 1983

Silverstone • Ralt RT3/83
Marlboro British F3 • 1st

Senna took a second successive pole with 1m 25.14s to Brundle's 1m 25.49s but as the start time approached, so did the rain, and everyone changed to wet tyres, as at the previous round.

Senna made another fine start but Brundle saw an opportunity at Becketts and went for it, diving through on the inside. His lead didn't last long. Senna repassed him around the outside of Stowe in a move that Brundle conceded was "quite brilliant".

When the rain became torrential after six laps the race was red-flagged and restarted. Brundle got away best this time but Senna drove round the outside of him at Becketts! "It was incredible," Brundle said. "He had two wheels on the wet grass and still kept his foot in..."

This time it was the West Surrey car running less wing and Brundle again had to be content with second place, 2sec behind. But with what we came to know of Senna's wet-weather ability, that small deficit – and a 5sec margin over third-placed Calvin Fish – was no shabby effort.

27 MARCH 1983

Donington • Ralt RT3/83
Marlboro British F3 • 1st

Just turned 23 and in his third successive year in the UK, Senna was now fully familiar with the British racing scene and knew, as it was still only March, that more rain was likely. Qualifying was once again held on a wet but drying track and Brundle (1m 18.19s) again did well to push Senna (1m 18.06s) hard for pole.

"It was like driving on oil out there," Senna said. Locals would always tell you that the surface could be treacherous at Donington, especially early in the day, due to kerosene from aircraft using adjacent East Midlands airport, and it was even worse in the wet. Ten years on, Senna would make a mockery of his F1 rivals at the same track in even worse conditions...

Ayrton took the lead on the first lap and opened out a 2sec margin. Brundle managed to peg the gap until affected by fourth and fifth gears jumping out, forcing him to hold the lever in. There was 5.5sec between them at the flag as they finished 1–2 for the fourth consecutive race.

⬇ Senna's rivals had a sense of humour. The answer to his dominance – the arrow directs Ayrton onto Silverstone's GP track while everyone else does the Club circuit...

📷 sutton-images.com

4 APRIL 1983

Thruxton • Ralt RT3/83
Marlboro British F3 • 1st

Ayrton was suffering a bout of flu and 'the guru', West Surrey Racing's Dick Bennetts, almost forbid his man to get into the cockpit, but Ayrton was having none of it. He wasn't so ill that he couldn't take another pole (1m 13.07s) while Davy Jones pipped Brundle (1m 13.30s) to the remaining front-row spot.

Senna missed his shift from first to second off the grid, allowing Jones to lead briefly before Senna came by. The American also had to give best to Brundle, who took fastest lap in his chase of Senna that resulted in the Eddie Jordan Racing Ralt being just over 1sec adrift at the chequered flag. "Why doesn't he ever make a serious mistake?" Brundle queried, after five races and five second places.

24 APRIL 1983

Silverstone • Ralt RT3/83
Marlboro British F3 • 1st

Senna equalled a record of Nelson Piquet's when he won again at Silverstone after a three-week break in the season. Counting back to the non-championship Thruxton TV race of the previous season, it was his seventh back-to-back F3 win – something Piquet had achieved in 1978.

Senna (53.30s) took pole ahead of Brundle (53.51s) once again. This time it was Martin who muffed his change from first to second allowing Senna to escape to a comfortable 5sec win over Davy Jones, with Brundle third. Ayrton now had a 20-point advantage in the championship table.

2 MAY 1983

Thruxton • Ralt RT3/83
Marlboro British F3 • 1st

Martin Brundle arrived at Thruxton having won the Donington 500kms European Touring Car round the previous day, sharing a Jaguar XJS with John Fitzpatrick and Enzo Calderari. But it still didn't help him halt Senna's run of F3 pole positions, Ayrton lapping Thruxton in 1m 13.55s to Martin's 1m 13.89s.

Senna converted his pole and led from the start but Brundle got a better run out of Thruxton's 'complex' and towed up alongside the West Surrey car on the approach to the chicane. Senna had the line, though, and gradually increased his lead to win by almost 3.5sec.

8 MAY 1983

Brands Hatch • Ralt RT3/83
Marlboro British F3 • 1st

Senna was in scintillating form and took pole by almost three tenths – around the Brands Hatch club circuit! Brundle was his nearest challenger once again.

In wet conditions with the cars on grooved rubber, away they went as one. Brundle commented, wryly, "I thought about trying to go round his outside at Paddock, but decided that was silly..."

Senna completed the 20-lap race 2.5sec ahead of Brundle, with nobody else within 10sec. Ayrton considered this his best win yet.

30 MAY 1983

Silverstone • Ralt RT3/83
Marlboro British F3 • 1st

Fresh from some time at home in Brazil, Senna set a fabulous 53.05s pole, his eighth in succession, and some half a second beneath his own lap record. David Leslie's Magnum was his closest challenger this time as Brundle suffered handling problems.

Leslie succumbed to clutch trouble and it was left to an oversteering Brundle to take second place, a massive 11sec adrift of Senna's West Surrey Racing car.

12 JUNE 1983

Silverstone • Ralt RT3/83 • Marlboro British F3
& European F3 • Retired, 7 laps, accident

Held on the grand prix circuit, this race was a combined round of the British and European F3 series, and boasted 44 entries.

The British series was run on control Avon tyres, while the Europeans used Yokohama and Michelin tyres. After testing a set of the 'Yokos' Senna realised that there was no hope of winning outright on Avons. Such was his lead in the British series that he elected to go for the outright victory.

Senna's speed in the wet first session was astonishing, the West Surrey Racing car lapping in 1m 32.27s. His closest challenger was reigning British F3 champion Tommy Byrne, now contesting the European series, with a lap in 1m 34.00s, while Davy Jones recorded 1m 34.49s and Brundle 1m 34.76s.

The second session of practice, however, was dry

← Senna's record-breaking sequence of nine F3 wins came to an end on 12 June at the European round at Silverstone.

📷 sutton-images.com

and Senna looked like taking his customary pole with a lap in 1m 24.08s. But, 15 minutes from the end, Brundle changed his mind about concentrating on British points, figuring that he was a comfortable second in the series anyway and unlikely to be able to do anything about Senna. He therefore discarded his Avons and bolted on a set of Yokohamas. With his Eddie Jordan Racing Ralt handling perfectly, he went round in 1m 23.99s to knock Senna off pole by nine hundredths.

Ayrton said that his car hadn't been perfect, with off-track moments at Stowe and Club illustrating the point. Considering that someone had actually gone quicker than him, though, he was uncharacteristically magnanimous.

"I'm pleased for Martin," he said, "because he's a very, very good driver and also because it shows how good the British series is because all the European series are well behind us." He was right, too. The quickest of them, Dane John Nielsen, was well over a second slower than Brundle.

Brundle held off Senna into the first corner, Copse, and led across the line at the end of the opening lap, with Senna's future Lotus team-mate Johnny Dumfries chasing the West Surrey Racing Ralt.

Senna had gone for a harder tyre on the left front in the interests of durability, against the advice of the Yokohama technicians, and it was soon obvious that he had a handling imbalance. With Brundle pulling out clear air, Senna had his hands full with Dumfries, who had qualified more than half a second slower.

When Dumfries pulled alongside on the Hangar Straight approaching Stowe at 150mph plus, Senna unceremoniously put him on the grass. Dumfries had the kind of moment that FF1600 rival Rick Morris would have been able to identify with two years earlier. And, as Senna had discovered with Morris, if you're going to do that to someone, it's probably best that you don't leave them on the circuit. Dumfries somehow managed to collect up an almighty tank-slapper and, very angry, was homing in on Ayrton's gearbox once again three laps later.

Senna, perhaps a bit flustered for once, dropped it at Club and spun onto the infield, resuming ninth behind a battling trio of Europeans – Carlos Abella, John Nielsen and Kris Nissen.

During the next couple of laps Senna passed both Danes but then spun backwards into the catch-fencing at Woodcote, to unsettlingly thunderous cheers from a very un-British crowd. Senna's 10-race winning streak, dating back to the 1982 Thruxton TV race, was at an end.

In a great day for Eddie Jordan, Tommy Byrne finished second to Brundle while Canadian Allen Berg, also running out of the Jordan stable, took the Avon-shod Marlboro British F3 series victory.

19 JUNE 1983

Cadwell Park • Ralt RT3/83 • Marlboro British F3
Did not start, qualifying accident

Just nine cars arrived for F3's single visit to the fabulous circuit in the Lincolnshire wolds. Despite the lap distance being just 2.25 miles, the twists and undulations have led to the track being dubbed the mini-Nürburgring.

The field was soon reduced to just eight. Senna and Brundle had been battling for pole position all the way through the first session and their nearest challenger, Calvin Fish, was over a second adrift. Senna was just a hundredth quicker when, overdoing it out of the right-hander at the bottom of The Mountain, he kept his boot in and ran straight into a marshals' post just over the brow.

"Looking at his car," recalls Brundle, "I could never understand how he didn't break his leg. Those cars were only pop rivets and aluminium."

Senna might have been all right but his banana-shaped Ralt most certainly wasn't. Ayrton was forced to sit out the race as Brundle took his second straight win in a week. In the championship, though, there was no need to panic. The Silverstone 'off' hadn't affected the British series and this was Ayrton's first non-score in the series, which he led with 88 points to Brundle's 64.

3 JULY 1983

Snetterton • Ralt RT3/83
Marlboro British F3 • Retired, 23 laps, accident

There was more trouble in store for Senna at Snetterton as he found himself mysteriously off the pace. He couldn't get within a second of a stunning 60.8s lap in testing and for the first time that season he failed to qualify on the front row.

Johnny Dumfries was quickest in the opening practice session on 1m 1.63s before a big shunt at the track's first corner, Riches, left the way clear for Brundle to take pole in the second session with 1m 1.59s. Davy Jones managed 1m 1.80s with Ayrton 0.01sec slower. Calvin Fish, Senna's old FF2000 foe, was fifth on 1m 1.85s.

The vacant grid slot for Dumfries worked in Senna's favour and the familiar white Ralt tucked in behind Brundle. Martin was able to open up a small margin before Senna began to edge closer as the race entered its closing stages, with Jones and Fish not far behind.

Out of the right-handed Sear onto the back straight on the penultimate lap, Senna claimed that Brundle

SENNA TESTS FOR WILLIAMS

T hree days after winning the British GP support race, Senna tested an F1 car for the first time: a Williams FW08 at Donington, overseen by Frank himself.

The team was stunned by Senna's immediate speed and consistency despite not being a good fit for the shorter, broader Keke Rosberg's cockpit. Senna only did just over 20 laps before stopping and reporting that the engine was losing its edge and he didn't want it to blow. By then he'd set the fastest ever Williams time around Donington, 60.1s, and lapped almost 1.5sec quicker than Jonathan Palmer, the 1981 British F3 champion who had tested a few weeks earlier and was on his way to winning the 1983 European F2 crown. Had Frank jettisoned Jacques Laffite in favour of Senna, F1 history would have been considerably different...

made a mistake and, immediately, Ayrton tried to come alongside on the left to get the inside line for the entry to the following Esses. Brundle (see 'Recollections of a rival', page 86) saw it differently, stating that he merely took the left-hand line without leaving room for Senna and left Ayrton to sort himself out, much as Ayrton himself had done to Calvin Fish the previous season in FF2000, also sparking a post-race enquiry.

Senna, as usual, kept his boot in and as the entry to the Esses loomed, the West Surrey Racing Ralt's right front wheel made contact with Brundle's left rear. Senna's car was launched into the air and ended its race in the tyre barrier, while Brundle continued to secure his hat-trick of F3 wins, ahead of Jones and Fish. A 90-minute post-race gathering in the stewards' room saw the collision declared a racing incident.

16 JULY 1983

Silverstone • Ralt RT3/83
Marlboro British F3 • 1st

Senna was determined to get his season back on track in the British GP support race but it was soon evident that he was going to have a fight on his hands as he claimed pole by just 0.04sec from Brundle.

Senna made the better start and led the opening lap. The pair were in a race of their own, averaging a second a lap quicker than third-placed Fish. Senna's decisiveness in traffic gave him the win in the season's most important encounter, though he also had better fortune in that traffic as Brundle came across Finnish backmarker Jorma Airaksinen, who had qualified six seconds off the pace, at an inopportune moment.

24 JULY 1983

Donington • Ralt RT3/83
Marlboro British F3 • 2nd

A week later, Brundle gained his revenge and, for the first time, beat Senna in a race that Ayrton finished.

It may or may not have been significant that Brundle's car now had an experimental twin-overhead-camshaft Toyota engine that was believed to give a marginal advantage over the standard unit. Used for the first time by Tommy Byrne at the Silverstone European round, this engine was fitted to Brundle's car after the British GP support race. It annoyed Senna that Eddie Jordan had agreed an exclusive engine-build deal with the Pedrazzani brothers for the British F3 series.

Although Ayrton took pole with 1m 08.42s to Martin's 1m 08.66s, Brundle made the better start but he came under severe pressure from Senna throughout. In the end Martin managed to hold off Ayrton by less than half a second after 30 laps, although Senna claimed the extra point for fastest lap.

"I've had enough of playing second fiddle," said a delighted Brundle, "and I think I showed today that I'm every bit as good as he is." Whether Martin truly believed it or not, that line was bound to register with Senna. The engine deal wasn't the only thing Jordan had done to destabilise the championship favourite (see 'Persecution complex?', page 74), and with some success!

But with 14 of the 20 championship rounds gone, Senna led the series by a still-comfortable 106 points to Brundle's 88.

6 AUGUST 1983

Oulton Park • Ralt RT3/83
Marlboro British F3 • Retired, 28 laps, accident

In the first of two visits to the fine Cheshire circuit in just five weeks, Senna got off to a bad start when he had a big testing shunt at the track two days before the race. A rear stub axle failure put his Ralt heavily into the barrier at the fast double-apex Druids corner, and a second chassis was destroyed in the space of seven weeks. Ayrton was fortunate to escape with a sore hand.

Dick Bennetts and the West Surrey Racing crew did a deal with fellow driver Richard Trott to hire his similar chassis and fitted the engine and rear end of Senna's car to it during the intervening day. Senna put this hybrid car on the grid but he was 0.34sec behind Brundle and said: "It was very difficult to drive. Very dangerous. I couldn't drive it on the limit."

But he tried to do precisely that in the race, after Brundle had made the better start and led for the first 27 of 35 laps. Martin, however, had some small brake concerns after sitting on the grid with his foot on the pedal. As he started the warm-up lap the fronts had locked on and it took most of the lap to free them off, with the result that they overheated.

Over a lap Brundle could keep Senna at bay but Ayrton noticed that he was better on the brakes at Foster's corner. Senna claimed the point for fastest lap as he closed in and, on lap 29, made his move.

"I was right up his gearbox into Cascades," Senna explained, "and going much quicker than him. I just braked later and went for the inside. I'm sure he didn't see me."

The two cars came to rest with Senna's car on top of Brundle's, Martin fortunate to escape unharmed. Most felt that Foster's wasn't a realistic overtaking place for evenly matched cars. Stewards endorsed Senna's licence and fined him £200.

29 AUGUST 1983

Silverstone • Ralt RT3/83
Marlboro British F3 • 1st

It was remarkable that Brundle was even on the grid for this race. On 13 August, at the Austrian GP, Martin won an F3 support race that West Surrey Racing and Senna didn't enter.

On the return journey to the UK, the Eddie Jordan Racing transporter went off the road and plunged 200ft down a ravine. Crew members thrown through the windscreen survived but Brundle's 27-year-old chief mechanic, Rob Bowden, who was asleep in the back of the truck, lost his life. Jordan's three chassis, engines and spares were all lost. Thankfully, however, Eddie Jordan Racing was up and running again two weeks later, with much owed to the support of lifelong fan Tim Clowes, the motorsport insurance specialist, and Ron Tauranac at Ralt.

On the Club circuit, Senna took pole with 53.18s to Brundle's 53.24s. In the race he was always just out of Martin's reach as he claimed his 11th win in 16 races and extended his championship advantage to 116 points versus 94, with four rounds remaining.

In the scrutineering bay, Brundle almost lost second place when one sidepod was found to be 1mm lower than the regulation 4cm. Eddie Jordan Racing claimed that the transgression was down to someone falling back onto the car during the champagne celebrations and a handy witness was duly found. In truth, nobody had the stomach for disqualifying the team after the tragedy it had just come through. As far as Senna was concerned, though, rules were rules and the verdict, coming on the back of his fine at Oulton, reinforced his feeling that he was taking on more than just Brundle.

11 SEPTEMBER 1983

Oulton Park • Ralt RT3/83
Marlboro British F3 • Retired, 7 laps, accident

Qualifying was another nip-and-tuck affair with Senna shading it on 57.24s to Brundle's 57.30s. But it was Martin who got away from the lights best and led throughout the 20 laps to finish 20sec clear of Calvin Fish.

← At Oulton Park on 6 August, Senna, in a car hired from Richard Trott after a testing shunt, was fined for this optimistic attempt to go inside Brundle at Foster's.
📷 sutton-images.com

Senna spent the first seven laps shadowing Brundle's car before trying an ambitious move round the outside of Druids, losing grip and slamming heavily into the barrier. Senna, by then in talks with several F1 teams about 1984, could have clinched the title but his non-score meant a decent championship gain for Brundle, whose slim hopes of the title were reignited.

18 SEPTEMBER 1983

Thruxton • Ralt RT3/83
Marlboro British F3 • Retired, 2 laps, engine

A maximum 10 points to Brundle for the win and fastest lap – and another non-score for Senna!

With a new chassis after his Oulton shunt, Senna took pole 0.05sec quicker than Brundle but he wasn't convinced about his Ralt's handling. Brundle made the better start but locked up at the 'Complex' and Senna scrabbled by. As Brundle tried to tow back past on the run into the chicane, Senna blocked, but compromised his exit, and Martin was able to take full advantage and claim back the lead.

Next time round it was all over for Ayrton as he detonated an engine with what was later discovered to be sub-standard fuel. It was the first time in 65 F3 races contested by West Surrey Racing that its car had retired with a mechanical problem.

Ayrton's championship lead was now down to just three points but with two rounds to go and only 17 of the 20 rounds to count, Brundle would have to drop a score.

2 OCTOBER 1983

Silverstone • Ralt RT3/83
Marlboro British F3 • 2nd

At this penultimate round Senna lost his championship lead for the first time all season! Eddie Jordan (see 'Persecution complex?', page 74) says that one of the 'mind games' his team used to play was always to have its cars first in the queue to get out onto the track. Normally, it was of no significance, but this time it was...

Drizzle was falling as the first qualifying session got underway, and it took time for cars to get onto the circuit as they were forced to stop for a scrutineer to check the 4cm sidepod clearance with his 'hockey stick'. Senna was quite a long way back in the queue and by the time he was on the circuit and up to speed, the two Eddie Jordan Racing cars of Martin Brundle and Allen Berg, along with American Davy Jones, had all got laps in before the rain intensified.

Senna's first flying lap on the GP circuit was a second

and a half down on Jones and then Ayrton lost it at Abbey trying to go quicker, damaging an upright and wishbone. The second session was completely wet, meaning no chance to improve, so Senna would start fourth.

Jones didn't get away well and Brundle leapt into the lead, with Senna following him through. On quick circuits such as Silverstone's GP track it was hard for F3 cars of the time to follow each other closely without losing aerodynamic performance and, with Brundle making no mistakes, Senna had to accept second place. Crucially, Brundle also claimed the additional point for fastest lap by 0.03sec, giving him 123 points to Senna's 122 with just the final round at Thruxton remaining.

23 OCTOBER 1983

Thruxton • Ralt RT3/83
Marlboro British F3 • 1st

Brundle came to the series finale with 'No 1' on his car after taking the points lead at the penultimate round. For this championship decider, however, the points situation was complicated. Only 17 of the 20 rounds counted and so if Martin repeated his Silverstone success and Ayrton was second, he would have to drop four points for a third place and that would put him level with Senna on points, but with Senna champion due to his greater number of wins. In order to win the title by one point, therefore, Brundle had to win the race and claim the additional point for fastest lap.

For some time, Van Diemen's Ralph Firman had been telling Senna that there was no way he should be losing races to Brundle and that he had an engine deficit, allowing the Eddie Jordan car to run more rear wing. Senna, therefore, got in his road car, drove down to the engine-building Pedrazzani brothers in Novaro, Italy, and demanded the same development-specification Novamotor engine that Brundle used. And he got his way.

In the meantime, Ron Tauranac at Ralt was producing development parts for 1984, as Brundle recalls: "There were some sidepods that generated less drag, which is pretty handy at Thruxton, and there was pushrod suspension, the sort of thing you need to test for two or three days. Senna got the sidepods and I got the suspension – I was pretty miffed about that. I'm not even sure now whether or not we ran the suspension in the end, but I think we tried it. I don't know how it was decided who got what, but I know which I'd rather have had if I'd been part of the decision-making process. But it was news to me until I got to Thruxton."

Senna and Bennetts had been thinking about the all-important opening laps and, to derive maximum power, they planned to tape up the radiators to get the oil up to

temperature immediately, rather than after the usual five or six laps. Obviously, though, it was crucial that Senna could reach out and remove the tape once the oil was up to temperature in order not to cook the engine. During testing Senna had practised loosening his belts and doing this.

The anticipated battle was somewhat diluted when Brundle blew his engine and was forced to fit an inferior one (see 'Recollections of a rival', page 87). In qualifying, with his engine pinking, Brundle could do no better than third, on 1m 13.88s, with Senna taking pole on 1m 13.36s and Davy Jones second on 1m 13.63s.

Senna made no mistake at the start, opened up a gap, reached out to take off his tape and, loose in the cockpit before he retightened his belts, sorted out a wiggle under braking for the chicane, and was gone.

"I was following him when he took the tape off," Brundle says. "He had to loosen his seat belt and reach out to his sidepod. I remember watching him do that going up to the chicane, and the car wiggling. I was third and I saw him moving around on the straight and thought, 'What's going on?'. He was leaning out, taking the tape off at full bore. Incredible. That was a new one on me."

Senna won the 15-lap race by 5.5sec from Jones, with a struggling Brundle a disappointed third, a further 3sec behind. A delighted Senna was finally champion and, on the podium, hailed his rival "the best British driver since Jim Clark". Which was a revealing insight into Ayrton's feelings about his own level. Sort of, blimey, if he can get that close to me, then he must be...

← Senna won Macau in a Marlboro-backed Ralt for Teddy Yip and Theodore Racing.
📷 sutton-images.com

20 NOVEMBER 1983

Macau • Ralt RT3/83 • Macau GP • 1st

Senna had his first experience of a street circuit in the Portuguese colony of Macau, as Dick Bennetts ran the West Surrey Racing Ralt in Marlboro colours under the Theodore Racing banner for local entrepreneur Teddy Yip. Eddie Jordan Racing also ran two Marlboro-Theodore cars for Brundle and Colombian Roberto Guerrero.

Despite heavy jetlag, Senna comfortably won both 15-lap heats of this showpiece event by an average of 7sec from Guerrero, with Gerhard Berger a similar distance further behind.

Brundle had completed a Marlboro-Theodore 1–2–3 on the grid but was clobbered by Pierluigi Martini as he tried to take the lead on the first lap of the opening heat and dropped to 18th. Brundle turned in a fine recovery drive but Senna, groggy or not, was totally imperious out front. Formula 1 beckoned for Ayrton but it wouldn't be with Bernie Ecclestone's Brabham, as was expected the week after Senna won at Macau.

PERSECUTION COMPLEX?

Ayrton Senna, many times, believed that the world was against him. Terry Fullerton referred to it, and so did Rick Morris, Dennis Rushen and Martin Brundle. Later, Alain Prost would say the same.

Eddie Jordan, recalling that epic F3 season in his autobiography, *An Independent Man*, admits that after his team's first mid-season victory in the European round at Silverstone, they did everything they could to get inside Ayrton's head.

"There was a lot of horseplay over the legality of the rear wings teams were using and how these wings could be made to flex in order to improve performance," Jordan says. "Each team was watching the others like hawks. We tried to have Ayrton's car excluded from a couple of races on dubious technicalities and we would feed non-attributable stories to the motorsport media about naughty things we were allegedly doing to our car, knowing that Ayrton devoured every written word because he had absolutely nothing else to do with his life at that time.

"We would employ the simplest of moves to upset him. Each car had to undergo scrutineering at the start of a race weekend. The trick was to be first in the queue in order to avoid wasting time. I knew Ayrton had a thing about that, so I drilled it into my guys that it was essential our cars were first in the queue – even if it meant staying up all night. In fact we used to arrive early, at about 6.30am. This would really irritate Ayrton and mess with his head.

First in the queue for scrutineering would do it to him let alone being first cars onto the track [which mattered at Silverstone on 2 October].

"We discovered that he hated coming to Silverstone because he knew it was Jordan's 'home' circuit and he thought we had some sort of advantage there. It was true that we knew everyone very well and got on famously with the scrutineers but, despite that, the officials were 100 per cent professional and would throw us out as quick as look at us if they thought we were doing something wrong [strictly speaking, when Brundle won at Silverstone on 29 August, they didn't, although there were the very best of extenuating circumstances]. Ayrton couldn't quite believe that.

"I would turn the screw by hiring the circuit exclusively for testing and charging the other F3 teams if they wanted to join in. However, I wasn't prepared for the number of people who didn't pay. It became such a serious problem that it jeopardised the entire running of F3 testing.

"So I made a deal with Silverstone Sid. I said, 'Sid, I'm gonna give you a little drink. Here's how it works. Everyone has to have a pass. You put one of your guys at the end of the pitlane with a flag. If a car turns up and it hasn't got a pass, the driver gets turned away. Simple.'

"It was fun to watch a car reach the end of the pitlane only for the driver to be told, 'Sorry, park up, your team hasn't paid, you haven't signed the form, therefore you're not insured. You'll have to forget about running today.'

"This really got under Senna's skin. Normally a driver wouldn't care about such details but Ayrton got involved in everything. And a driver would usually react angrily when he reached the end of the pitlane only to be prevented from going about his business. The sound of other cars roaring into Copse Corner would heighten the frustration enormously. You can imagine the explosion if he discovered that a rival, particularly Jordan, was preventing him from doing the one thing in his life that mattered most – driving a racing car!

"We discovered that he hated coming to Silverstone because he knew it was Jordan's 'home' circuit and he thought we had some sort of advantage there"

↑ Eddie Jordan with
Martin Brundle:
no wonder Ayrton
feared a conspiracy.

📷 sutton-images.com

"Poor Ayrton was easy to play mind games with: you could see it in his face. We would put the word around that we had people watching him and it would get back to him. Of course, we were doing no such thing, but if a person happened to be standing in all innocence by his garage door, Ayrton would start getting twitchy. You could see it happening.

"Now that was extending to his driving. We realised Senna was suspect under pressure, so Martin pushed him like crazy, and it worked."

Jordan also admits to pulling a tremendous flanker to get the development Novamotor engine deal.

"I focused on the fact that John Brundle [Martin's father] was a Toyota main dealer in Norfolk," Jordan explains. "I approached Toyota in Japan. They said they were not making engines for F3 but suggested that I speak to the Pedrazzani brothers at Novamotor in Italy. I flew to Turin and did a deal that would quickly irritate Senna.

"Ayrton was driving for Dick Bennetts and their Novamotor engines were built in England. Almost from the start Senna became upset because he always claimed that we had a better engine. Just to rub salt in, part of my engine deal with Novamotor was that they couldn't build an engine for anyone

else in England. I argued that Martin was a Toyota dealer and the name needed protecting. I was being a chancer and it took a lot of persuading. The net result was an exclusive deal between Novamotor [Italy] and Jordan for the British championship.

"This was typical of the mind games that could be played in order to manipulate your position. You did it in the knowledge that the opposition would do everything to screw you. I loved it!"

Senna didn't. Of that there is little doubt. At the time, Simon Arron was a young journalist with *Motoring News*. In the midst of a problematic period for Ayrton, they spoke at Oulton Park in an interview that was never published. What Senna had to say speaks volumes of his mindset:

"Two days before the first Oulton round [6 August] we were testing here, the car was quite good, everything was going very well and then suddenly at Druids, the rear stub axle broke. It's fifth gear there and I crashed heavily. I thought for a while that it would be a big one, nose first, but just before I hit, it went to a 45 per cent angle. But I still hurt my right hand and the car was finished.

"Dick [Bennetts] decided to hire Richard Trott's car and through Friday they put it together and worked hard halfway through the night. We went straight into early-morning practice and the car wasn't handling well at all but we managed to be second. Martin got the lead at the start and I started pushing and pushing all race. We had 35 laps and with seven or eight to go I was quite close to him through Cascades and I tried to overtake him. Unfortunately things went wrong, he didn't see me and we both touched and went off.

"Afterwards I wasn't even thinking anything about the accident because it was a racing incident but somehow the stewards decided it wasn't and I was very disappointed because what they did to me that day was very unfair. I felt, again, that I was in England racing against Britain.

"We'd also had a big moment at Snetterton and it was very clear the way that they got together with the marshals and nothing was done there.

"I even talked to Dick and said that we have to take a lot of care and just do things differently. We couldn't afford to be close to him any more because anything that could happen would be our fault and they would get us, maybe with disqualification or taking points away. I must say I felt that things had changed quite a lot and if we were not very careful they would do everything to take away our championship.

"But after that we had a two-week break and I was looking around at a few F1 contacts. That takes a lot of attention from the F3 programme because next year is very important to me and believing that it's possible to be in F1, I'm putting in a great effort to get into a good team, and it's not easy, at all. We have to wait for others to play around and that disturbs my concentration on F3 quite a lot. I really found that.

"After that we went to Silverstone to the Club track, we were on pole, I did a good start and we won the race. It wasn't easy at all, but not as hard as I was expecting. And there again, I will make another point. After official practice the clerk of the course called me, Dick was with me, and he was complaining that I had stopped the car in the pitlane on the other

side of the yellow line, which everybody does. That was for 30 seconds, not more than that, and just to make a practice start at the end of the session. That wasn't fair because most of the drivers did that. Again I said to Dick, 'We have to be careful, they are pushing hard!'

"They are just pushing, pushing, pushing to try to disturb you. And try to take some advantage from that when it gets to the critical moment, you see, because the pressure just builds up, builds up, builds up. Then in the race we got the lead, it was never close and they couldn't do anything really.

"Mind you, even after that Martin's car was below 4cm, that was very clear, they did several measurements in different spots and both sides were down, not only one side. Dick was there watching all the time and they lifted the car up so much from the ground, which is not allowed. The scrutineers had turned down the car and disqualified it and Eddie put in an appeal in a very smooth way and the stewards, after a very long meeting, somehow decided that the car was legal. How, I don't know, honestly. It is a simple measurement. There was nothing to be discussed. It is either in or out. And it was out.

"Apparently Eddie had said that when I sprayed the champagne one of the photographers fell over on Martin's car, and he put in a witness who was from King's Lynn [Brundle is from Norfolk]. The coincidence was that he was a journalist who was doing a piece on Martin. He was the witness who had fallen onto the car when I sprayed the champagne. They were very wrong because when I got the champagne it was already opened and I sprayed it behind me, not to the front or the side, where the cars were. So nothing happened. But they are just playing around. They are not doing a serious job. They are joking. That's not so good, I must say.

"If things were done fair and square he should be out. Not losing 18 points as the rules would say, three times what you have scored. I don't think that's right, but they should lose the points from that day. And we'd have the championship already in hand. That's not the way to win the championship but there are rules and you must follow them. One of the stewards said to Dick that the car wasn't that far out. But, if it's bit low, it's low...

"In Formula 1 if the ballast is 1kg below, it's out, like happened to McLaren last year. And if your airbox is half a millimetre bigger, you are out, otherwise why have rules? But that was just to save his six points; they couldn't do anything about me. I'm only telling you all these things because after Snetterton I thought maybe it was a one-off, it can happen, but to come here and have them do wrong, I thought, that's not coincidence – there's something going on. Then Silverstone again...

"It was a racing incident but somehow the stewards decided it wasn't… what they did to me that day was very unfair. I felt, again, that I was in England racing against Britain"

It's just not fair. I'm just pointing that out. Not for you to write everything I am saying, but just to point out the feeling that I have. But even like that we are leading the championship and maybe we clinch it today. And if not, it doesn't matter. Next race."

Senna then moved on to talking about his F1 hopes for 1984.

"I'll just keep going with my Formula 1 contacts. I thought I would have something already sorted out last week or two weeks ago but things didn't quite work out as I planned and things are still quite open.

"What can I say? The contacts with F1 teams have increased during the last month but again not one of them has reached a decision and we are still waiting a few days perhaps to have something definitely done. It's already later than I expected so it can happen any time, maybe even tomorrow, maybe the end of the week, but any day now. It's very close. But I will try to keep as many doors open as I can until it is done."

In fact, Senna's 1984 F1 deal with Toleman wasn't done for some time. There is little doubt that in his mind, Senna saw himself at Brabham in 1984. Nelson Piquet was on his way to his second World Championship with Bernie Ecclestone's team and in his mind Senna would have been sure that he could

handle Nelson. Ecclestone wanted him too, but Piquet most certainly didn't, and brought pressure to bear on Parmalat, the sponsor.

Before Simon Arron's interview concluded, though, Senna wanted to make sure that his interviewer had fully grasped the depth of his feeling about F3.

"Martin is a very good driver," he said. Which is revealing in itself. It was Martin, note, not Brundle. Later, whenever Senna had an issue with a driver, it was always Piquet, Prost or Schumacher, not Nelson, Alain or Michael.

"He tries very hard," Ayrton went on, "and is very concentrated and consistent. He has a very good car, like I have, and he behaves well. But the way that people around him are dealing with us is just a joke. And that doesn't make me very happy at all. Unfortunately he is the one involved with that, but nothing against him, as I say, nothing personal at all. He is just the opposition.

"What I'm dead against is the organisation and the stewards on those three occasions – Snetterton, Oulton and Silverstone. By coincidence one of those stewards was the same and I know, don't ask me how, that he was the one pushing hard to give me the problem on every occasion. Fortunately, he's not here today."

DICK BENNETTS
ON SENNA

I was first told about Senna by Ralph Firman and Dennis Rushen. Dennis introduced me in 1982 because EJ [Eddie Jordan] was trying to get hold of him and offering the world, as he does. Eddie had given him a test, which I didn't know about then, and we gave him a run at the end of the season.

"Ayrton was quick straight out of the box in Quique Mansilla's car at a half-day Snetterton test. Because he was so happy, we did the non-championship Thruxton TV race and he just blitzed everyone.

"I said to him, 'Surely Jordan will offer you a better deal for '83 than I can?'

"He said, 'No, no, I want to come to you because of how you operate. Let me know the budget. That car is fantastic compared to the Jordan one.'

"What impressed him was that Mansilla had finished second in the F3 championship with us that year. 'He's a rock ape!' Ayrton said, having driven against him in FF1600. 'If he's second in the championship, I want to run with you!'

"I said, 'Give the bloke a chance! He ran Tommy Byrne close.'

"The thing was, we'd struggled with Quique at first because he didn't detect understeer. He kept cranking lock on until the front bit, then complained about oversteer! There I was trying to dial out oversteer, getting nowhere. So I went out and watched him on the track... 'You've got bloody understeer, not oversteer!' He said, 'Oh, have I?'

"So we changed springs, ride heights, wing settings, everything.

"He said, 'That's much better', and we were on the right track. The Falklands War didn't help him either. Poor bloke...

"Anyway, Ayrton shook hands and said he was off to Brazil.

"I said, 'Woah… We need to sit down and work out a contract.'

"He said, 'No, no. I've agreed the money. Trust me.'

"That's not how I worked. I liked a signed contract and four staged payments, in advance. His first one was cash, US dollars in London. Go and meet this man on the corner of a street, at 2pm, and he'll have a newspaper under his arm... It was coming from one of the sponsors or something.

"I said, 'Look, we've got to do it by cheque or bank transfer, Ayrton.' But eventually I said, 'OK, if it helps you.' I drove there in my Cortina estate, arrived 10 minutes early, parked, stood on the street corner, a bloke came up and said, 'Are you Dick?', and thrust me a thick packet containing $25,000 in cash. 'What do I do with this?' I thought. I got back in the car, locked all the doors, and drove away looking in the mirror...

"Ayrton himself came back over quite late and I was panicking that we wouldn't have time to sort the new car. He came round, had a seat fitting and said, 'Where's the car I drove in the TV race?'

"I said, 'That was an '82 car and we're selling it. We have a new car every year.'

"He said, 'But that was a good car, I liked it.'

"I said, 'Well, I wish you'd said, because I'd have saved myself a whole lot of money!'

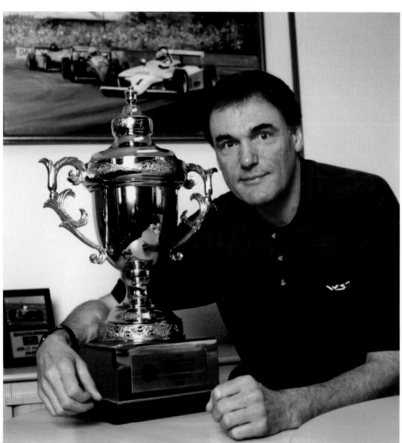

Dick Bennetts – that 1983 F3 season will always be special to him.

sutton-images.com

"We were in the groove with the new car after the first week and he went and won the first nine races. I knew the bubble had to burst some time and it was when we opted for the 'open' round at Silverstone and went to the Yokohama tyres.

"I did know that Tommy Byrne had used Yokos with EJ in Europe, so not only did they know the characteristics of the tyres but they also knew the Yoko people. So obviously Martin's car was set up a bit better than ours. Ayrton was adamant he picked up a puncture that day at Club Corner and when he arrived at Woodcote and turned right, it didn't grip and spun into the fence.

"Then, at Cadwell, he was quickest in qualifying when he stopped. I was timing him, Martin and Davy Jones, and told him he was P1, but only by a tenth. He said he could go much quicker but had a bit of understeer. There were only four minutes to go so I changed the front wing half a degree and told him to get going.

"Someone timing halfway around the lap said he was way quicker but he didn't make it round. He dropped a wheel off at The Mountain, kept his foot buried and hammered straight into a concrete marshals' post. He was lucky. The car was like a banana. His girlfriend said, 'Can't you fix it?' I don't think she understood concrete and aluminium...

"It was 9.30am Sunday morning and I was back in the King's Head pub in Shepperton at 2 o'clock for a Sunday roast. My mates said, 'Thought you were racing today...' 'Yeah,' I said, 'So did I...'

"This was the point of the season where the momentum shifted towards Martin and we didn't know why. We didn't know about Jordan's upgraded engine and later, when we did, EJ said it was hardly any improvement. He was having his engines rebuilt by Novamotor in Italy and I'd done a deal with John Nicholson to rebuild ours in the UK to save a bit of money. They were reliable but we had a head gasket

↑ **Bennetts: "I didn't make any money that year because I didn't have damage insurance. He was so good that I'd figured he wouldn't crash..."**

📷 sutton-images.com

"I drove there in my Cortina estate... a bloke came up and said, 'Are you Dick?', and thrust me a thick packet containing $25,000 in cash. 'What do I do with this?' I thought."

go late in the season at Thruxton so we took an engine out to Novamotor before the final round. What EJ says about an exclusive Novamotor deal for F3 in the UK in '83 is wrong – we'd been using Novamotor since 1980 with Stefan Johansson for Ron Dennis.

"It was bugging me that we had to run less rear wing to keep up on the straight, as you then lose a bit of cornering speed. So I did a bit of digging, and kicked myself for not being a bit sharper.

"I phoned Novamotor and said, 'Look, we can't keep up on the straight, the chassis is handling fine but we're finishing second. My driver's pretty damned good and he thinks we should be finishing first!' We sent Ayrton out to Italy because it's harder to say 'no' when the guy is standing there. After all, we'd won all these races, were the leading team and all of that...

"After Ayrton got back, we went for a test at Snetterton and were so much quicker than Martin. We also had development '84 sidepods that Ron Tauranac at Ralt said should be better but he couldn't guarantee it. He said, 'Test them, then it's up to you.' Tauranac also had a steering geometry mod as well as the new pods. I asked him what he reckoned and he said he honestly didn't know. But I had first call. An Aussie helping a Kiwi – doesn't happen very often!

"I figured that the steering wouldn't do a lot but the aero was interesting, and I knew Ron was always in close dialogue with Patrick Head at Williams about what they were developing. So I thought that was worth a punt, to at least test them. So we went to Snett with the new engine and, in the morning, with the old pods, we were very quick. Martin and EJ were at the opposite end of the pitlane and we were timing each other's every lap. We were a couple of tenths faster and I wondered if they were sandbagging. It goes through your mind with the championship at stake.

"About half hour before lunch I said to Ayrton, 'Right, we'll put the new pods on and do a run, so we can think over lunch about whether we have to rebalance the set-up.' Ron had said it might move the centre of pressure. So we bolted them on, didn't touch the car, and he banged in one quick lap as fast as he'd gone all morning. The flag was out for the lunch break and he came in and just nodded.

"I said, 'But you haven't gone any quicker.'

"He said, 'I'm not trying yet. This is good. It gives me more confidence in the fast corners.'

"So already the engine is a tick in the box and the sidepods are a tick in the box. We had lunch, put some better tyres on and went back out. Bang. Hell! Where did that time come from?

"We're happy – and now it's all about preparation for Thruxton. Strip the car, rebuild it again and double-check

everything. That was my main worry – that this guy was going to lose the championship because of unreliability, that we were going to let him down. But then I reminded myself how many times he'd crashed!

"We got to Thruxton for the decider, took pole comfortably, and just walked away with it. It was a huge relief but not without a little drama. Muggins me was trying to get the extra bit. The RT3s didn't have oil coolers. They had a round aluminium oil tank and the sidepod had a slot where air came through to cool the tank. Good old Tauranac, clever, but it took a while to get the oil temperature up.

"So we did a test at Snetterton with the hole taped up, and the temperature obviously came up quickly because it wasn't being cooled. We thought, right, for the first couple of laps of the final round, we'll have it taped up. We'll get more power, which could be crucial, then we'll take the tape off before the engine overheats. We tried this at Snett but, of course, we didn't try it at high speed.

"For Thruxton I put the tape on with a fold at the back so Ayrton could lean out and pull it off. Of course, going up to the Thruxton chicane he's doing 150mph and he

can't get his arm out! He had to loosen his seat belt and still he couldn't get at it. The tape fold was hard down. I should have packed it out with something.

"Next lap, the oil temperature is really climbing and a couple of people asked me afterwards if he'd had a problem because he was all over the place in the chicane. What he'd done was loosen his belts right off to get his arm out and he wasn't holding the wheel properly. He finally managed to get the tape off and retighten his belts. My heart rate returned to something more normal... We were trying to find the important advantage for the first couple of laps but we could have blown it.

"Generally Ayrton and I got on great, but early in the second half of the season he was getting a bit jumpy. I sat him down and told him we had a 36-point lead, and if he finished second Martin was only going to pull in three or four points. I told Ayrton to stop crashing trying to beat Martin and just finish second a few times. 'Yeah, yeah.' Then he goes and chucks it off at the next race!

"He just couldn't handle not being the best. That was one of very few weaknesses. His crashes put more pressure on us and I didn't make any money that year because I didn't have damage insurance. He was so good that I'd figured he wouldn't crash...

"Then there was one test we did at Silverstone where he was off the pace and I was a bit perplexed. Then someone walked down the pitlane and said, 'Jesus, he had a big shunt yesterday!'

"I said, 'We weren't testing yesterday...'

"It turned out he'd been at Snetterton driving Ralph Firman's new FF2000 car for the Anglia TV cameras. A rear wheel broke going into Riches and he barrel-rolled it into the field, right in front of the cameras!"

"He bloody well hadn't told me, so I waited, we finished testing and I said, 'We're a bit off the pace, Arry.'

"He said, 'Oh yeah, I'm not quite feeling the best...'

"I said, 'Not surprised, I've just found out something you haven't told me...' He looked a bit sheepish. I said, 'Why the hell didn't you tell me so I didn't waste all day looking for something wrong with the car that's not there?'

There was no data-logging in those days, so you couldn't measure anything, it was all feel. Generally his memory recall was astounding. It was like having a data-logger in the car. But that day he was a bit sore and every time he came to a fast corner he just eased off a bit. Which isn't great at Silverstone...

"I was particularly pleased about winning Macau at the end of the year because F3 had never been there, so it was a clean sheet of paper. He arrived very late. He didn't even get a chance to walk the track. He'd tested a Brabham at Paul Ricard on the Tuesday, flew to Paris, then to Hong Kong, then Macau, arrived knackered, went out, stuck it on pole and won both races.

"We didn't run on Saturday because the 'bikes were out. So apparently he'd gone out on Friday night and rumour had it that someone spiked his drink. I'd agreed to meet him at lunchtime on Saturday to discuss what we were doing with the car and he turned up at 6pm, looking dreadful.

"I said, 'This isn't lunchtime, Arry... Have you been on the bottle?'

"He said, 'No, I just feel awful.'

"On Sunday we did race 1 and won it, but he was knackered. It wasn't like him at all. He needed to sit down and said, 'Don't touch the car, just refuel it, I've got to go back to the hotel for a sleep.' What? It was two aggregated heats in those days, so I was a bit worried... But he came back half an hour before race 2 and blew everyone away again.

"Afterwards, he kept in touch. When he was driving for Lotus in '85 and we were winning the F3 championship with Mauricio [Gugelmin], his friend, he came to the final

round at Silverstone. We'd done two full test days and I'd really got the car working well with low downforce.

"Ayrton came out onto the grid. 'Dickie! You haven't got enough wing on. All the cars behind you are running loads more!'

"I told him not to worry, we'd tested for two days and I was comfortable. All Mauricio had to do was get off the line ahead of Andy Wallace and we'd be gone. That's the way it worked out and I could grin at him and say, 'Told you so!'"

↑ As meticulous a man as there is in racing, only after the Thruxton finale could Bennetts enjoy the moment.

📷 sutton-images.com

"He'd tested a Brabham at Paul Ricard on the Tuesday, flew to Paris, then to Hong Kong, then Macau, arrived knackered, went out, stuck it on pole and won both races"

MARTIN BRUNDLE
RECOLLECTIONS OF A RIVAL

At the end of 1982 I'd done one season of British F3 with Dave Price's team and BP backing and the idea was that we would do the European F3 series in '83. Calvin Fish was pencilled in for the British F3 drive I'd had that year. But then the budget for Europe got pulled and, because Calvin had won an FF2000 race against Ayrton, I think he was perceived as the only man who might beat him.

"And so I ended up out of a drive. I remember sitting in Pricey's office and he said, 'I'm sorry Martin, I haven't got anything for you. The budget's gone and they want to put Calvin in our car for British F3.'

"Almost as a last thing, a throw-away, he said, 'I'm going to ring a man who might be able to help you.' And the man he rang was Eddie Jordan. So I went straight from Dave Price's to Eddie's, stayed the night, we got talking. I hadn't any money and neither had Eddie from what I could work out.

"Ayrton's reputation preceded him – from his Formula Ford success and the way he went about his business. I'd seen him race because sometimes FF1600 had been supporting F3 and he was a hot story. Everyone was looking out for Ayrton Senna. And how much he was going to win by. Everyone pretty much had him down as the champion before we'd even started.

"It surprised me a bit that it was perceived he was going to walk it. I'd had a difficult '82 but by the end of it I was very strong. But then he went and won the first nine races...

"I had some good races with Ayrton and led him off the line on several occasions. Though he won those first nine I was always in the hunt. He wasn't walking away and leaving me. There were times I was leading. It was

⬇ **"How did you do that?" Brundle quizzes Senna about his outside pass at Silverstone's Stowe Corner.**

📷 sutton-images.com

close but he was just edging it. I was second eight times in those first nine.

"I was a very good starter, always was throughout my career, and carried that through into F1, but he was strong at qualifying and sticking it on pole. But he wasn't dropping me for dead on the first lap. He just had all the credentials – the qualifying, the start, the first lap, the race pace, the consistency.

"Neither of us was fit enough. I've got a picture on the wall at home, when I'd won at Donington. It was a very intense race and we both look battered, but it was only half an hour or whatever. In terms of being professional drivers we'd done nothing.

"He was good in traffic and he was very good in the rain. He just had the full deck of cards. And he also had the confidence that he could beat me. I had the exact opposite of that. I didn't have the confidence I could beat him until that day at Silverstone in June. He had me covered, but not by much.

"I remember leading a race early season at Silverstone in the pouring rain. We were going down Hangar Straight to Stowe, in the pouring rain, and he went right down the outside of me. I'm like, 'See you, but I wouldn't want to be you out there', but he went all the way round the outside of me on the karting line – I never did any karting – and came out of Stowe in front.

Then there was a shunt and the race got red-flagged.

Going to the grid for the restart, I thought I'd try his line. Well... I hit this puddle of water and very nearly stuck it in the barrier. I survived that and Ayrton won it, though not by much. I said to him on the podium, 'Your line into Stowe didn't work in the second race, did it?' He replied: 'I don't know, I didn't try. It was too wet...'

"To this day it annoys me that he knew that and I didn't! It's something that you saw all the way through his F1 career. He had a sixth sense and a gift for knowing where the grip was.

"He was right. It had been raining hard when they were cleaning up the mess, he'd taken a look at the surface and decided there was no point in trying it again. But he just knew, that was the thing...

↑ The Senna/ Brundle F3 rivalry truly grabbed the British public.

📷 sutton-images.com

"Everyone was looking out for Ayrton Senna. And how much he was going to win by. Everyone pretty much had him down as the champion before we'd even started"

"We spent a lot of time racing at close quarters and there was contact at times, but he wasn't a dirty driver. I remember Thruxton one time. He had an engine problem and I was passing him coming down the pit straight. They had to move all the pit boards pretty damn quick because there was a Ralt's width available and I took it and passed him. He could have had me off there if he'd wanted to, but didn't. Perhaps he never believed I'd go for the gap…

"He could be pretty ruthless but the accidents we had together weren't out of bloody-mindedness. They were in really aggressive, competitive situations. There was no weaving, diving across the road at me or just being bloody-minded and having me off. Well, maybe just once.

"When we contacted at Snetterton I was on pole and led away. He got a good run on me coming out of Sear and I moved to the left-hand side of the straight to make him go the long way round into the Esses – but he didn't go the long way round. He carried on down my left-hand side, where there wasn't a full car's width. He touched the back of my car. Some people say I ran him off the road but I didn't. I moved there and left him to make up his own mind. The last I saw of him were the rivets of his undertray. When he landed he kept his foot in and tried to T-bone me, but he just missed as I went into the left at the Esses – which, ironically, is now called Brundle!

"That was bloody-mindedness but it was after the

event. He landed on my head at Oulton Park but that was through an over-ambitious overtake, not bloody-mindedness. Not like I experienced with Schumacher when I was his team-mate in '92, and others experienced. The harshest example of that was Budapest with Rubens Barrichello on the pit straight. That was the instinctive default: 'You're not coming past me, I'll have you off the road.'

"I just didn't have that with Ayrton. Obviously he had his adventures with Prost later on, particularly at Suzuka in 1990, but I'd say he was a tough and hard racer. I didn't find him unfair.

"Ayrton was a man driven from his heart rather than his head. When people ask me the difference between Schumacher and Senna, two of the greatest of all time, I think Schumacher was cerebral, driven from his head, and Senna was driven from his heart, supported by his head. I'm not saying he wasn't a clever guy, because he was, but for me his primary energy was his emotions. Suzuka '90 was an emotional decision. I saw it in '83 quite a lot. This feeling that the world was against him.

"When we sat in stewards' inquiries post-race at Oulton Park and Snetterton, his demeanour, words and expressions were all… 'It's the British, it's F3, it's the system. You're all against me.' And I think that's exactly how it was in F1. It was no longer the British system, British F3 and British stewards, it was Jean-Marie Balestre, the French and the FIA.

"And I think that's why he went so wobbly in the middle of '83. He allowed that to dominate his mind.

"Two things happened: one, he realised I could beat him, and two, I realised I could beat him. Those two things just swapped over and mentally it softened him up. I just took off: I can beat this guy, I'm good enough to beat this guy! It all just kept going my way after that. I took chances and it worked out for me. He took chances and it didn't. You go through those phases sometimes but suddenly I just had that supreme confidence that I could beat him.

"The thing was, when he'd been winning all those early races, I'd finished second all but once and then he started having accidents and not finishing and the points gap closed right up. And I actually did the last race with number one on my car as the championship leader.

"I'd heard he'd got a new engine for the last race. I was a bit gutted because Ayrton didn't do the European rounds. He came to watch. I won in Austria and then our truck went over the edge of a cliff on the way home and killed my number one mechanic, Rob Bowden. All our cars were lying at the bottom of a ravine and it was an extraordinary effort to get back on track.

"So I get a bit miffed when I hear that we had more money and all the right goodies. I mean, I'd have to go to EJ's factory via Allied Irish bank in Northampton and put five hundred quid in, or just anything I could get!

"It was a tough year but I won at Donington, in Austria

⬇ **There was mutual respect in the Thruxton handshake after Senna clinched the F3 crown.**

📷 sutton-images.com

↑ In F1 Senna
was blessed with
championship-
winning machinery;
Brundle was not.

📷 sutton-images.com

and the Silverstone European round. Then I detonated
my engine and we only had two really old ones left. For
the Thruxton decider we tried one and it was rubbish, so
we fitted the reserve engine in desperation. We knew it
was rubbish really. I was only third on the grid and I only
finished third in the race.

"So there were two aspects at the last race. Ayrton
got a new engine and he drove well. And if I'm honest
I think I suffered under the pressure a tiny bit. I'll never
forget sitting on the grid. There was talk that I could have
won the championship by just taking him out of the race.
I remember Sid Offord, a big bloke, standing in front of
my car, saying, 'Any monkey business and I'll have you!'
Because Rupert Keegan had done it a few years earlier
with Bruno Giacomelli – took him off at the first corner, got
out of the car and stuck his arms up in the air to celebrate!
So that didn't do my head an awful lot of good...

"History tells you that the best man won the
championship because of what he went on to achieve. But
I don't know whether I'd have been better off dominating
the championship or – because of his reputation – running
him close. I mean, 30 years later it's still talked about in
pubs around race tracks in hushed tones.

"In Formula 1, of course, we were never that close on
the track with the way our respective careers went but
I do remember a little incident at Spa in practice, in '91,

when we tripped over each other. I was in my debrief in the
Brabham motorhome and he came bursting in. All of my
guys had an intake of breath: 'Oh, look, it's Ayrton Senna!'

"With the old Bus Stop chicane at Spa you used to have
to back up through Blanchimont and find yourself a gap
before you started the lap. And, like me, he was trying to
find some space and wanted to jump me, so I beat him
into the chicane. I didn't block him, I just stopped him from
being able to steal my space. So he comes in, moaning
and groaning and swearing, and so I later went and found
him at McLaren and returned the compliment."

"Two things happened: one, he realised I could beat him, and two, I realised I could beat him… It all just kept going my way after that. I took chances and it worked out for me. He took chances and it didn't"

1984

FORMULA 1 BAPTISM

Senna's F1 graduation took longer to finalise than he imagined. At the top of the Constructors' Championship in 1983 were Ferrari and Renault. Ferrari had replaced Patrick Tambay with Michele Alboreto for '84, while Renault would field Tambay and Derek Warwick, the latter signed to replace Alain Prost, who had committed a couple of indiscretions during '83 while losing out to Nelson Piquet by a single point at the final round in the quest for the World Championship.

Piquet had thus clinched his second title in three years for Bernie Ecclestone's Brabham team, which tested Senna at Paul Ricard and was very keen. Piquet, though, wasn't. He put pressure on Brabham, via Italian sponsors Parmalat, to sign Riccardo Patrese.

Williams was shut too. Frank had been highly impressed by Senna's first F1 test for his team in July '83, but was already committed to Keke Rosberg and Jacques Laffite.

Ron Dennis at McLaren, meanwhile, suddenly found a cut-price Prost on the market and snapped him up, dropping John Watson.

At Lotus, Peter Warr desperately wanted Senna but already had Elio de Angelis and sponsor John Player wanted to keep Nigel Mansell in the second car.

And so it was that Toleman, ninth in the 1983 Constructors' Championship with just 10 points, brought one of motor racing's all-time greats into the Big League.

← In the Toleman-Hart TG184 on the way to that stunning second place in the rain-soaked Monaco GP on 3 June 1984. Senna looked set to take the lead just when the race was stopped, after 31 of 77 laps.

📷 sutton-images.com

25 MARCH 1984

Brazilian GP (Jacarepagua)
Toleman-Hart TG183B • Retired, 8 laps, turbo failure

On his F1 debut, Ayrton was the best-placed Pirelli runner on the grid, qualifying the Toleman-Hart TG183B 16th out of 26. His impressive qualifying time was 1.78sec quicker than team-mate Johnny Cecotto, the Venezuelan former motorcycle ace, but both were troubled by a rogue batch of Pirelli tyres that delaminated.

Senna also suffered an engine failure that engine builder Brian Hart attributed to over-enthusiastic application of revs.

Ayrton made a good start to run 13th but was passed by Stefan Bellof's Tyrrell, Jacques Laffite's Williams (which had qualified 2sec quicker) and the recovering Brabham of World Champion Nelson Piquet, who'd stalled on the grid. Ayrton then posted the race's first retirement after eight laps, with no turbo boost pressure.

7 APRIL 1984

South African GP (Kyalami)
Toleman-Hart TG183B • 6th

Low oil pressure and an electrical misfire spoiled much of the opening day of practice. The turbo boost pressure problems that affected Senna in Brazil, however, had been tracked to faulty parts supplied to turbo builder Holset, enabling Ayrton to finally qualify 13th.

Planning to complete the race without a pit stop, Senna hit more boost problems early on and ran over debris on the main straight while glancing at his gauges. The impact damaged the Toleman's front wing, robbed it of downforce and made the steering feel even heavier; the slightly-built Ayrton had been quite shocked by the steering weight on first acquaintance. Over the 90-minute race the heavy steering extracted a considerable physical toll and Senna was exhausted when he crossed the line to score his first F1 World Championship point. He was treated for dehydration.

29 APRIL 1984

Belgian GP (Zolder)
Toleman-Hart TG183B • 7th

Ayrton qualified 19th, half a second and three slots adrift of Toleman team-mate Johnny Cecotto after more electrically-induced engine misfire problems. With the track surface at Zolder bumpy and the Toleman's radiators nose-mounted, it was necessary to raise the ride height, which did little for the handling.

After a tough race Ayrton was two laps down among the 10 finishers, ahead of Patrick Tambay's Renault, Marc Surer's Arrows and Jonathan Palmer's RAM.

6 MAY 1984

San Marino GP (Imola)
Toleman-Hart TG183B • Did not qualify

On Senna's first visit to Imola, politics between Toleman and Pirelli came into play, with an edict from base that the team wasn't to take part in Friday practice. Whether to believe that the reason was an unpaid bill from testing or an impending switch to Michelin was a matter of personal choice!

More misfire trouble struck when Ayrton finally took to the circuit on a wet Saturday morning, and then a fuel-pressure problem in final qualifying meant that an unimpressed Senna was reduced to the role of spectator on race day.

12 MAY 1984

Nürburgring (Race of Champions)
Mercedes-Benz 190 2.3-16 • 1st

To celebrate the opening of the new Nürburgring, Mercedes invited every living World Champion to race its new sports saloon, the 190 2.3-16, in the 'Race of Champions'.

They all accepted apart from five: Juan Fangio, at 72, said he was too old but attended as a Mercedes ambassador; Jackie Stewart had vowed never to race again after retiring 11 years earlier; Mario Andretti and Emerson Fittipaldi were busy qualifying for the Indy 500; and Nelson Piquet declined. Senna, as a friend of Mercedes' Gerd Kremer and very much a coming-man, took Fittipaldi's place.

Most of the drivers treated it as a bit of fun, as much as naturally competitive animals ever do, but Senna saw it as a great opportunity to beat esteemed competition in equal equipment. It was at this event that Ayrton met Alain Prost for the first time as, ironically, Kremer asked Prost to pick up Senna from Frankfurt Airport. They spent about half a day together and got on well, with Prost finding it amusing that Senna didn't know any of the other drivers.

After following Carlos Reutemann for the first couple

of laps, Senna comfortably won the race, beating Niki Lauda into second place by a couple of seconds, ahead of Reutemann, Keke Rosberg and John Watson. John Surtees was so impressed that he later told his former team boss, Enzo Ferrari, that Senna was the driver he should have.

One man not keen to mix it with Senna was Hans Herrmann, who finished a distant last, his wife telling everyone that he'd done a good deal to buy the car and wanted all its panels intact!

20 MAY 1984

French GP (Dijon)
Toleman-Hart TG184 • Retired, 35 laps, turbo failure

Delighted with the team's new TG184 and his Michelin tyres, Senna qualified 13th, which could have been even better had he not bolted on a set of qualifying tyres just as Niki Lauda's engine expired and coated the track in oil.

"You can't compare the handling of this car with the previous one," Senna enthused. "I feel I can take time off anyone in the corners." A wet session should have provided a first glimpse of Senna's wet-weather prowess, but of four wet compounds available, Toleman had only

the slowest. But there wasn't long to wait for Formula 1 to see what Senna could do in the wet…

After qualifying 13th Ayrton managed to work the TG184 up to ninth position before, on lap 36, suffering the same turbo failure that afflicted team-mate Johnny Cecotto 14 laps earlier.

3 JUNE 1984

Monaco GP (Monte Carlo)
Toleman-Hart TG184 • 2nd

On his first visit to Monte Carlo, Senna qualified the Toleman 13th. But race day dawned grey and wet: it was the perfect stage for Senna to announce a stunning talent to the world.

Ninth at the end of lap 1, he then passed Jacques Laffite, Manfred Winkelhock, Keke Rosberg, René Arnoux and Niki Lauda. Early leader Nigel Mansell spun in treacherous conditions and after 19 laps, with others having fallen by the wayside, Senna was second. Relentlessly, he closed down Prost's leading McLaren, surviving damaged suspension after solid contact with the chicane kerbing.

At times, the Toleman was 3sec per lap quicker than the McLaren in a stunning display. The outcome looked inevitable and Prost, not overly confident in the McLaren's brakes, had already determined that he wouldn't fight the Toleman when it arrived.

As Prost crossed the line at the end of lap 31, he was greeted by the red flag and the chequered flag together, and immediately backed off. Senna flashed by into what he thought was the lead, but the race was over, clerk of the course Jacky Ickx ruling that it was too dangerous to continue. Although the rain had worsened, the timing was cruel. It should have been Ayrton's first victory. He had been robbed.

17 JUNE 1984

Canadian GP (Montréal)
Toleman-Hart TG184 • 7th

Buoyed by his Monaco headlines, Ayrton qualified in the top 10 for the first time in Montréal. The Hart engines had electronic ignition with twin injectors per cylinder, which was useful for qualifying but, in the absence of fuel consumption data, couldn't be used for the race. Some faulty valve gear problems on Saturday also meant that Senna's time, ninth quickest and just 2sec from Nelson

Piquet's Brabham-BMW BT53 on pole, came at the wheel of the spare Toleman.

With the Toleman's Hart engine lacking power in comparison to BMW, Ferrari and TAG Porsche turbo rivals, Senna's performances were now attracting universal interest. Canada resulted in a seventh place, just one place outside the points.

24 JUNE 1984

United States GP (Detroit)
Toleman-Hart TG184 • Retired, 21 laps, accident

On a circuit at which he thought he'd be able to make more of a difference, Senna was a bit over-ambitious at the chicane before the pits in Friday practice. Among the quickest, he took too much kerb on the way in, lost it and slammed heavily into the wall.

A significant rebuild was needed before qualifying, when Ayrton used the electronically injected development Hart engine to good effect and put the Toleman seventh, his best qualifying performance so far.

A multiple shunt at the start saw the right rear wheel ripped from Nelson Piquet's Brabham. The wheel landed

⬇ **In atrocious conditions, Ayrton's performance in Monte Carlo was simply astonishing...**

📷 sutton-images.com

squarely on the front suspension and sidepod of Senna's car, meaning he had to take the spare TG184 for a restart.

That lasted 21 laps. Senna was running ahead of Rosberg's Williams and Martin Brundle's Tyrrell, which finished second, when a front suspension wishbone broke at the first corner and he hit the tyre barrier.

United States GP (Dallas)
Toleman-Hart TG184 • Retired, 47 laps, driveshaft

The heat of Texas in July brought it home to Senna that he needed to work on his strength and fitness. Once he realised how it impacted on performance his physical condition would become a strength but, for now, extended lappery in Dallas required revival with ice packs and cold compresses! Despite that, Senna again improved on his best F1 qualifying performance when he was sixth quickest, just 1.2sec adrift of Nigel Mansell's pole position in the Lotus-Renault 95T.

Senna crossed the line fourth at the end of the opening lap but then clipped one of Dallas's unforgiving concrete walls and spun. He pitted for fresh tyres, then repeated the mistake and fell to the tail of the field. He was out 20 laps from the end with a broken driveshaft.

⬇ Ayrton shared a Joest Racing Porsche 956 with Henri Pescarolo and Stefan Johansson in the Nürburgring 1,000kms – his only sports car race.

📷 sutton-images.com

Nürburgring (World Endurance Championship)
Porsche 956 • 8th

Back at the Nürburgring just two months after his Mercedes 190E victory, Senna partnered Stefan Johansson and Henri Pescarolo in a New Man Joest Racing Porsche 956 in the World Endurance Championship. Senna had never driven a pukka closed racing car before and only got to drive the Porsche for the first time in the wet afternoon practice after the other two drivers had monopolised the car in the dry morning session. He was back in after only one lap for some instruction on the cockpit dials and switches!

Senna set the team's best wet-weather time in the afternoon, seventh quickest overall, and they started ninth. In the race the car ran comfortably in the top 10 until a clutch problem cost it eight laps. It rejoined 12th and ultimately finished eighth.

Team boss Reinhold Joest told *Autosport*: "Ayrton was immediately very fast, especially in the rain in both practice and race. He was also very interested in every technical aspect of the car. He asked the engineers many questions. He told us that he had some ideas and came back with a three-page report!"

"There were some very good ideas and we did use some. The Porsche 956 always had an understeer problem but we made some changes based on what he said and it was a help."

22 JULY 1984

British GP (Brands Hatch)
Toleman-Hart TG184 • 3rd

Ayrton liked Brands Hatch and was fastest of all in Friday's untimed practice but Toleman team-mate Johnny Cecotto suffered a serious leg-breaking accident. The Brazilian was fourth quickest in Friday qualifying, despite the Toleman feeling a bit twitchy over some of the Kent circuit's bumps.

The team softened off the car a bit for Saturday but Senna found his first qualifying run compromised by René Arnoux's Ferrari and his second by Niki Lauda's McLaren. With his Friday time he was still seventh, just 1.03sec from Nelson Piquet's Brabham-BMW pole, the Toleman benefiting from the fitment of larger Holset turbos.

Ayrton didn't get the best of starts and was ninth at the end of the opening lap, but soon gained a place by passing Mansell's Lotus at Paddock Bend. As the race wore on and some of the leading contenders hit trouble, it suddenly looked as if Senna's first dry-weather F1 podium was a possibility if he could get the better of Elio de Angelis in the second Lotus. The Italian did all he could to resist but Senna dived inside at Paddock Bend and, when Piquet's Brabham had problems with turbo boost pressure, Ayrton picked up another position to finish third.

5 AUGUST 1984

German GP (Hockenheim)
Toleman-Hart TG184 • Retired, 4 laps, accident

Just one Toleman was entered in Germany after Cecotto's Brands Hatch accident. If there was a circuit that penalised lack of power it was the old Hockenheim and Senna, even though he put the TG184 solidly into the top 10, was 2.38sec adrift of Prost's TAG Porsche-powered McLaren MP4/2 in pole position.

Meanwhile, there were yet stronger rumours linking him to Lotus for 1985. It added a certain coolness to the team atmosphere as the press claimed he'd actually signed on the Saturday night.

⬆ **Seven weeks after the heroics in Monaco, Senna scored his first dry-weather podium at Brands Hatch, behind Niki Lauda and Derek Warwick.**

📷 sutton-images.com

Sixth on the opening lap, Senna took fifth from Patrick Tambay's Renault and was running competitively when the Toleman's rear wing detached itself, without warning, while Ayrton was flat-out in top on the run down to the first chicane. The Toleman spun backwards into the barrier but Senna was unhurt. The team's investigations showed that the wing's mounting bracket was broken as a result of vibrations from the engine at higher revs than it had previously been running.

19 AUGUST 1984

Austrian GP (Osterreichring)
Toleman-Hart TG184 • Retired, 35 laps, engine

The Osterreichring saw Ayrton 3sec from Piquet's pole position time but the Toleman was in the top 10 yet again. He found that his race car handled well but was 300rpm down and short of power, while the spare Toleman had a decent engine but not so benign handling. He felt he'd done all he could but he was far from happy. The engine from the T-car was installed for the race.

Seventh across the line on the opening lap, he passed Elio de Angelis before the Italian repassed, then closed in and got the better of Derek Warwick's Renault RE50 as he raced in a Lotus sandwich, with Mansell behind. But he was out with engine failure after 35 of 51 laps.

26 AUGUST 1984

Dutch GP (Zandvoort)
Toleman-Hart TG184 • Retired, 19 laps, engine

Track action was limited by a misfire on Friday and a blown engine on Saturday, so Senna could qualify no higher than 13th. Off-track it was a different matter: Lotus announced that Senna had signed a contract. The reception from Toleman was understandably frosty, the team having signed Ayrton to a three-year contract. It contained a £100,000 buy-out clause but, Toleman's Alex Hawkridge insisted, that was supposed to be exercised before indulging in negotiations elsewhere. Lotus boss Peter Warr did little to endear himself to

Toleman or, indeed, Nigel Mansell, when he made the Senna announcement an hour before the race!

There were to be no heroics in the race, however, with Ayrton running a lonely ninth before succumbing to engine failure before one-third distance.

7 OCTOBER 1984

European GP (Nürburgring)
Toleman-Hart TG184 • Retired, 0 laps, accident

Although legal proceedings continued after Toleman suspended Ayrton for Monza (see page 98), he was reinstated in time for the European GP, where Brian Hart had fitted his engine with larger Holset turbos. Unfortunately, an ECU failure meant that Ayrton was unable to get the best from the revised engine, which explained the 12th place and 3.56sec deficit to Nelson Piquet's pole position Brabham.

The race was all over for the Toleman on the opening lap when Senna was nudged and rode over the back of Rosberg's Williams, eliminating both cars on the spot.

21 OCTOBER 1984

Portuguese GP (Estoril)
Toleman-Hart TG184 • 3rd

Senna's final race for Toleman was a revelation. Since the switch to Michelins, Toleman hadn't been entitled to the top-specification tyres, with McLaren boss Ron Dennis ensuring that contractual stipulations were followed. When Michelin made the surprise decision to pull out at the end of the year, however, the French decided to give Toleman the best rubber anyway. The result was third on the grid at Estoril, with Ayrton just 0.23sec from Nelson Piquet's pole position Brabham!

The race was all about the title showdown between McLaren team-mates Prost and Lauda. Prost won at a canter but Lauda secured his third World Championship title by half a point with a drive through the field from 11th on the grid to second. En route, Niki passed Senna's Toleman on lap 33 of the 70. When the chequered flag fell, Senna was just 6sec behind the new champion and 1sec clear of Michele Alboreto's Ferrari.

⬇ Senna, with Michelin slick parity for the first time, mixes it with Nelson Piquet, Alain Prost and Keke Rosberg in Portugal.

📷 sutton-images.com

TOLEMAN STANDS DOWN SENNA!

In response to Lotus's announcement on 26 August at the Dutch GP that it had signed Senna for 1985–86, Toleman claimed that Senna was in breach of article 19 of his contract and suspended him 'until further notice'. Post-race that same day, Toleman issued a statement:

'Ayrton Senna is under a three-year contract with Toleman which is still in full force and specifically states that "he will not enter into negotiation with any party regarding sponsorship of Mr Senna or the team or future prospects"…

'Throughout the currency of this agreement, and, to date, despite press speculation, Senna has continually denied to the team that he has negotiated or signed or intended to sign with another team.

'John Player Special Team Lotus has chosen to ignore public warnings from Toleman not to create a breach of contract between Toleman and Senna. The Toleman team has not been informed by Senna that he has signed or negotiated with Lotus. The Toleman team does not appreciate the press release from Lotus stating that Senna will, of course, continue to drive for Toleman for the rest of the season. Lotus has never consulted Toleman concerning Senna and therefore cannot know the terms of the contract. Toleman will exercise its contractual rights and will take action for damages against Senna and others.

'This statement by John Player Special Team Lotus puts at risk Toleman's future participation in motor sport. Our sponsorship prospects are based on our three-year contract with Senna, and at this late stage it may be difficult to maintain our current sponsors and to interest new sponsors as most leading drivers have now completed their contracts for next year.'

Senna turned up at Monza to watch Stefan Johansson finish fourth in 'his' car, while Toleman also fielded a second car for the first time since Cecotto's accident, for Italian Pierluigi Martini, who failed to qualify.

Senna's own version of events was somewhat at odds with Toleman's. Selected excerpts from Ayrton's own statement in Monza read as follows:

'The implication that Senna has broken a three-year commitment to Toleman is utterly unjustified.

'On a number of occasions since at least June 1984,

→ Stefan Johansson got his chance in Senna's Toleman when the team suspended Ayrton at Monza.

sutton-images.com

Senna and Toleman have had detailed discussions about whether and on what conditions Senna would agree to drive for Toleman during 1985. In talking to Toleman Senna has never made a secret of the fact that he had received offers from other teams and remained until recently, uncommitted.

'Senna advised Toleman immediately after the Austrian GP on August 19 that he had decided not to continue racing with them after the 1984 season and that he would exercise his rights under the contract accordingly.

'On August 22, Mr Hawkridge confirmed to Senna in a letter that "over the course of last weekend you have made it clear to me that you had reached an agreement to drive for another team next season and you confirmed to [team manager] Peter Gethin that you would not be driving for the Toleman team next season."

'On August 22 Senna's solicitors formally confirmed to Toleman in writing that Senna proposed to cease driving for the team as from the end of the 1984 season. Toleman's press release of August 26 creates the false and damaging impression that Senna had failed to advise Toleman of his decision to leave the team until the Team Lotus announcement on that date.

'Toleman have said that Senna is not permitted to discuss "future prospects" with any other team. Whilst there is a clause that could be read to say that he will not (whilst part of the Toleman team) negotiate future sponsorship prospects for himself or Toleman, there is no clause, agreement or any other reason to prevent him discussing his career as a driver for seasons subsequent to the exercise of his right to terminate the Toleman contract.

'Although he had decided to leave for 1985 Senna wished and fully intended to complete the 1984 season with Toleman – and felt morally bound to do so. However, he didn't want to wait until after the last Grand Prix in 1984 before exercising the so-called 'buy out' for obvious reasons. Naturally he decided to tell Toleman of his intentions as soon as practicable after he had made his choice – expecting that his lawyers would be able to make arrangements for him to pay the £100,000 whilst still racing in the last three races. In view of the reaction of the Toleman team and their lawyers, Senna now wonders whether he was wise to tell Toleman of his decision so soon.

'Senna has been advised that legal proceedings will be commenced. He will strongly resist any claims that may be made against him, and will if necessary counter-claim for substantial damages for the injury to his career and reputation.'

↑ Toleman didn't appreciate it when Peter Warr announced at the Dutch GP that Team Lotus had a contract with Senna for 1985.

📷 sutton-images.com

ALEX HAWKRIDGE
ON SENNA

The gamble wasn't so much taking him straight out of F3 but making him number one driver.

"My sons were involved in karting and had kept me pretty well informed about what was going on. Ayrton Senna was the guy my eldest son James talked about the most. Despite the fact that he never won the world championship, the drives that he'd had, everyone talked about him. He told me later that he didn't win it because he stayed loyal to his chassis manufacturer, DAP, and I soon got the impression it wasn't going to be a mistake he made twice!

"I met him when he was with Rushen Green. I was at Snetterton on a cold, horrible day and he was thrashing round. I talked to Dennis Rushen and later in the day the session was over, everyone was clearing up, I bumped into him and introduced myself. His English wasn't great in those days and so it wasn't exactly a conversation, more a case of saying 'hello'.

"He was just so dominant in FF2000 and in the wet at the Hockenheim F1 round he was about 2sec a lap quicker than everyone, so Chris Witty, my PR guy, and I had a chat about him and decided we needed to keep in contact. Later in the year we had a meeting, asked what his plans were and subsequent to that I made him an offer of a fully paid F3 drive on the basis that as soon as he got his superlicence he came into our F1 team.

"Very politely, he said he'd like to choose the team he drove for in F1. He just kind of waved us out of the way. I wasn't shocked because that's the kind of character he was. He had his plan in his head. When I pushed him a bit harder he said he wouldn't be ready and didn't want to make the move too soon.

"I organised a dinner with him one evening and he said he'd like to come to the factory, meet everyone and have a look around. We agreed a date and he rang me up a few hours before and said he couldn't make it.

"He had a really good F3 battle with Martin Brundle – they were the two stand-out guys. I spoke to Rory Byrne, our designer, and said that one of these guys could well fill our slot, because we knew Derek Warwick was moving to Renault, but Rory wasn't convinced that anyone from F3 could lead the team.

"Small teams can't go and buy established drivers and so you have to take more of a risk. So we went to a Silverstone test with Ayrton and the same day Martin was driving a Tyrrell. Both drove absolutely fantastically and were quicker than the regular drivers at the track earlier in the year. I made my mind up that day Ayrton was the guy we wanted, and if we couldn't get him we'd go for Brundle.

"The team was completely bowled over by him at that test. Afterwards I was getting phone calls every five minutes from initial sceptics like Rory and Roger Silman, asking if he'd signed yet!

"It wasn't just the speed, it was his recall. He could pick up so much detail in a very short time and relay it very succinctly, and with the right level of priority. For an engineer, that's the kind of stuff that keeps you alive. And it wasn't an easy car to drive, whereas it was pretty easy for Brundle to jump into a Cosworth car and pedal it quickly. In '83 we didn't have engine management on our cars, but Zytek was working on a digital system, which we had in '84, and it transformed the car.

"Ayrton was being kind of wooed. He was talking to Frank Williams and Ron Dennis, and to Brabham, but none of them would take on an F3 driver. They had the budgets for established stars so why take a risk when you didn't have to? A bit short-sighted maybe, but they had the money and the best driver for them was the established guy who was more likely to win a championship for them quickly. Their view of a second driver was someone who was still capable of winning a championship. They wouldn't go for anyone who was just bringing a budget or was there to learn the ropes.

"When we were talking to Senna he was almost forlorn. We were certainly not his first choice, by miles, and for a while I didn't think he was going to sign for us. He was a very shrewd guy and if Ayrton hadn't wanted to be a grand prix driver he could have been president of Brazil. He had the intellect and focus to make things happen.

"When we were talking to Senna he was almost forlorn. We were certainly not his first choice, by miles, and for a while I didn't think he was going to sign for us"

"His performance at Monaco in '84 was astonishing because he had less experience than anyone else and yet, technically, he drove so much better than everyone else, using the gears to control his traction and the throttle to keep up turbo pressure. The combination of those two things meant that at times he was 5sec quicker than Prost over a lap – ridiculous.

"With the turbo, you knew it was Senna from a mile away, especially at a place like Monaco. He was the only guy constantly blipping the throttle through corners and keeping his turbo revs up, so he had less lag coming off the corners. That worked astonishingly well for him in the wet. And the fact that he was short-shifting much more than anybody else.

"To blip the throttle he was slipping the clutch, which would have been quite a dangerous strategy if you didn't have the touch of an angel. He knew just where the clutch was going to engage and could blip the throttle. When you were out of the power band on a turbo the boost didn't come on until, let's say, 8,000rpm. So below that you've got no power to the rear wheels anyway. So if you could keep the revs up to that level you are going to keep the turbo spinning and very close to the point where it started delivering torque.

"There were two techniques involved: one involved slipping the clutch like you do at a race start and modulating the throttle, and the other was knowing how much throttle you could keep blipping before you would break traction. It was a combination of the two. At the Loews Hairpin he was slipping the clutch and in other places, like Rascasse, he was using a throttle blip just below the torque curve. Nobody told him how to do that, or taught him, he just did it. For him it was just an obvious thing to do, but nobody else was doing it.

"Those are the kind of things that people didn't realise about Senna. We knew because he was driving for us but even people who were supposedly watching and taking notice of him didn't really have a clue how good he was. He was obviously judged by results but nobody really knew how he was getting the results.

"His Toleman buy-out was £100,000 but it wasn't a buy-out clause in the strict sense of the term. The critical part was that he had to give us an opportunity, before he spoke to any other team, of rectifying any shortcomings he thought the team or the car or engine or tyres might have. And, earlier, he'd kicked up a hell of a stink about Pirelli and almost threatened to go home unless we got some Michelins on the car. We knew that if we didn't do the change and take all the flak that came with it, we'd lose him at the end of the year anyway.

"An interesting part of the story is that we went to Dijon with Pierre Dupasquier, the Michelin boss at the time, for a secret test while still under contract to Pirelli – which says something about what Dupasquier thought of Senna.

⬆ **Toleman's Alex Hawkridge was the man who brought Senna into F1, then lost him to Lotus.**

📷 sutton-images.com

Michelin took two truckloads of old tyres – all old ones – because they had a contract with McLaren that stopped them providing a new team with the same specification of tyres. Dupasquier, who was pretty shrewd, basically went down there to mix and match tyres and see if there was anything in the old inventory that might work. He had an idea of which combinations might work but they'd never had time to do any development because they were always forging on with new development.

"Michelin is an incredibly scientific tyre company, I'd say the only one at the time, and nothing was left to chance. They used to send squads to overseas races to dig up bits of tarmac and bring them back. Pirelli were almost amateurs by comparison.

"At the end of the day Ayrton was setting quicker times than McLaren had done on the latest rubber at their tyre test about three weeks previously. So we felt pretty confident that if we could mix and match tyres we'd be in good shape.

"Announcing a change from Pirelli to Michelin at Imola didn't go down at all well, and wasn't what we'd planned to do, but it was driven by logistics, circumstances and notice periods. We arrived there and unfortunately it wasn't how we'd naively thought it would be, with Michelin

bringing loads and loads of tyres that we'd be able to mix and match. It came down to Dupasquier bringing what he thought would work. Which was a bit different from what we imagined. And from what Senna imagined. So on a race-by-race basis we never quite had the tyre performance from Michelin that we expected.

"I think Dupasquier knew that, so when we got to Monaco and it was raining, he gave us new tyres, the same as McLaren. Ron Dennis went absolutely ape shit, threatened to get an injunction and all sorts of things – not the sort of thing you'd normally say to a tyre manufacturer you're in bed with! I think Dupasquier told Ron that Michelin hadn't brought any older wet tyres, but we knew they had. Short of emptying all the trucks, there was no way for Ron to argue with them...

"It happened again with the slicks in Portugal at the last race of the season. There, Michelin really had only brought new tyres. They told us that with Ayrton in the car, on the same rubber, we might be quicker than McLaren.

"But it's a big change when they turn up with a brand new tyre and you've been working with year-old rubber all season. Set-up wise, it's a massive job to get on top of. We ended up third in Portugal, on the podium, and Lauda in the McLaren had to pass Ayrton to win the title.

"After the race Michelin stayed on so that we could do some driver testing, because by then it was known that Senna was going and I think Dupasquier wanted to know just what was possible with Ayrton on the right tyres!

"We'd had the choice of tyre that McLaren had in Portugal but Michelin had a lot of other stuff in the truck. So we went into the mix and match again with their '84 compounds. I think we went a second quicker than we'd gone in qualifying [Senna had qualified third, just 0.16sec behind Prost's McLaren and well ahead of Lauda] and the tyres we were testing were able to do a race distance!

"It was a real shame that we weren't able to carry on with Senna and Michelin in '85 and have a real crack at it, because I think we had a much better package at the end of '84 than people realised.

"Ayrton was pretty pissed off when I suspended him for Monza over the Lotus situation, but nothing other than taking his toys away would have affected him. You couldn't fine him and it was shooting ourselves in the foot suspending him, but I felt it was a matter of principle that someone who breaks their contract shouldn't get away with it scot-free.

"We knew that it was going to cost us our sponsorship and possibly our future in F1. People thought our reaction was disproportionate but they wouldn't have if they knew the facts. He buried our team when he did that. And we knew it. I think if I could have done something worse, I would have!

"I wouldn't say any of us were ever really friends with Ayrton. It was a kind of healthy respect. I met him several years later when he'd won championships. Believe it or not he was walking Silverstone on his own. He wandered over and we chatted for about half an hour. It was as if there hadn't been a break. So I don't think he had any kind of grudge or animosity. We didn't do anything wrong. And he knew that he had.

"When he kind of apologised he said that Lotus had let the cat out of the bag and blamed them. I said, 'No, you broke the contract first and then they let the cat out of the bag.' He couldn't see that it was his fault. If they hadn't opened their big mouths he'd have been all right – that was his attitude.

"It was the most unpleasant episode I ever encountered with a driver. All he had to say to us was, 'I don't think you're going to be competitive next year, I've got a more competitive option.' That would have been sufficient grounds for him to go. The contract wasn't that strong. If we'd challenged his decision to go, the courts would have supported him. Unless you can prove that it's the end of the world, which you never can, they're always going to go with the employee. That's the situation we were in."

"His performance at Monaco in '84 was astonishing because he had less experience than anyone else and yet, technically, he drove so much better than everyone else… at times he was 5sec quicker than Prost over a lap"

PAT SYMONDS
ON SENNA

I had followed Ayrton's career through Formula Ford because I wasn't long out of it – 1980 was my last year. So you do follow because you know the people and it was a case of 'which Brazilian has Ralph Firman imported this year to milk him of money? Oh, actually, this one seems to be pretty good!'

"Equally, when Ayrton did F3 in '83 I followed the battle with Martin Brundle quite closely, from afar. I was off doing F1 races by then. I think everyone thought he was quite a talent but, as an aside, I think they totally underestimated Martin at the time, which was really sad because he was an awful lot better that most people realised.

"But Alex Hawkridge was the one who had the balls to sign him for Toleman. It's easy with hindsight, but at the time Ayrton had only done a test in the Williams. Alex and all of us, if we're honest, were pretty hesitant about taking someone straight out of F3. It wasn't the done thing then. We were a young team and it could have gone awfully wrong. But Alex had always had a lot of foresight.

"Ayrton was so quick, so intelligent, and the only problem he had at that time was that he was staggeringly unfit. You have to remember that things were so much less professional than now. We did a bit of testing prior to the start of the season but not with anything like the rigidity we have now – three race distances before the season, and so forth. You'd just go out and do some quick laps, stop for a chat and so forth. And we didn't have data to pore over.

"We tested in South Africa before the start of the season. One of the reasons we didn't get much done in the way of race distances, even had we wanted to, was that we just kept destroying cars. We weren't terribly certain

how to repair them because this was our first carbonfibre monocoque, but our chief fabricator, John Love, found a workshop in Jo'burg where he could do repairs. As soon as he'd finished one monocoque, we'd give him another that had hit the wall. It wasn't just Ayrton, we had Johnny Cecotto as well. So we hadn't got a lot of distance in.

"At the end of the first race Ayrton was just a heap of jelly. I don't think we really appreciated how unfit he was. But, ability-wise, you realised immediately that the guy was exceptional.

"In those days we didn't have much data, so the role of a driver was quite different. It was necessary for a driver to be able to give a level of technical reporting that we don't need these days – now we know more about what the car's doing than the drivers do. Ayrton was just staggeringly good at that. It was remembering to look at the gauges, remembering the revs everywhere – to get the gear ratios right – and then describing what the car was doing in terms of handling. He was very good and very disciplined. He'd come in and just rattle off the numbers, always in the same order, and then he'd go through the car balance. I'm talking about very simple things, such as giving us water temperature readings so that we could get the radiator blanking right – people now wouldn't even conceive of it!

"He did a little bit of, 'Why don't we try this, why don't we try that?' I prefer the engineers to decide as they generally understand all the interactions better, but he was also very good in that respect. It was obvious from the start that the guy was a bit different.

"That Monaco race was absolutely thrilling for us. The history of the team had been quite difficult. Our '81 season had been almost an embarrassment – an absolute triumph of enthusiasm over knowledge. In '82 it wasn't much better: we learned an awful lot about racing but we still had a difficult car. In '83 we were just starting to spread our wings a bit and we got some credibility. We turned up with a car that was actually very quick, especially at the start of the season, but it was stunningly difficult to set up. When you got it right it was fantastic but when you got it wrong it was miles away. We never quite proved ourselves but we got our first point at Zandvoort and we were starting to knock on the door. But we weren't there."

The '84 car was a big step forward, but we were waiting for the Michelins to launch it all off properly, and we weren't

> "He was distraught and really couldn't understand how he'd hit the wall. We were sitting talking, debriefing, and he said: 'It's impossible I hit the wall. The wall moved'"

↑ Rory Byrne
(left) and Pat
Symonds were
soon convinced
by Senna's novice
prowess.

📷 sutton-images.com

going to give Ayrton the new car and leave Johnny Cecotto in the old one. So for the first few races it was a case of having this new car and the tyres in the wings, and knowing that things were going to get much better.

"The anticipation was fantastic and Monaco [the second race with the new car] was our first real play with the big boys. It was thrilling. I still remember coming home and thinking, did that really happen? We so nearly won a grand prix! It was something I'd never felt before.

"Ayrton clobbered a kerb early in that race [a moment captured in the *Senna* movie]. The car had pull-rod front suspension with machined aluminium rockers and the impact cracked one of those rockers. Would that rocker have lasted to the end of the race? It's a question I'll still ask myself on my death bed. I'll tell myself, yes it would. But I'm not sure...

"We were aware that they were thinking of stopping the race because Prost was gesticulating. We had incredibly mixed emotions. I think the overriding one was 'we nearly won a race!' rather than 'we've been robbed of a race'. And I'm always a glass-half-full person. So I think I was very satisfied that we'd given Prost and McLaren a run for their money.

"I think Ayrton had very similar emotions. I think there was first the euphoria of what we'd done and then later the analysis of what we might have done dragged it down a bit.

"But my favourite Ayrton memory is from Dallas. It was very hot and a terribly difficult race. Ayrton had had a bit of a mixed bag: he'd qualified all right, thought the car was

OK, he'd spun early in the race and had to work his way back, but was heading towards a reasonable if not stunning finish. Then he clipped the wall, damaged a wheel and broke a driveshaft.

"After the race he was distraught and really couldn't understand how he'd hit the wall. We were sitting talking, debriefing, and he said: 'It's impossible I hit the wall. The wall moved'.

"I said, 'Yeah, sure it did...' They were huge great concrete blocks...

"But he was so insistent, and I had so much confidence in the guy, that I said, 'OK, we've just got to go and look at this.' I did think he was talking bollocks but he needed to go and see it.

"So we walked out to where he'd hit the wall and do you know what? The wall had moved. It was made of the great big concrete blocks that they used to delineate the circuit, but what had happened was that someone had hit the far end of a block and pushed it, which made the leading edge come out a few millimetres. He was driving with such precision that those few millimetres, and I'm talking probably ten millimetres, were enough for him to hit the wall that time rather than just miss it.

"That really opened my eyes. I knew the guy was good but that really told me how special. Not just the driving but this total conviction, the analysis and then the conclusion: I cannot be wrong, so the wall must have moved. Everyone else would say, 'Bollocks, how on earth did I do that?' But the conviction he had was just staggering. And he was right."

1985

SHAKING THINGS UP

Midway through 1984 Lotus boss Peter Warr got his way and Ayrton Senna put his signature to a Team Lotus contract. Senna joined Elio de Angelis as Nigel Mansell departed for Williams, a move that would be the making of him after four disappointing seasons at Lotus.

De Angelis had finished third in the World Championship in 1984 as the McLaren-TAG/Porsche turbos dominated, Niki Lauda beating team-mate Alain Prost by half a point to win his third world title. McLaren won 12 of 16 races while Elio was best of the rest. But the Roman was about to get a shock...

← Ayrton's first grand prix win, in the Portuguese GP on 21 April 1985, came in only his second race in the Lotus-Renault 97T and again confirmed his brilliance in wet conditions. A delighted Peter Warr, Team Lotus boss, welcomes Ayrton back to the collecting area at Estoril.

📷 LAT

↑ In Brazil Senna
and Elio de Angelis
shared the second
row for Ayrton's
first Lotus start.

📷 sutton-images.com

7 APRIL 1985

Brazilian GP (Jacarepagua)
Lotus-Renault 97T • Retired, 48 laps, electrics

There was a great sense of expectation greeting Senna
in Rio as he prepared for his first start with John Player
Special Team Lotus. The new Lotus-Renault 97T from
Gérard Ducarouge handled well but it was Michele
Alboreto's Ferrari 156 that took pole position. Senna
qualified fourth, 0.62sec adrift and three tenths from
team-mate Elio de Angelis, after being held up on both of
his quick qualifying laps.

Senna had qualified ahead of both McLarens but in
the race the Marlboro cars had more speed and first
Prost, then Lauda, went by. Lauda was destined not to
finish and as the race entered its second half, Senna's
Lotus was third. Realising that a conservative choice of
Goodyears and heavy fuel consumption (cars now had

to complete the distance on 195 litres of fuel) would limit
his competitiveness, Ayrton drove a measured race until
the engine cut out with 13 laps to go. A pump in the fuel
system had caused a short circuit.

21 APRIL 1985

Portuguese GP (Estoril)
Lotus-Renault 97T • 1st

This milestone race signalled Senna's true arrival as
an F1 superstar. Team-mate de Angelis was quickest
in the first session of Friday practice but then Senna
took over. He took his first pole position as spots of rain
arrived, with a later downpour ensuring that nobody
could go quicker.

The inclement weather remained for race day, when
Ayrton was in a class by himself. In appalling conditions

he drove away from de Angelis at 1sec a lap in the early stages. And when Alboreto's Ferrari took over in second place, he kept on doing it. With 30 of the scheduled 69 laps gone, he led by more than half a minute. Conditions were such that the two-hour time limit intervened after 67 laps, when the chequered flag greeted Ayrton in what was his 17th grand prix.

"It was difficult even to keep the car in a straight line," Senna admitted. "For sure the race should have been stopped. It was much worse than Monaco last year. Once I nearly spun in front of the pits, like Prost, and was lucky to stay on the road."

The bitter feeling at his treatment in the Principality a year earlier was now at least partially compensated…

5 MAY 1985

San Marino GP (Imola)
Lotus-Renault 97T • 7th

Ayrton had had precious little circuit time at Imola the previous year thanks to the Toleman/Pirelli dispute, but when he did get extended lappery he topped both timed sessions to take his second successive pole position. He was no great fan of the place, though, thinking that the proliferation of chicanes lacked interest and the overall layout placed too much emphasis on power.

The use of power was set to dictate the race, with F1 amid a controversial phase during which the 195-litre fuel capacity limit proved difficult to manage. Ayrton led the early laps from de Angelis in the sister Lotus, which he outqualified by half a second. Crucially, though, the Italian had the latest, more fuel-efficient EF15 specification Renault V6 turbo and he was able to finish second behind Prost, while Ayrton had the older EF4 engine and had to moderate his pace severely.

It wasn't enough. Three laps from the end, while still leading from Johansson's Ferrari and Prost's McLaren, Ayrton's Lotus ground to a halt – out of fuel. The same fate befell Johansson a lap later, much to the disappointment of the partisan Ferrari faithful. After the race, Prost's winning car was found to be 2kg underweight and Alain was disqualified, so de Angelis inherited victory, making Ayrton's bitter pill even more difficult to swallow.

⬇ **At Estoril Senna claimed his first pole position and then dominated a wet race to take his first grand prix win.**

📷 sutton-images.com

19 MAY 1985

Monaco GP (Monte Carlo)
Lotus-Renault 97T • Retired, 13 laps, engine

A third successive pole position, by 0.08sec from Nigel Mansell's Williams-Honda FW10, was the result of some spectacular driving around Monaco's confines, but Senna upset a number of his colleagues when he ran an unusually high number of laps – 16 – in final qualifying, prompting accusations that he was on track principally to baulk his rivals after setting quickest time.

Michele Alboreto was among the most vociferous and Niki Lauda had a go too, although the triple World Champion would later apologise to Senna at the subsequent Paul Ricard test, "for going a little over the top."

In the warm-up Ayrton buzzed the Renault engine when changing from fifth to second – an error that would come back to haunt him. He also had to contend with his tyre blankets short-circuiting and overheating his fronts to the point of blistering, which meant they had to be changed just before the start. Thus he went into the race with cold front tyres and warm rears, not that it seemed to make much difference as he powered away in front, tracked by Alboreto's Ferrari. But after 13 laps the engine let go and Senna trailed disconsolately into the pits.

16 JUNE 1985

Canadian GP (Montréal)
Lotus-Renault 97T • 16th

Although a fan of Montréal, Senna was beaten in qualifying by team-mate de Angelis, who lined up a quarter of a second quicker as Lotus locked out the front row.

The black and gold cars led the race but after five laps Senna was in the pits, a problem with the turbo collector box causing him to lose boost. He lost almost five laps before being sent back into the fray without the need to worry about fuel consumption!

In a similar situation, although not so far back, was Keke Rosberg, who also had boost problems with his Williams-Honda FW10 and then flat-spotted a set of tyres and pitted for new ones. Running together but separated by five laps, Rosberg and Senna attacked hard for the rest of the race, Keke in pursuit of points – he finished fourth – and Ayrton for the hell of it. Senna set the quickest lap of the race, Rosberg the second.

Afterwards, they formed something of a mutual admiration society. "I really enjoyed it," Senna told

Autosport. "Keke is fantastic, driving on the limit all the time. It was a good experience for me, we were very even – my car was better on braking and quick corners and his was better on acceleration and slow corners. He takes some amazing chances…"

Rosberg responded: "He's really good. I was impressed, but Jesus… he takes some risks!" For Ayrton, it had all been for 16th place, which said it all.

23 JUNE 1985

United States GP (Detroit)
Lotus-Renault 97T • Retired, 51 laps, accident

On a circuit that was by no means popular with the F1 fraternity but required some 'acrobatics', Senna was in a class of his own once again as he secured his fourth pole of the season. De Angelis, in the same car, was 2.7sec slower! The nearest challenger to Ayrton was Nigel Mansell's Williams, and even that was more than a second away.

Mansell beat Senna off the line but Ayrton slammed

the Lotus down the inside of Turn 3 to take over. Rosberg passed Prost and Mansell on the first lap too, and suddenly it was Montréal all over again, with Ayrton and Keke doing battle.

Senna was soon regretting his tyre choice and could only keep the Williams at bay for seven laps. The Lotus came in for more rubber and Ayrton rejoined 12th. These tyres lasted just 20 laps before Senna stopped again for a different compound, which improved the Lotus dramatically.

With these tyres Ayrton charged back up to fourth place, often lapping 3sec faster than the leaders. He had the Ferraris, in second and third places, in his sights, and there was even an outside chance he could catch Rosberg, who had stopped for tyres. But then he made a mistake…

Drivers had been faced with the choice of carbon or steel brake discs. Carbon brakes were stronger but it was a gamble whether they would last 63 laps of Detroit, so many had opted for steel brakes – but not Senna. Late in the race he was having to pump the pedal but on lap 52, trying to pass Alboreto's Ferrari up the inside of Turn 3, he forgot and went into the wall, suffering a sprained wrist from the steering.

French GP (Paul Ricard)
Lotus-Renault 97T • Retired, 26 laps, accident

At Paul Ricard, Ayrton was still in pain with the wrist he'd hurt in Detroit but said it didn't affect him in the car. He was quickest on Friday but, trying to defend pole from Keke Rosberg on Saturday, suffered an engine failure and so started from the front row alongside the Williams.

Senna ran second until he was forced into the pits early with gear-selection problems. The problem righted, he ran hard until another engine let go just as he approached the fast Signes corner at the end of the Mistral Straight. The car went off on its own oil and destroyed the catch fencing, but Senna escaped without injury.

British GP (Silverstone)
Lotus-Renault 97T • 10th

Ayrton was favourite to be the first man to lap Silverstone at 160mph but the honour fell to Rosberg when Senna had troubles with his qualifying car and had to use the spare Lotus. This was fitted with the more fuel-efficient EF15 Renault V6 turbo, which didn't accept as much boost.

Lining up on the second row, Ayrton made a stupendous start to lead and, as the race progressed, pulled away along with Rosberg's Williams. Keke reckoned he couldn't run at the Lotus's pace without killing his tyres, so backed off. On the move now, however, was Alain Prost, who had topped the race morning warm-up, as he so often did. Prost caught Senna and they ran together until, with 15 laps to go, the Lotus started to misfire. Prost passed him but, as the Renault engine cleared itself, Senna fought back and retook the lead with five laps to go. But then the Lotus coughed again and this time it didn't recover. Senna pulled off, out of fuel.

German GP (Nürburgring)
Lotus-Renault 97T • Retired, 27 laps, CV joint

Senna topped the early part of Friday qualifying but the engine refused to run cleanly when he attempted to go out for a second run, the problem traced to remnants of a rubber washer blocking a valve in the fuel system. Mild frustration was setting in for Ayrton as his only points so far were the nine for that Estoril win, whereas team-mate de Angelis had 26 points and his car seemed to be a beacon of reliability.

Senna made a strong start from the third row and

⬇ With Senna in the car, Team Lotus soon became a regular presence at the top of the qualifying-time monitors.

📷 sutton-images.com

Another wet race, another dominant drive. Senna leading Piquet and Prost into Spa's La Source, and (opposite) on the podium celebrating his second GP victory of 1985.

sutton-images.com

fought another first-lap battle with Rosberg. The Lotus tracked the Williams for the first 15 laps and then took the lead. Senna looked to be in good shape but a broken CV joint put him out well before half distance.

18 AUGUST 1985

Austrian GP (Osterreichring)
Lotus-Renault 97T • 2nd

Unlike most of the opposition, Lotus hadn't tested in Austria prior to the race and, on Friday, paid the penalty as Senna found both his race car and the spare almost impossible. Things improved overnight, with third quickest on Saturday morning suggesting that a decent grid position was likely. But no sooner had Senna gone out than one of the Renault engine's cylinder banks lost boost pressure. Then came the rain. It all translated into a lowly 14th grid slot.

Unlikely as it seemed, Senna then salvaged his best result of the season since Portugal. Tenth on the opening lap, he benefited from the retirements of Rosberg, Tambay, Piquet, Mansell and Lauda, and passed de Angelis and Fabi, so that by the time the chequered flag fell he was runner-up, albeit half a minute adrift of Prost's victorious McLaren.

25 AUGUST 1985

Dutch GP (Zandvoort)
Lotus-Renault 97T • 3rd

In Friday practice Senna's Lotus caught fire and he drove down the slip road at the exit of the circuit's Hugenholtz hairpin in an attempt to get back to the paddock quickly. But Dutch stewards felt he'd acted dangerously and fined him $5,000, much to Ayrton's annoyance. He qualified fourth, behind Piquet, Rosberg and Prost.

At the start Piquet stalled and the Lotus made a strong getaway, so Senna was soon up to second place, slotting in behind Rosberg. But Senna felt that his engine was off-song from the start and, as the McLarens began to demonstrate their customary race pace, there was nothing he could do to resist.

By the time the chequered flag fell the McLarens were in a race of their own and for Senna it was all about defending third place from Alboreto's Ferrari. Starting the last lap they were together and duly made contact at the chicane. The Italian claimed that the Brazilian had blocked him, Senna said that Michele had simply driven into the back of him. They both finished, in the same order.

8 SEPTEMBER 1985

Italian GP (Monza)
Lotus-Renault 97T • 3rd

Driving at Monza for the first time, Ayrton took his fifth pole position of the season with an on-the-limit lap that deposed Rosberg despite the Lotus running off the track at the first Lesmo and losing an estimated 0.3sec!

On the first lap Rosberg chopped across the Lotus's bows into the first chicane, causing Senna also to drop a place to Mansell's Williams. Ayrton later lost another position to Lauda's McLaren as the Marlboro cars ran their customarily strong race pace.

For much of the race Senna was frustrated by a tyre choice that was a mite too hard. When the likes of Rosberg and Nelson Piquet retired, Ayrton picked up his third consecutive podium but, fully a minute behind Prost's victorious McLaren, it wasn't the kind of race he enjoyed.

15 SEPTEMBER 1985

Belgian GP (Spa-Francorchamps)
Lotus-Renault 97T • 1st

After a problematic Friday with both his race chassis and the spare 97T, Senna hit back on Saturday and qualified second, within a tenth of Prost's McLaren.

Race day brought mixed conditions and, as in the rain at Estoril, Ayrton was in a class of his own. Although Nigel Mansell gave chase, Ayrton was always in control and even a misfire, which grew worse as the race wore on, couldn't prevent him from extending his advantage, which stood at almost half a minute by the end. The nine points moved Senna up to third in the World Championship table, one point ahead of Lotus team-mate de Angelis.

6 OCTOBER 1985

European GP (Brands Hatch)
Lotus-Renault 97T • 2nd

The combination of Brands Hatch, which Senna loved, and a Lotus 97T that he felt was the best it had been all year, meant that Ayrton set a stunning pole position, seeing off the challenge of Piquet's Brabham despite Nelson reckoning that his car's BMW engine gave in excess of 1,200bhp when running qualifying boost!

In the race, though, Williams proved too strong.

Rosberg complained that Senna was adopting F3 weaving tactics on the straight and as he tried to go inside the Lotus at Surtees on lap 7 Senna closed the door. Rosberg spun and was clipped by Piquet's Brabham, which was out on the spot, while Rosberg limped round to the pits with a punctured tyre.

Rejoining just in front of Senna and Williams team-mate Nigel Mansell, Keke gave Ayrton a taste of his own medicine at the same corner, causing him to momentarily lift. Mansell didn't hesitate and took a lead he never lost en route to his first grand prix victory. Senna was 21sec behind at the finish.

← Senna and Mansell battling into Paddock Bend on the first lap of the European GP at Brands Hatch: Ayrton took one of his many 1985 pole positions and Nigel won his first grand prix.

📷 sutton-images.com

19 OCTOBER 1985

South African GP (Kyalami)
Lotus-Renault 97T • Retired, 8 laps, engine

With Honda making progress all the time in the power stakes, it was becoming harder for Senna to challenge the Williams duo for pole position, and at Kyalami he ended up almost half a second adrift of Mansell's time, despite going almost 1.3sec quicker than team-mate de Angelis. Through the main straight speed trap Senna was also 10mph down on Piquet's Brabham-BMW.

The race itself proved a Williams benefit, with Mansell taking a second successive win. Senna ran fourth until his engine expired on lap 9.

3 NOVEMBER 1985

Australian GP (Adelaide)
Lotus-Renault 97T • Retired, 62 laps, engine

The inaugural Australian GP was held around Adelaide's 2.234-mile Victoria Park Circuit, which required more input from the drivers than mere power and brawn. Senna duly delivered another pole position, fully 0.7sec clear of Mansell's Williams-Honda.

Ayrton was beaten away by Mansell and then incurred Nigel's wrath when he barged past on the opening lap, making contact with the Williams. The race then developed into a battle between Ayrton and Keke Rosberg, who both led while the other made stops for tyres. With his Lotus ahead, Senna had a couple of spectacular off-track moments as he coped with fading brakes, and then went out with 20 laps to go after a second successive engine failure.

Senna finished his first season with Lotus fourth in the World Championship with 38 points, behind Prost (73), Michele Alboreto (53) and Rosberg (40).

STEVE HALLAM
ON SENNA

Steve Hallam started in F1 as race engineer with Team Lotus in 1982 and ran Nigel Mansell in 1982–84 and then Senna in 1985–87. At the end of the 1990 season he moved to McLaren, where he remained until 2008, heading the race team from 1998.

"We had obviously been watching Ayrton pretty closely, as had a lot of people, from Monaco time in '84, but I'd first encountered him at Donington in '82 when we were testing a Lotus there in an open test day – something that would never happen nowadays! Tim Densham and I were the race engineers at Lotus and we both commented that he was probably going to be one of the coming-men.

"We shared a test with Toleman early in the second half of '84. Gérard Ducarouge and I were there and we spent quite a lot of time watching Ayrton – his pace and what was going on. Peter Warr then signed him and we first met him formally in early '85, after he'd been back in Brazil for the winter, when he had that spell of Bell's Palsy that paralysed part of his face.

"I'm not saying this just with the benefit of hindsight, but I genuinely found him a very friendly and professional person. He obviously wanted to make a good impression and so did we, so that we got off on the right foot. He was very engaging and I found him easy to talk to and get on with.

"He was interested in the cars to a level that, in my relatively short career, was unlike both drivers I'd been used to [Nigel Mansell and Elio de Angelis]. He was very interested in the technical side, not actually crunching numbers but understanding why we were doing things and what the benefit was going to be.

"He was very keen to absorb anything and everything about the cars. Everything that was relevant or interesting would be parked in his mind and later, if we were wrestling with the set-up, he would often recall something and comment on it.

"When we started testing, it was clear that in the Type 97 we had a good car and that he was going to be very, very quick. And he was. We scored a lot of pole positions but we didn't win enough races. It was very clear that we were letting him down far more than he was letting us down.

"In terms of his thinking when he was behind the wheel he was a much more clever driver than people generally imagined. Some years ago Martin Brundle made an observation during a TV commentary about Räikkönen and Montoya at McLaren, saying that he felt Kimi had far more mental capacity to think about the race and needed, say, 95 per cent of his capacity to drive, which left him 5 per cent to think about what was going on in the race; he felt that Montoya needed more to drive and had less left over. I would say Ayrton wasn't dissimilar to Kimi, and perhaps even marginally in front of him. He had the capacity to think during the race as well as to drive at the pace he was going. I only worked with Fernando Alonso for one year but he's like that too: a very, very powerful driver, on all fronts – very fast, thinks really clearly, never gets flustered.

"Ayrton also immersed himself with the team. He still stayed with Ralph and Angie Firman, or close by, and used to come into work. He'd go running with the boys at lunchtime or come to the pub with us.

"At Lotus he took the space that Elio de Angelis had inherited over the years. We'd see Elio at the factory three or four times a year but Ayrton doubled that in his first two weeks. We even gave him a desk. He'd come in, put his briefcase on it and sometimes sit and do some paperwork. Other times he'd just be hanging around at the factory and everybody got to know him and like him. He was just good to be around – an easy person.

"As a result, the boys couldn't do enough for him.

> "He always gave 100 per cent in the car. Absolutely always. And he always expected 100 per cent of everyone around him, but he expected it in a good way and people wanted to work for him… He was a magnet"

And had we had a more reliable car there's absolutely no doubt that we'd have won a lot more races that first year. We only won two, Estoril and Spa. He led a huge number of races and there were many times when he dropped out near the end while leading. The car was very quick and the engines were very powerful but sometimes a bit fragile. And we didn't have the fuel consumption of the Honda so were handicapped, even though Ayrton was well able to compensate on a lot of circuits.

"That's what I mean about him having the capacity to understand. He could work out how to balance the strengths and weaknesses of the car. The set-ups he liked weren't particularly unusual – if a set-up was faster, he liked it. We had qualifying engines in those days too, with unlimited boost, which is how he was able to do his stunning qualifying laps. But fuel capacity was the problem and the major barrier to race performance.

"Speed-wise, he was just phenomenal. Absolutely phenomenal. I recall that John Watson stood in for Niki Lauda at the European GP that year and talked about seeing in his mirrors this black-and-gold apparition with the yellow helmet, and suddenly it was past him and gone. And, John thought, that applied to his own time in F1…

"Ayrton's own reaction to his ability was interesting. The only time I ever saw him fret, just a little, was right at the beginning, in Brazil, where we qualified fourth. We retired from the race because of an electric fuel pump problem but that was the only time I saw him really 'wanting' to do well. From that point on I think he knew that he had the ability and was very comfortable in his own skin.

"It was just about doing the job and doing it correctly. He was the absolute master of 'get the process right and the results will come'. I don't know if he did it consciously but that's what it was. He always gave 100 per cent in the car. Absolutely always. And he always expected 100 per cent of everyone around him, but he expected it in a good way and people wanted to work for him, and to work on his car and be part of the team he was in. It was a self-generating process. He was a magnet.

"One of the French journalists once gave Ayrton a smiley face badge with the word 'magic' written on it. And that's what it felt like at the time. It was magic."

⬆ **Steve Hallam engineered Senna throughout the Team Lotus years, 1985–87, and later worked with him at McLaren.**

📷 sutton-images.com

119

1986

MORE WINS AND POLES

Fourth in the World Championship in his first full F1 season with Lotus in 1985, and with his first two GP victories under his belt, Senna wanted to 'kick on'. But, if the McLaren-TAG/Porsches were less dominant than in 1984, the team closing the gap wasn't Lotus, but Williams.

This was the year Frank Williams suffered his life-changing car accident on the way back from a pre-season Paul Ricard test. But his team now had potent and super-competitive Honda V6 turbos, far removed from those that had suffered severe turbo lag in 1984. Senna was in for a frustrating year with Alain Prost winning again at the final round to secure his second World Championship title, but the Williams pair, Nigel Mansell and Nelson Piquet, were formidably quick.

Ayrton had a new team-mate in Johnny Dumfries, Elio de Angelis having moved to Brabham-BMW because he felt that Team Lotus was increasingly directing its efforts towards Senna. Dumfries had won the Marlboro British F3 Championship in 1984, the year after Ayrton, driving for David Price Racing.

← Senna's Lotus 98T climbs Eau Rouge during the Belgian GP at Spa and sends sparks flying – rival teams had suspected Lotus of generating ground effect by running the car too low.

📷 sutton-images.com

↑ Senna wouldn't have Derek Warwick at Lotus in 1986. He didn't fear Warwick, but just felt that with a top British driver Lotus would have to split its efforts, and didn't have enough resource. So Johnny Dumfries (right) got his chance. It drove a wedge between Ayrton and the British media.

23 MARCH 1986

Brazilian GP (Jacarepagua)
Lotus-Renault 98T • 2nd

Senna, who had just turned 26, delighted his fans by taking pole position by 0.72sec in the Lotus-Renault 98T from the other home hero, new Williams signing Nelson Piquet. But on the first lap it was the other Williams driver, Nigel Mansell, who tried to go inside the Lotus and relieve Senna of the lead, but Ayrton wasn't giving way and Mansell ended up in the barrier.

In race trim the Williams-Honda FW11 was clearly the superior car and it took Piquet only as long as lap 3 to get past Senna and start pulling away at a second a lap. Senna came under threat from Prost's McLaren MP4/2C, as usual quicker in race trim, but Alain was destined to retire with engine failure, leaving Ayrton a comfortable second, but 35sec behind the winning Williams.

13 APRIL 1986

Spanish GP (Jerez)
Lotus-Renault 98T • 1st

The first grand prix run at the newly built Jerez de la Frontera circuit, in sherry-producing territory, brought another emphatic pole position for Senna – and the 100th for Team Lotus – with a time 0.83sec clear of Piquet's Williams-Honda. The hydraulic-valve Renault V6 was now producing prodigious horsepower in qualifying spec but the stiffly-suspended car was showering sparks and leading rivals to suspect that the team was generating ground effect by running the car too low. In the cockpit Ayrton took such a pounding that, post-race, he booked himself in for a physio session with Austrian fitness guru Willi Dungl.

Senna led for 39 of the 72 laps before being passed by Mansell's Williams. Shortly afterwards, Nigel picked up a slow puncture and the Lotus retook the lead midway through lap 63. Mansell, re-shod, was 20sec behind Senna with eight laps to go but put in a heroic charge. Senna only just fended him off to take the chequered flag by a margin of just 0.014sec, the closest F1 finish since Peter Gethin – Senna's team manager at Toleman – famously won the Italian GP at Monza in 1971.

27 APRIL 1986

San Marino GP (Imola)
Lotus-Renault 98T • Retired, 11 laps, wheel bearing

Once again Senna took a decisive pole position, half a second clear of Piquet's Williams-Honda and a full second ahead of Mansell's sister car. And again there were dark mutterings about ground effect. Rivals wondered how a supposedly flat-bottomed car was sparking from the sides rather than the middle. But FISA stewards inspected the Lotus and cleared it.

Piquet got the jump on Senna on the run down to Tosa and started to pull away, while Ayrton soon lost further places to the McLarens of Prost and Rosberg. Senna could feel a vibration from the back of the Lotus and posted an early retirement with a broken right wheel bearing, a similar affliction also ending the race of team-mate Johnny Dumfries.

11 MAY 1986

Monaco GP (Monte Carlo)
Lotus-Renault 98T • 3rd

Senna was quickest of all on the first day of qualifying on Thursday and then raised the bar with conclusively the quickest time in Saturday morning's practice – 1m 22.340s. Nobody could beat that when it mattered, not even Senna himself, but Prost's 1m 22.627s was enough to claim the all-important pole position for the annual thread-the-needle contest that is Monte Carlo. Mansell also managed to squeak ahead, with Ayrton having to content himself with third fastest time – 1m 23.175s.

⬇ When Senna beat Mansell by 0.014sec to win the first grand prix at Jerez, it was the closest finish since Peter Gethin's victory in the 1971 Italian GP at Monza.

📷 sutton-images.com

SENNA vs PROST: ROLE REVERSAL

With the rivalry that would develop over time between Senna and Alain Prost, it became accepted that Ayrton was usually the aggressor, Alain the more passive.

In his *Autosport* report of the 1986 Canadian GP, however, Nigel Roebuck wrote of Prost's removal of Senna from second place in Montréal:

"Prost put a move on Senna which helps to explain why the man is a double World Champion. As the two of them went for the right-left-right sweepers at the beginning of lap five, Alain had the McLaren up alongside, to Ayrton's right. As they shaped up for the left-hand portion he was drawing ahead and, into it, calmly moved across to claim the line, obliging the Brazilian to lift and drive over the kerbing.

"It was done with the ruthless precision of a meat slicer: I'm coming through, so you'd better make your own arrangements. Moreover, Prost took the rest of the queue with him, for Senna lifting off allowed Rosberg, Piquet and Arnoux to get momentum on the Lotus down to the next corner. In a matter of seconds Ayrton had gone from second to sixth."

Senna, being Senna, won't have appreciated that…

⬇ **Prost shapes up for his pass of Senna's Lotus.**

📷 sutton-images.com

Senna managed to get through Ste Devote, the first corner, in second place but there was no holding Prost, who had a 5sec advantage after the opening 10 laps. Alain motored away to a comfortable 25sec win and Senna had to concede second place to Rosberg in the second McLaren, eventually finishing 28sec behind the Finn.

25 MAY 1986

Belgian GP (Spa-Francorchamps)
Lotus-Renault 98T • 2nd

As F1 re-assembled in Belgium, it was mourning the death of Ayrton's former team-mate Elio de Angelis, who died in a testing accident at Paul Ricard a week earlier.

At Spa, Senna's pole position challenge was affected by reversion to the old-specification Lotus rear suspension in a bid to avoid the wheel-bearing failure that hampered him at Imola. He lined up fourth behind Nelson Piquet's Williams-Honda, Gerhard Berger's Benetton-BMW and Alain Prost's McLaren-TAG/Porsche.

Ayrton attempted to go round the outside of Berger and Prost at La Source on the opening lap, squeezing his rivals, who made contact. Senna took full advantage as he sprinted through Eau Rouge in second place.

When Piquet retired early, Senna led for five laps with Nigel Mansell's sister Williams closing in. The Williams

pitted first and when Senna emerged from his own stop, Nigel was already in front. Mansell took the flag a comfortable 20sec clear but Ayrton's second place took him to the top of the World Championship table for the first time, two points clear of defending champion Prost.

15 JUNE 1986

Canadian GP (Montréal)
Lotus-Renault 98T • 2nd

Senna and Mansell fought out pole position at the Ile Notre-Dame track with the Englishman ultimately prevailing by just 0.07sec.

Mansell drove a fine opening lap to lead by 3sec, with Senna under threat from Prost's McLaren. Prost's overtaking move on lap 5 lost the Lotus so much momentum that Ayrton dropped to sixth (see panel, 'Role reversal').

Senna then spent much of the race battling with Arnoux's Ligier JS27, which was on hard-compound Pirelli tyres as René intended to run through without a pit stop. Senna finally found a way by with just 10 laps remaining, but then he and Arnoux were lapped by the flying Mansell. That was a measure of the Williams-Honda race superiority that now saw Nigel win his second successive race.

↑ **Senna and Peter Warr contemplate the fact that with the Williams-Hondas fully into their stride, even Ayrton's genius could only put the Lotus on the second row at Monaco.**

sutton-images.com

125

22 JUNE 1986

United States GP (Detroit)
Lotus-Renault 98T • 1st

Pole for the unpopular Detroit race was another battle with Nigel Mansell, which Senna won. He then hurried off to his hotel room to watch the Brazil v France World Cup game, leaving a tape of his thoughts to be played at the press conference. That didn't go down well with a largely American audience…

Still, Ayrton impressed them on race day. After leading the first couple of laps, he was passed by Mansell when he missed a gear and it looked as if Nigel would motor off into the distance for a hat-trick of wins. Soon, though, the Williams-Honda had brake problems and Senna retook the lead, which lasted for only four laps until the Lotus got a punctured left rear tyre and Ayrton shot into the pits for new rubber. He rejoined eighth, quickly passed the Ferraris of Stefan Johansson and Michele Alboreto, and started to chase down the leading pack. His fresher rubber meant he could go longer before his scheduled mid-race tyre stop. When, on lap 40 of the 63, Piquet crashed while trying to prevent the Lotus taking the lead after his stop, Senna hit the front again. He pulled away to win by more than half a minute, putting himself back at the top of the championship table, three points clear of defending champion Prost.

6 JULY 1986

French GP (Paul Ricard)
Lotus-Renault 98T • Retired, 3 laps, accident

For this race Senna had the latest EF15C engine, which, Renault's Jean Sage explained, had new cylinder heads that were intended to improve combustion, and thus fuel consumption. Since dispensing with valve springs, the key disadvantage of the Renault V6 compared with the likes of Honda and TAG was its inferior fuel consumption. Testing with the new engine at Silverstone the previous week, however, had proved problematic due to the car's telemetry interfering with the V6's electronic injection system.

Tyres were expected to be a significant factor for the race, but Senna didn't get far enough to find out. Mansell's Williams and the Lotus ran first and second for the first three laps but then Andrea de Cesaris blew up his Minardi-Motori on the long Mistral Straight – and continued through Signes on the racing line. Mansell's car twitched when it hit the oil but got away with it. Senna wasn't so fortunate. He flew off the road and went hard into the tyre barrier. It spelled the end of his championship lead. Prost, second to Mansell at Ricard, now led with 39 points to Nigel's 38 and Ayrton's 36.

13 JULY 1986

British GP (Brands Hatch)
Lotus-Renault 98T • Retired, 27 laps, gearbox

Ayrton had taken pole position for the European GP at the same circuit nine months earlier but this time he couldn't stop the Williams-Hondas. With Frank Williams back at a circuit for the first time since the March car accident that confined him to a wheelchair, it was fitting that his drivers claimed the front row. Senna's Lotus looked twitchy and difficult, and he had to be content with third, 0.56sec behind Piquet's pole.

At the start Mansell broke a driveshaft as he grabbed second gear after outdoing Piquet, but behind him there was chaos as Thierry Boutsen triggered a multiple accident that resulted in a leg-breaking shunt for Jacques Laffite, whose Ligier went into the inside barrier on the run to Paddock Bend. A restarted race was an opportunity for Mansell in the spare Williams, which he drove to a great 5sec victory over his pole-winning team-mate. Senna had to give best to Berger's Benetton in the early laps but moved up to third when the Austrian retired after 22 laps. It was short-lived, Ayrton himself out of the race five laps later when the Lotus broke fourth gear.

Mansell now led the World Championship with 47 points to Prost's 43 and Ayrton's 36.

27 JULY 1986

German GP (Hockenheim)
Lotus-Renault 98T • 2nd

Ayrton wasn't happy with his Lotus's balance on Friday and when a fuel-pump problem manifested itself at the start of final qualifying, he was forced to use his race car and engine rather than their qualifying counterparts. The Lotus team worked wonders to change the pump in time for his final run, which netted third on the grid behind Rosberg and Prost. It was Rosberg's first pole for McLaren, on the back of announcing that he would retire at the end of the year.

Senna speared his Lotus between the two McLarens to lead, nudging Prost's right front wheel as he did so, but Ayrton could only remain there until the second lap, when Rosberg came by. Senna knew that single-lap pace was one thing, but also that he was unlikely to have the economy to race McLaren and Williams to the end.

He was wrong about McLaren, passing Prost for third with two laps to go as the Frenchman glanced anxiously at his fuel read-out, which was telling him he didn't have enough to resist. Rosberg, also with concerns about fuel,

lost the lead to Piquet with five laps to go. When Keke ran dry on the final run down to the first chicane, Ayrton swooped by to take second place.

10 AUGUST 1986

Hungarian GP (Hungaroring)
Lotus-Renault 98T • 2nd

This was Formula 1's first trip behind the Iron Curtain, to the new Hungaroring. Despite the average Hungarian wage being £75 a month and race day admission costing £13, over 200,000 flocked to a circuit that, in many respects, was similar to Jerez.

With hot, dry weather and much dust, there wasn't a lot of grip. Ayrton took pole, 0.33sec ahead of Piquet's Williams, but said: "I think I've spun here more times than in the rest of my career..."

Senna led the first 11 laps but could do little to stop Piquet going by because the Honda-powered Williams

was quicker on the straight. Nelson led until lap 35 of the 76, when he made a tyre stop, Senna staying out seven laps longer. Ayrton got his stop done without losing the lead and looked in good shape until Piquet started to close rapidly. After some hairy stuff into Turn 1, which didn't impress Piquet, the Williams took the lead again and held onto it comfortably, taking the flag 17sec in front of the Lotus. World Championship points were now Mansell on 55, Senna on 48 and Piquet on 47.

17 AUGUST 1986

Austrian GP (Osterreichring)
Lotus-Renault 98T • Retired, 13 laps, engine

Power is what's needed at the Osterreichring and qualifying saw a front row lock-out for the Benetton-BMWs, with Italian Teo Fabi silencing the locals when he beat Austrian Gerhard Berger to pole.

Senna had problems with a leak in the Renault

engine's pneumatic valve system in the first qualifying session and took over Johnny Dumfries's car after the Scot had done his first run. It took Ayrton a considerable time to go quicker, however, and when back in his own car on Saturday he could only improve a single place to eighth, 1.7sec from pole.

The race was little better. Senna struggled to run ahead of Arnoux's Ligier JS27 in seventh place before making an early stop for a blistered front tyre. He was back in the pits for good five laps later, the engine misfiring chronically.

7 SEPTEMBER 1986

Italian GP (Monza)
Lotus-Renault 98T • Retired, 0 laps, transmission

Ayrton was quickest in the opening session of qualifying but on Saturday the engine blew and he was knocked back to fifth on the grid. Sunday was worse, the transmission failing before Senna had done a lap. His thin championship chances had receded further and he was now fourth with 48 points behind Mansell on 61, Piquet on 56 and Prost on 53.

21 SEPTEMBER 1986

Portuguese GP (Estoril)
Lotus-Renault 98T • 4th

At first it looked like a repeat of Monza, Ayrton unhappy with his car's balance on the first day and then blowing an engine early on the second. But with the Renault V6 changed in time for qualifying, Senna's first run was good enough for pole, until beaten by Mansell, Berger, Prost and Fabi.

The team changed to a different type of turbo in time for the second run and after a spectacular, snaking, sparking lap, Senna improved from 1m 18.34s to 1m 16.67s to beat Mansell to pole by more than eight tenths.

Up and down pitlane there were mutterings about sidepod stays being lowered and the car running lower than it should to maximise downforce, with the undertray producing showers of sparks.

"When you do a good lap and then have a car come along and beat it by almost a second, going nearly two seconds quicker than it's gone before, you must draw your own conclusions," Mansell said. "You have to congratulate Lotus, I suppose. If they're as quick as that tomorrow, then I'll worry..."

After the race morning warm-up, the four

championship contenders – Mansell, Piquet, Senna and Prost – all posed for a photograph that was to become iconic. "All great buddies," one of their rivals jested. "Alain gets on with Nigel, Nigel gets on with Alain, and that's about it..."

With his stunning debut win the previous year still in the front of many minds, not least his own, Senna was hoping for another wet race, but didn't get it. He didn't think he'd be able to match the Honda's fuel efficiency in the race, and he was right.

Mansell beat the Lotus off the line, led the first lap and was never headed. As the race wore on, Piquet in the second Williams put Senna under pressure but Ayrton resisted, and used the traffic well. Piquet eventually spun in frustration, allowing Prost through into third.

Cruelly, though, Senna ran out of fuel on the last lap and dropped to fourth. At his tyre stop his read-out was telling him he was just the wrong side of making the finish, but he adapted and at the time he ran out, his display told him he had enough fuel for another lap and a half...

The championship was now Mansell on 70, Piquet on 60 and Prost on 59, with two rounds to go. Ayrton, with 51, was no longer in the fight.

12 OCTOBER 1986

Mexican GP (Autodromo Hermanos Rodriguez)
Lotus-Renault 98T • 3rd

Grand Prix racing returned to Mexico City for the first time since 1970 and it was all about whether Nigel Mansell, with a 10-point advantage, could seal the World Championship.

Senna took a second successive pole with a superb lap, after which Lotus announced that anyone muttering about a 'cheat' qualifying set-up needed to put up – and risk being sued – or shut up!

Disastrously for his title aspirations, Mansell was unable to get the Williams into gear on the grid and was 18th at the end of the opening lap. Senna locked up at Turn 1, meanwhile, letting Piquet through to lead. Berger's Benetton and Prost's McLaren were next.

The Benetton, with its hugely powerful BMW turbo, had turned in some impressive performances, the team finally getting its reward on the bumpy Hermanos Rodriguez track when Berger won after running a non-stop race with his durable Pirelli rubber. Prost finished second after Senna needed a second tyre stop, while Piquet and Mansell finished fourth and fifth, keeping a three-way title fight with Prost alive to the Adelaide season finale.

➜ In Portugal, with three rounds to go, Senna, Prost, Mansell and Piquet were all in contention for the world title. The bonhomie was no doubt a little forced...

📷 sutton-images.com

26 OCTOBER 1986

Australian GP (Adelaide)
Lotus-Renault 98T • Retired, 43 laps, engine

Senna's removal from the title fight didn't curb his enthusiasm for a hat-trick of poles. On Friday he clipped a kerb and spun. In the final session an awesome lap was spoiled by yellow flags and he had to be content with third.

Mansell, who needed only to finish in the first three to win the championship, converted his pole and led, with Senna running second ahead of Piquet, until Nigel left a gap for the pair of them, not wanting to run too hard early on. Nelson then outbraked Ayrton and Rosberg was on the move too. Prost had to win the race in order to stand any chance of the championship and McLaren's plan was for Rosberg to set a fast pace on full tanks to encourage Prost's championship rivals to burn fuel in pursuit. Prost moved quietly though to third, ahead of Mansell, as Piquet spun and resumed behind his team-mate.

The McLarens were soon 1–2 and, with Rosberg bound to cede the lead, Prost's outside chance of the title was still alive. But Mansell, a comfortable third, was doing all he needed. Prost could have done with Ayrton giving Nigel a fight but, on lap 44 of 82, the Lotus blew up.

Prost, meanwhile, had what turned out to be a stroke of good fortune. Lapping Berger, he clipped the Benetton and suffered a punctured front tyre and pitted for fresh tyres on lap 32. The Goodyear technicians, expecting a tyre stop to be necessary for everyone, changed their minds after examining the condition of Prost's discarded set.

Rosberg, leading his last grand prix in his McLaren, suffered delamination of the right rear Goodyear tyre and his race ended on lap 63. On the very next lap, with just 18 laps to go, Mansell's left rear Goodyear exploded at 180mph as the Williams was lapping Philippe Alliot's Ligier. Nigel manfully wrestled the car to a stop in the escape road at the end of Decquetteville Avenue.

Nigel's hated team-mate now led, but dare Piquet stay out? If he won he would become World Champion but, responsibly, in view of what they'd just seen, Williams called him in for fresh rubber.

Prost now led but his fuel read-out was telling him that he was five litres short – about two laps' worth. Piquet, with no such worries and a new set of Goodyears, was setting the track alight in pursuit. Prost, therefore, couldn't slow down too much and was certain he would run dry. But his McLaren kept going and a jubilant Alain took the flag 4sec clear of Nelson. Williams, through no fault of their own, had managed to snatch defeat from the jaws of victory and Prost was the first back-to-back World Champion for a quarter of a century. Senna looked forward to having a Honda engine in his Lotus...

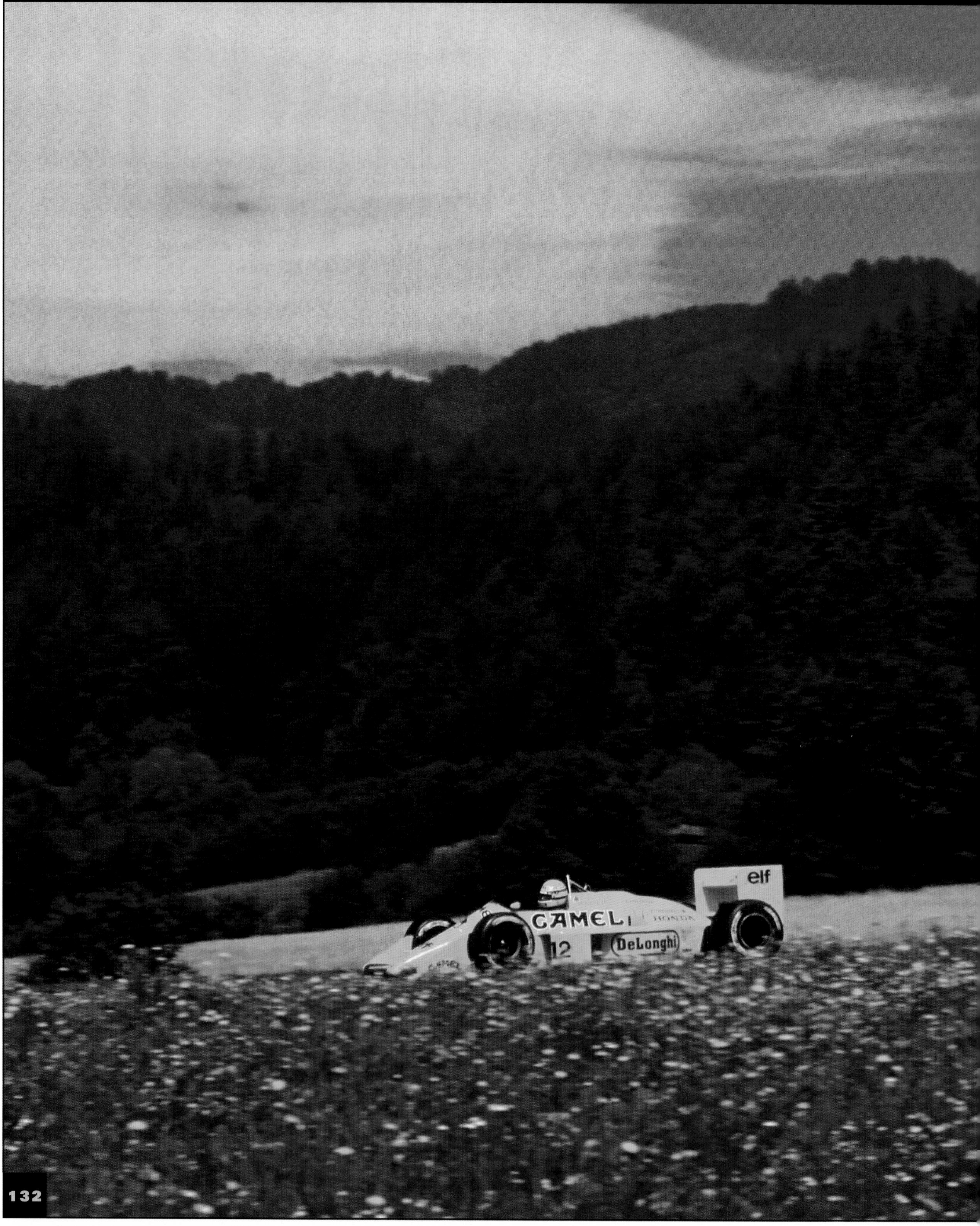
elf
CAMEL
HONDA
12
DeLonghi

1987

FRUSTRATION AT LOTUS

In 1986, some of the BMW turbo engines were reputedly developing 1,500bhp in qualifying trim! To limit power figures ahead of a return to normally aspirated engines in 1989, therefore, the turbos were fitted with a pop-off valve that would open if boost pressure exceeded 4 bar.

For a time it looked as if there would be no tyres as Goodyear pulled out and Pirelli withdrew its support. But a change of heart by Goodyear meant single supply and the end of qualifying tyres and multiple compounds at each race.

After the strong results for Williams at the end of 1985 and throughout '86, it was assumed that a Honda engine was a guarantee of success, so when Lotus clinched a deal to swap from Renault to Honda (with Satoru Nakajima joining as Senna's team-mate), it was assumed that Ayrton would be challenging the Williams-Hondas.

It didn't quite work out like that. Lotus raced its active-ride system, the result of six years' development, and at bumpy tracks like Monaco and Detroit, both won by Ayrton, the benefits were self-evident. But the active system came with an inherent weight penalty and, aerodynamically, the Lotus 99T was no Williams FW11B.

There was a different look about the team too. After 15 years of black-and-gold livery, John Player (Imperial Tobacco) withdrew from sponsorship, to be replaced by the RJ Reynolds Camel brand and its yellow colours.

← The frustrations of the 1987 season, the last of Senna's three with Team Lotus, were typified at the majestic Osterreichring, where Ayrton finished fifth after a push-start on the grid and a pitstop for a new nosecone following a tangle with Alboreto's Ferrari.

🖸 sutton-images.com

133

↑ For 1987 the
black-and-gold
JPS branding was
gone from Team
Lotus. Senna's new
team-mate, Satoru
Nakajima, signalled
the arrival of Honda
turbos in place of
Renault engines.

📷 sutton-images.com

12 APRIL 1987

Brazilian GP (Jacarepagua)
Lotus-Honda 99T • Retired, 50 laps, engine

Brazil gave an early indication that the 1987 season
wasn't going to be the tour de force many had predicted
for Senna and Lotus-Honda. The Lotus 99T's active-ride
system gave the drivers a torrid time on the opening day,
with team boss Peter Warr reckoning that the discomfort
it was delivering was more suited to the Safari Rally than
the Brazilian GP!

Reversion to a previous active set-up on Saturday was
better, but Senna, having started the previous year's race
on pole, had to be content with third this time. And not a
close third either: his 1m 28.408s compared badly with
Nigel Mansell's 1m 26.128s in the Williams-Honda...

Piquet, also a front-row starter in the other Williams,
took the lead with Senna second as Mansell made a poor
getaway. Ayrton, though, was destined not to finish,
forced to switch off when an oil tank separator broke 50
laps into the 61.

3 MAY 1987

San Marino GP (Imola)
Lotus-Honda 99T • 2nd

In better shape at Imola, Senna pipped Mansell's Williams
to pole by just 0.12sec, while Piquet didn't start after an
enormous accident at Tamburello. In the race, however,
the Lotus had no answer to the Williams. Senna duly
converted his pole and led the opening lap but, next time
round, Mansell imperiously went round the outside into
the tight Tosa corner.

Senna also had to give best to Prost's McLaren MP4/3
but the Frenchman suffered a rare retirement and it was
left to Ayrton to give vain chase of Mansell. By the end
Senna was half a minute down in second place, his
Lotus one of only four cars on the lead lap.

17 MAY 1987

Belgian GP (Spa-Francorchamps)
Lotus-Honda 99T • Retired, 0 laps, accident

There was no answer to Mansell's Williams in qualifying. Nigel took pole with 1m 52.026s but Ayrton, on 1m 53.426s, failed by just 0.01sec to pip Piquet's sister car to the other front-row spot. It was a good effort but it could have been better: someone had failed to remove the blanking tape from the brake ducts, so Senna's quickest lap was affected by overheating brakes, then a misfire.

In the race it was tempers that were running hot. Mansell rounded La Source hairpin and headed the field through the famous Eau Rouge but an accident to Philippe Streiff's Tyrrell led to the race being stopped.

At the restart, Senna grabbed the lead from Mansell at La Source. Nigel tracked him until the exit of Pouhon, then jinked out and blasted alongside. At the next corner they made contact. Ayrton finished his race in the gravel trap, while Nigel soldiered on for 17 laps before retiring the Williams. He then sought out Ayrton for a 'little chat'.

31 MAY 1987

Monaco GP (Monte Carlo)
Lotus-Honda 99T • 1st

Lotus suspected that Monte Carlo would play to the strengths of its active ride and tested at Donington the previous week in an attempt to fine-tune the system. But there was no stopping Mansell. Ayrton's skills were always showcased by Monte Carlo but even he was seven-tenths away from the ultra-confident Brit in the Williams.

With the Spa altercation fresh in the memory, eyes were on Nigel and Ayrton at the start, but Mansell it was who blasted through Ste Devote with Senna in pursuit. There was no holding the Williams as it disappeared at around a second a lap, only to suffer a turbo wastegate problem before half distance.

After Mansell's retirement Senna took a comfortable victory, over half a minute clear of Piquet, moving himself up to second in the championship table, three points behind defending double champion Prost.

⬇ **After Mansell retired from the lead, Senna took a comfortable victory in the Monaco GP.**
📷 sutton-images.com

MANSELL GETS PHYSICAL AT SPA

Predictably, there were two different versions of the coming-together between Senna and Mansell at Spa.

"I don't know whether he missed a gear or the engine hesitated but there was a sudden flame-out from the Lotus exhaust," Mansell claimed. "I moved left, it was the logical thing to do, and I passed him so easily that I was sure he was in trouble. I wouldn't have tried to pass him there normally but I had the line into the corner. The next thing I knew, I was being pushed off the circuit. There is no doubt that I was ahead."

And Senna's explanation: "I can tell you that nothing happened to my car at the previous corner. I took it flat. Maybe you find the car in front appears to slow if you hit the boost button on your steering wheel and have an extra 100bhp! But I couldn't believe what he was trying to do – overtake on the outside of a place like that...

"I tried to get out of the way, braked as much as possible, but you can only do so much in a situation like that. I was committed to the corner, there was no way I could stop. Then he came down and we had a bit of an argument about it."

Mansell, in fact, moved F1 from the back pages to the front when he came marching into the Lotus pit after finally retiring, by which time Ayrton was changed.

"I knew he hadn't come to apologise," Senna said. "His face wasn't right for that. "And you are not apologising when you get hold of somebody by the throat..."

Eventually three Lotus mechanics managed to drag Mansell away.

⬇ **After Senna and Mansell tangled on the first lap of the restarted Spa race, Nigel went to the Lotus pit to seek out Ayrton.**

📷 sutton-images.com

21 JUNE 1987

United States GP (Detroit)
Lotus-Honda 99T • 1st

Mansell continued his dominant qualifying form with a lap in 1m 39.264s compared with Senna's 1m 40.607s, which again was good enough for the front row, 0.3sec clear of Piquet's Williams.

As in Monaco, Williams-Honda utilised its superiority to drop Lotus-Honda by a second a lap at the start. When Mansell made his tyre stop after 21 laps a rear wheel nut jammed and he lost 10sec in the pits. He immediately started to lap 2sec quicker than anyone but the canny Senna, now in front, began to contemplate going through without a stop.

The information from Mansell's stop was that the tyres were in reasonable shape and as the fuel load lightened Senna carried on. The strategy worked and Ayrton won his second consecutive grand prix, ahead of Piquet. Mansell battled severe leg cramps to finish a lapped fifth. Ayrton now led the championship by two points from Prost, who finished third in Detroit.

5 JULY 1987

French GP (Paul Ricard)
Lotus-Honda 99T • 4th

Senna qualified third at Ricard, behind – yet again – Mansell's Williams-Honda on pole and Prost's McLaren in second spot. Qualifying was problematic for Ayrton, however, with Friday affected by lost time with a gearbox check after a failure on Satoru Nakajima's sister 99T, as well as inconsistent handling that was traced to incorrect tyre pressures. The following day, the Honda started to misfire just as Senna began a hot lap, so he switched off and accepted he wasn't going to start from the front row.

Both Monaco and Detroit had been bumpy tracks where Lotus's active-ride system had been a help but this wasn't the case at Ricard. Although Lotus hoped they had made progress in a Silverstone test, the car simply didn't have the speed to offer a challenge. Ayrton's quickest lap was only seventh best and almost 3sec from the Williams's pace. He finished a lapped fourth and, with Prost third, his two-point championship lead was halved.

→ **Senna and the active-ride Lotus 99T proved an unbeatable combination in Detroit.**

📷 sutton-images.com

↑ Although Senna
still narrowly led
the championship,
the Lotus-Honda
combination was
2sec slower than the
Williams-Hondas
at Silverstone.

📷 sutton-images.com

12 JULY 1987

British GP (Silverstone)
Lotus-Honda 99T • 3rd

The Williams-Honda domination continued with
Nelson Piquet turning the tables on Nigel Mansell
– in qualifying at least. Ayrton was third but again unhappy
with the Lotus balance, although a few inputs into the
computer-controlled active ride improved things a little.
Senna was also fortunate when Mansell's Williams kicked
up a piece of metal – from Christian Danner's Zakspeed
– that badly damaged the Lotus's front wing before
narrowly missing Ayrton's head.

The story of the race was a simple one: a Williams-
Honda benefit with Mansell pulling off his famous dummy
on Piquet at Stowe Corner to snatch victory from his
team-mate with two laps to go. Nobody else finished
on the same lap. Ayrton's best race lap on the way to
third place was almost two full seconds down on Nigel's,
which told you all you needed to know about the
Lotus/Williams contest – despite both teams having
the same engine.

Amazingly, Senna still led the championship by
a point, with 31 to the 30 of Mansell and Piquet, but
that advantage couldn't last much longer...

26 JULY 1987

German GP (Hockenheim)
Lotus-Honda 99T • 3rd

In pre-race testing at the flat-out Hockenheim autodrome,
Senna's Lotus suffered a tyre blow-out at almost 200mph
on the run to the first chicane. The active ride tried to make
amends – which was asking too much! – and Senna was
fortunate not to hit anything.

Although Senna's fine qualifying effort (1m 42.873s)
was just a quarter of a second from Mansell's Williams and
good enough for the front row, once again the performance
wasn't there in the race. Although Ayrton led off the start
and round the first lap, Mansell passed him on the run to the
first chicane second time around, then Prost demoted him
into the Stadium section and Piquet soon went by too.

It wasn't long before Senna was experiencing mechanical
dramas. A loose bolt in the turbo housing robbed him of
boost control, followed by a sudden loss of grip that a pit
stop was unable to explain, followed by a third stop to have
a damaged nose replaced. And as he left pitlane the last
time, the Lotus mechanics noticed leaking hydraulic fluid.

Senna made it to the end in third place, behind Piquet
and Stefan Johannson's McLaren, but for the second
successive race he stood on the podium beside drivers

who'd lapped him. His championship lead was gone too, Piquet now four points in front. While publicly he was happy with Lotus, privately, he wasn't...

9 AUGUST 1987

Hungarian GP (Hungaroring)
Lotus-Honda 99T • 2nd

Lotus had some revisions to the 99T in time for the Hungarian GP, including a more aerodynamic engine cover and sidepods, but it was lack of mechanical grip that Ayrton was complaining about most when he could only qualify sixth, behind Mansell, Berger, Piquet, Prost and Alboreto. The engine pop-off valve was also cutting in too soon and Ayrton found himself 2.3sec away from pole.

Senna passed Prost at the start and ran fifth in the early laps, picking up another place when Berger struck mechanical trouble. That became third when Alboreto's engine failed and second six laps from home when Mansell, having led all the way, cruelly fell victim to a loose right-rear wheel nut, leaving the win to Piquet. Ayrton was now 11 points clear of the season's undoubted pacesetter, but seven behind Piquet.

16 AUGUST 1987

Austrian GP (Osterreichring)
Lotus-Honda 99T • 5th

Once again Senna was more than 2sec behind the Williams pole time and reduced to sharing the fourth row when rain intervened and Lotus was unable to assess changes made to the active-ride system.

There was enormous drama as two startline shunts meant three attempts to start the race. At the third time of asking Senna stalled the Lotus and had to be push-started, meaning that he came around 18th at the end of the opening lap.

After a battling drive through the field, Senna encountered Michele Alboreto, who wasn't keen for his Ferrari to be overtaken. Into the Hella Licht chicane the pair touched and Senna was forced to pit for a new nose.

"He was weaving," Senna claimed, "and then braked in front of me. There was nothing I could do."

Ayrton rejoined ninth and fought back to finish fifth, benefiting when Prost and Alboreto hit problems. The championship deficit to Piquet was now 12 points after Nelson finished second to his team-mate.

⬇ Senna and Lotus designer Gérard Ducarouge. The Honda engine hadn't put Senna into a championship-challenging position and Ayrton, by now, was looking elsewhere.

📷 sutton-images.com

THE END OF THE ROAD FOR LOTUS AND SENNA

Halfway through his third season with Team Lotus, Senna still hadn't had a car that would allow him to compete for the World Championship. If he thought it was a Honda turbo that was making the Williams what it was, he was mistaken.

Shortly after the German GP, Senna's lawyers sent a letter to Lotus team boss Peter Warr informing him that Ayrton would be exercising a release clause in his contract. Honda was going to supply McLaren in 1988 and Ayrton was part of the deal.

Playing the politics shrewdly,

meanwhile, was Nelson Piquet, Senna's arch-rival and fellow countryman. While Mansell was regularly blowing Piquet away at Williams, Nigel was also suffering the lion's share of the failures, allowing Nelson to retain a semblance of credibility and respectability. Quite rightly, though, Piquet was having no luck in persuading Frank Williams that he was deserving of number one status. That being the case, and knowing that Honda was dissatisfied that Williams won most of the battles in 1986 but lost the war to Prost and McLaren at the final round, Piquet worked out that if he signed for

Lotus he would guarantee the supply of Honda engines for Lotus – and ensure that Williams lost theirs.

And so, although rumours were rife of Senna's impending McLaren deal to go head-to-head with Prost, it was Lotus that made the first move, announcing at the Hungarian GP that Piquet would drive for the team in 1988, alongside Satoru Nakajima.

⬇ Second places, including here in Hungary, were the limit of the Lotus capability and by now Senna was being linked to McLaren for 1988.

📷 sutton-images.com

6 SEPTEMBER 1987

Italian GP (Monza)
Lotus-Honda 99T • 2nd

At Monza, Senna wasn't the only one with an active car. Williams brought their active FW11B after an encouraging test at Imola by Piquet, who elected to race the car while Mansell stayed with his regular chassis.

Piquet used the car to good effect by pipping Mansell to pole by a tenth, while Ayrton started fourth, nearly a second and a half adrift of the Williams pace.

Senna didn't make a great start but was into the lead just before half distance in the 50-lapper as everyone else peeled into the pits. Ayrton contemplated the possibility of repeating his Monaco/Detroit non-stop tactic. The message from the pits was that it would be marginal. He went for it.

As the race reached its closing stages it looked as if the Lotus would hang on, but with seven laps left Senna got on the marbles as he lapped Piercarlo Ghinzani's Ligier going into Parabolica. He slid wide through the gravel trap and by the time he collected everything together Piquet was through.

Ayrton mounted a charge and was less than 2sec adrift as they crossed the line. His outside chance of the championship was fading fast as he was now 14 points behind Piquet.

21 SEPTEMBER 1987

Portuguese GP (Estoril)
Lotus-Honda 99T • 7th

Qualifying was a messy affair. On the Friday Ayrton spun in avoidance of Philippe Alliot's Lola, and on the Saturday he clipped a barrier, damaging a front wheel, and then suffered an engine fire with the spare car. That consigned him to fifth on the grid, behind Berger's Ferrari, Mansell, Prost and Piquet.

His fortune was no better in the race, which had a chaotic start when Alboreto and Piquet collided at Turn 1, triggering a multiple shunt. Piquet's Williams was damaged in the incident but a red flag gave him a second chance.

At the restart Berger and Mansell led with Ayrton running third, ahead of Piquet, who passed the 99T after 11 laps. Three laps later the Lotus slowed with a faulty throttle sensor. By the time it was replaced, Ayrton was three laps down but that didn't stop him fighting back to seventh as a victorious Alain Prost scored his 28th grand prix win, beating Jackie Stewart's record 27.

27 SEPTEMBER 1987

Spanish GP (Jerez)
Lotus-Honda 99T • 5th

Senna qualified fifth, almost 2sec down on the Williams pace, after being forced to change cars on Friday when the engine cut out.

Ayrton got up to third at the start as the Williams pair indulged in their own race. He then became a mobile chicane in a 99T that was handling badly in the corners but quick down the straights. To the frustration of all those stacked up behind (including Piquet, who'd had a slow tyre stop), Ayrton was again trying to go through non-stop.

Ten laps from the end, though, his Goodyears gave out and Senna fell victim to an attack from Piquet that put the Lotus off-line and also allowed Thierry Boutsen's Benetton and Prost through. Johansson's McLaren soon went by too, leaving Ayrton to fall away and acknowledge that his gamble had backfired.

18 OCTOBER 1987

Mexican GP (Autodromo Hermanos Rodriguez)
Lotus-Honda 99T • Retired, 54 laps, spin/clutch

Qualifying was a frustrating affair for Ayrton. The previous year he'd taken a superb on-the-limit pole but this time the track surface was even bumpier, despite the race organisers' claim to the contrary. The bumpiness confounded his Lotus's active-ride system to such an extent that Senna, going for it in Saturday qualifying, first spun and then put the car heavily into the tyres at Peraltada. He lined up seventh, 0.7sec from Mansell's pole.

Nigel didn't make a good start, however, and Berger's Ferrari F1-87 led from Boutsen's Benetton B187, with Senna up to fourth by the second lap and third by lap 16. When both Berger and Boutsen fell victim to mechanical problems, Senna's Lotus was second but under pressure from Andrea de Cesaris in the Brabham BT56.

De Cesaris was soon in the gravel trap and claimed: "Senna missed a gear and when I got alongside him he just drove me off the road!"

Ayrton had driven much of the race without a clutch and, running third behind the Williams twins with nine laps to go, locked up the rears and spun. The marshals tried to usher him into the escape road and didn't respond wholeheartedly to Ayrton's frantic gestures for a push. When the car rolled to a halt Senna angrily jumped out and remonstrated, which earned him a $15,000 fine for striking a marshal. It spelled the end of his slim championship hopes: he was now 22 points behind Piquet with just 18 to play for.

1 NOVEMBER 1987

Japanese GP (Suzuka)
Lotus-Honda 99T • 2nd

This was F1's first return to Japan for a decade, since James Hunt beat Carlos Reutemann at Fuji in 1977, but there was disappointment in Friday's first qualifying session when Mansell, who'd won his sixth race of the year in Mexico, crashed heavily and injured his back, effectively handing a third World Championship to team-mate Piquet.

There was much local interest in the Lotus-Hondas in Japan with Satoru Nakajima the home hero. But Senna was only ninth on the opening day when a driveshaft broke and could do no better than seventh when afflicted by a misfire towards the end of his best Saturday lap.

Berger led convincingly in the Ferrari but, happier with his race set-up, Senna battled his way up to second place by lap 12, having a spirited tussle with Piquet. Both lost out when Stefan Johansson's McLaren made an earlier tyre stop but Ayrton regained second place on the last lap as Stefan nursed his car, low on fuel, to the line.

15 NOVEMBER 1987

Australian GP (Adelaide)
Lotus-Honda 99T • Disqualified (2nd)

After winning in Japan, Berger's Ferrari again set the pace in Adelaide with Senna on the second row, alongside Piquet.

Running fourth in the 82-lap race, Senna pulled off a great move around half distance when he outbraked both Prost and Michele Alboreto as René Arnoux baulked them in his Ligier JS29C. Prost, however, was unimpressed with both Alboreto and his forthcoming new team-mate. "They both banged wheels with me and if I hadn't backed off they'd both have been off," he complained.

Unfortunately, Ayrton's hard-won second place didn't survive Benetton's post-race protest, after which scrutineers found that extra brake cooling ducts fitted by Lotus were an inch outside the regulation dimensions.

← **Senna was disqualified from second place in his last race for Lotus in Adelaide, for a brake duct infringement; Thierry Boutsen's Benetton follows.**

sutton-images.com

TOSSING A COIN FOR A MILLION STERLING!

Ron Dennis recalls an unconventional end to protracted negotiations to bring Senna to McLaren for 1988.

"Ayrton had struggled with some things in the initial period of his career but when we got together and started negotiating, he mentally prepared himself for those negotiations.

"He was a fine negotiator and, as with his driving, he would spend a lot of time thinking about it. He was renting a house in Esher, Surrey, which was about 15 minutes from our factory and when we were negotiating the meetings always seemed to be at midday. It was a series of days going backwards and forwards. I would go back and do other things and he would sit for 24 hours deciding how he was going to position himself for the next round of negotiations.

"How we structured the contract regarding non-fiscal matters was quickly established. It was the fiscal issues that were difficult and we were stuck between a rock and a hard place over half a million dollars. It seems flippant to imply that half a million dollars was trivial but it became more a point of principle about who was going to win that part of the negotiations.

"In essence, he was sat there thinking, 'I'm going to drive for McLaren even if I have to drive for half a million less.' And I was sat thinking, 'I'm going to give him

the half million extra because we want him to drive for McLaren.' So neither of us was concerned about the actual money, but about losing the last part of the negotiation.

"His English wasn't perfect at that stage but the moment came when I suggested that because we both had a very firm position, we should break the deadlock by tossing a coin. But tossing a coin doesn't happen in Brazil and it took quite a while to explain. Then, of course, it got quite serious, we had to be very clear about the rules, and so I literally had to draw a picture of a head and a tail, select a coin and say 'this is you' and 'this is me'.

"We went over the rules several times to make sure there was no misunderstanding and then we got into who was actually going to toss the coin.

And were we going to catch it or let it fall to the ground?

"We had a couple of practice runs. I had a very small office with a brown shag-pile carpet, so it wasn't a particularly good surface on which the coin was going to land. We threw it and it rolled under the curtain. As we were both jumping up, I said, 'Remember, if it's on its side it doesn't count.'

"He lifted the corner of the curtain and the coin was clear-cut flat. I won but I honestly can't remember whether I was heads or tails – and I'm not going to make it up. But I remember, later, realising that in fact we'd tossed a coin for $1.5 million because it was a three-year contract!

"It sounds as if we were disrespectful of money but it was actually nothing to do with that – just a simple means of breaking the deadlock."

→ **Ron Dennis was the victor in an unusual manner of contract resolution that gave his team F1's strongest-ever driver line-up.**

sutton-images.com

1988
THE FIRST WORLD TITLE

This was the final year of the turbo engine in F1 – until 2014. The 1989 season would see only normally aspirated engines but, for '88, there was a mixture, with the turbos expected to dominate despite being restricted to 150 litres of fuel and boost of 2.5 bar.

McLaren's MP4/4 broke cover late, the team heading for an Imola test not long before the freight had to leave for round 1 in Brazil. The car's lap times stunned the F1 establishment. Finally, Ayrton had reached the Holy Grail – a car that could win him the World Championship and a seat alongside the acknowledged world number one, Alain Prost. If he could beat Alain, that would say it all...

← After the first test of the MP4/4 Ron Dennis told McLaren personnel that with the car and drivers they had, he believed they could win every race. He was very nearly right...

📷 sutton-images.com

PIQUET QUESTIONS SENNA'S SEXUALITY

When the F1 circus arrived in Brazil for the start of the new season, Nelson Piquet had been up to mischief.

The World Champion had two principal enemies: Nigel Mansell and Ayrton Senna. Although Piquet had sealed his third world title in 1987, the reality was that for two years Mansell had blown him away at Williams. With just a modicum of good fortune, Nigel would have won back-to-back world titles in 1986 and '87.

Ayrton, meanwhile, was the emerging Brazilian superstar, the man who was poised to steal Piquet's

⬇ **Piquet – mischievous.**

📷 sutton-images.com

thunder in his homeland. And so, predictably perhaps, it was Ayrton and Nigel who were the targets of Nelson's destabilisation tactics.

In a Rio newspaper Nelson said that Senna was homosexual and that his much-photographed dalliances with women weren't for real. He repeated the allegation in Brazilian *Playboy* where, unforgivably, he described Mansell as an uneducated fool with an ugly wife. On reflection, given Nigel's physical strength, Piquet was probably fortunate to remain alive...

On the subject of the allegations made about Ayrton, Ron Dennis says:

"If you are passionate about something, whether you win or lose, it generates emotions. And if you are engaged in that person's life you are sharing the emotions and supporting each other through the success and failures – it's the same in any human relationship.

"But when another driver [Piquet] constructed a view that Ayrton had male relationships that went beyond normal male relationships, it was built and spun to affect that particular World Championship. It was surgical in its delivery, timed to perfection, meant to destabilise, and it did.

"When we talked it through, Ayrton actually said, 'How do I handle this?' I guided him through it and actually it ended up having a positive influence, part of the explanation being this embracing of individuals of both sexes and having the ability to express strong friendship and a deep commitment to it.

"He was a real friend. If you had adversity in your life, irrespective of

where it came from, he wanted to make it better and therefore he didn't have the aggressive harshness that most men have. He was soft in that position and tried desperately to be compassionate. That compassion was spun in a very bad way.

"I watched all of that through a significant period of time, the various girlfriends he had and how he built relationships that were not always right, as we all do. But he wasn't skilled in initially dealing with all the girlfriends. It goes back to something that you constantly see in drivers. They are dedicated to motorsport from day one. They go through karting, Formula Ford and so on, and get completely obsessive. It is to the detriment of their development as a human being.

"It really is to the exclusion of all things, as I know from personal experience. I got married very late. Girlfriends were not of interest to me for ages. My nose was up an exhaust pipe. I was working seven days a week, initially at Cooper, then Brabham, and girlfriends were unimportant. You are always trailing three to five years behind.

"It's the same with some drivers. Very often the ones obsessed with being great racing drivers, it's to the detriment of life skills and communication. So Ayrton wasn't polished in his initial handling of girls but these things were spun primarily to harm his popularity in Brazil. The driver concerned was vying to be the prominent sportsman in the country and it was a good way to spin the situation. When I explained that to him and what the motivation was, he then became very skilful in turning it round the other way."

Brazilian GP (Jacarepagua)
McLaren-Honda MP4/4 • Disqualified, 31 laps

Ayrton was on a mission to win the psychological battle with Prost from the outset and was quickest in both qualifying sessions, taking pole position with a lap in 1m 28.096s. Nigel Mansell, on his return after the Suzuka shunt that spelled the end of his 1987 title challenge, somehow managed to split the McLaren-Hondas with his normally aspirated Judd-powered Williams! Prost lined up third on the grid, nearly seven-tenths from Senna's pole, but had been forced to qualify in the T-car after a problem with his race chassis. This was the start Senna wanted, but in the race their fortunes reversed.

On the formation lap there was anger when Senna led the field round at practically walking pace. There was plenty of cooling for a 1.5-litre engine at that speed, but the normally aspirated brigade – most significantly Mansell's front-row Williams-Judd – could reasonably be expected to overheat, leading to fist-waving.

But this wasn't dastardly tactics – Senna's car was stuck in first gear! Realising that pitting was fruitless, he brought the car onto pole position and started waving frantically, which achieved a 'start delayed' signal and gave him time to get strapped into the spare car and start from pitlane.

Prost therefore began the year with a comfortable win and Senna failed to score. Ayrton was 18th by lap 2, eighth by lap 10 and second by lap 20 – such was the superiority of McLaren's MP4/4. At his tyre stop six laps later, however, Senna stalled as a result of a flat battery and fell back to sixth. But it was immaterial. The officials ruled that as the race had been merely delayed rather than restarted, Senna shouldn't have been allowed to take the T-car at all. Ron Dennis argued the case but after 30 of the 60 laps Senna was black-flagged.

San Marino GP (Imola)
McLaren-Honda MP4/4 • 1st

Senna, 1 May and Imola were to become synonymous with one of the blackest moments in the sport's history but, ironically, six years to the day before the awful events of that weekend, Senna won his first race for McLaren at the same track.

In Brazil he had conclusively outqualified Prost but Alain had been forced to take the spare car. At Imola they claimed the front row by a huge margin – Ayrton's pole time was almost three and a half seconds quicker than Nelson Piquet's third-place Lotus! But that didn't matter

↑ Imola and 1 May define one of F1's blackest days, but were also the place and date of Senna's first McLaren victory.
📷 sutton-images.com

PROST STUNNED BY SENNA'S SPEED

Mexican Jo Ramirez has been around motor racing all his life, first recruited as a 'gofer' by Ferrari team boss Eugenio Dragoni. In early 1988 he was 46 and working for Ron Dennis as McLaren's team co-ordinator. In the tricky position of being a friend to both Senna and Prost, few had closer experience of what really went on between them.

"Ron had tried to get Ayrton from Lotus the previous year but didn't manage it. When he eventually did, I wouldn't say that Alain was overly welcoming but Ayrton's reputation didn't bother him either. Actually, Keke Rosberg, who had been Alain's team-mate with us in 1986, reckoned that Ayrton joining our team was the best thing that could happen to Alain. Keke believed that alongside Alain, Ayrton would be nobody. Keke thought that Alain was just the greatest thing – so unbelievably quick yet barely touching the equipment.

"Keke was always very honest and at Monaco in '86, when he was second to Alain but almost half a minute behind, he let his frustration get to him a bit. 'You know,' he said, 'the harder I try, the further away that little frog gets!' Keke must have been astonished to see just how quick Ayrton was..."

So, it seems, was Prost himself.

"From the very first time Ayrton drove the MP4/4, he had an obsession about Alain. He wanted to know what rear wing he had, which front springs, which tyres. Every time he came into the pits the first thing he would ask was what time Alain had done. It was all the time. He didn't care about anyone else.

"Alain was pretty cool about it. He used to laugh. But he soon realised how serious a threat Ayrton was. It was at Imola, at the end of qualifying.

"Alain always used to get back to the truck and change quickly. Ayrton was a bit more methodical. When he changed he'd fold things up and put them away. Then he'd always sit in the truck and kind of meditate. I remember, Alain had finished changing and, just as he was walking out of the truck, he stopped where I was standing, looking at the times.

"Alain was resting on the cabinet with his back to Ayrton, who was sitting on the floor a bit further up the truck. Ayrton was a lot quicker and Alain just didn't understand how he was so fast. He looked at the split times and then half turned to me and whispered. 'Shit, he's quick!'

"But Ayrton heard it. And he just looked up at me and winked. At that moment I thought to myself, OK Ayrton, you're halfway there..."

← Prost knew straight off that he faced an altogether different kind of threat from Senna. Jo Ramirez was in the tricky position of being a friend to both.

sutton-images.com

to Senna. What mattered was that, as in Rio, he was more than 0.7sec quicker than Prost – a fact that shook the Frenchman (see facing page).

This time there were no mechanical dramas and no stopping Senna, who dominated the race from first to last, heading home Prost in a McLaren 1–2.

↑ Senna set out to annihilate Prost at the beginning of 1988. He did so for qualifying pace but failed to turn it into a points advantage through unreliability in Brazil and a devastating mistake at Monaco.

📷 sutton-images.com

15 MAY 1988

Monaco GP (Monte Carlo)
McLaren-Honda MP4/4 • Retired, 66 laps, crash

Anyone who thought that Senna couldn't have a more memorable Monaco GP than 1984 was made to think again by his first visit in a McLaren.

Qualifying was extraordinary. It had been hoped by the normally aspirated brigade, somewhat forlornly, that tight, tortuous places like Monte Carlo and Detroit would play to their strengths against the turbo cars. Predictably, the first 'atmo' car on the grid, in fifth place, was Nigel Mansell's Williams FW12 with a time of 1m 27.665s. Although then best known for his 'white line' accident when leading at Monaco in '84, Nigel was always absolutely superb at the street circuit, though destined never to win there.

The McLarens were in a different league. Behind them Gerhard Berger's Ferrari was the best of the rest, on 1m 26.685s. Prost, on the front row, was more than 1.2sec clear of Berger with 1m 25.425s.

But from the moment practice began, Senna was on another level entirely, sometimes as much as 2sec a lap quicker than Prost. Nobody imagined for a moment that a similar margin would still be there at the end of qualifying. There was stunned disbelief, therefore, when Ayrton stopped the clocks in 1m 23.998s!

It's the most talked about lap of Senna's career, when he spoke of 'coming out of himself', of having a spiritual experience and driving with such intensity that perhaps he even frightened himself (see 'Monaco: the most stunning lap of all', page 150).

And then came the race. Ayrton led off the start while Prost was beaten into the first corner by Berger. It meant that Senna disappeared at around a second a lap for the first half of the race. It took Prost until lap 54 of the 78 to find a way past Berger's Ferrari, by which time Senna led by more than 50sec. But some 12 laps later, with just another 12 to go, Ayrton clipped the barrier on the inside of Portier while accelerating out onto the harbour front and his McLaren was sent across the road into the outside barrier.

Unable to take in what had happened and not wishing to contemplate its consequences (see 'Monaco: what happened at Portier?', page 151), Senna walked straight back to his nearby apartment, where he was uncontactable for hours. Prost duly won and picked up the nine points. Despite Ayrton having been demonstrably the superior driver for the first three races, the score was now 24 points to Prost versus Senna's nine...

MONACO: THE MOST STUNNING LAP OF ALL

Senna's qualifying lap at Monte Carlo in 1988 has been used to support the theory that he wasn't content merely to beat Prost, but wanted to humiliate him. And it has been cited as evidence that Senna, through his religious beliefs, could sometimes elevate his driving to a totally different level, during which he was effectively having an out-of-body experience, as daft as that may sound.

Prost's reaction was simple enough: "Ayrton's time was fantastic but you have to take risks for a lap like that and I'm not prepared to do that so much any more." The implication was that, once, he could have done. Few agree.

In his 1990 book *Grand Prix People*, Canadian journalist Gerald Donaldson quoted Senna at length on this topic:

"When I am competing against the watch and against other competitors, the feeling of expectation, of getting it done and doing the best and being the best, gives me a kind of power that, some moments when I'm driving, actually detaches me completely from anything else as I'm doing it... corner after corner, lap after lap. I can give you a true example and relate it.

"Monte Carlo, '88, the last qualifying session. I was already on pole and I was going faster and faster. One lap after the other, quicker, and quicker, and quicker. I was at one stage just on pole, then by half a second, then one second... and I kept going. Suddenly I was nearly two seconds faster than anybody else, including my team-mate with the same car. And I suddenly realised that I was no longer driving the car consciously.

"I was kind of driving it by instinct, only I was in a different dimension. It was like I was in a tunnel, not only the tunnel under the hotel, but the whole circuit for me was a tunnel. I was just going, going – more, and more, and more. I was way over the limit, but still trying to find even more. Then, suddenly, something just kicked me. I kind of woke up and realised that I was in a different atmosphere than you normally are. Immediately my reaction was to back off, slow down. I drove back to the pits slowly and I didn't want to go out any more that day.

"It frightened me because I realised that I was well beyond my conscious understanding. It happens rarely, but I keep these experiences very much alive because it's something that's important for self-preservation."

At the time reaction to Senna's discourse was polarised. Some were awestruck, taking in the words and hanging on them as evidence that here, indeed, was some kind of other-worldly talent performing on an entirely different plane. Others dismissed it as just Senna trying to further turn the psychological screw on Prost. But he was doing that anyway...

← Ayrton does a scooter recce at Monaco before the famous 'out-of-body experience' qualifying lap.

📷 sutton-images.com

Monaco: what happened at Portier?

Senna's crash at the innocuous second-gear Portier corner at Monte Carlo, when leading the race by almost a minute with 12 laps to go, is one of the most notorious episodes of his career.

Over time, much drivel has been written and spoken on the subject. Quite unbelievably, some have suggested that Senna was panicked into losing the race when team-mate Prost, who had been trapped behind Gerhard Berger's Ferrari for the first 53 laps, suddenly got himself into second place and started going quickly. Was a man who had outqualified Prost by a second and a half, and was leading by more than half a lap, going to be remotely concerned about that? Even if Prost had been up Senna's exhaust pipe, Ayrton wouldn't have cared less, at Monaco of all places. Witness four years later with Nigel Mansell, who was in a far quicker car.

But Senna's mindset was such that he didn't so much want to beat Prost as destroy him. He was still fresh in the process of establishing himself unequivocally as the Main Man in a team seen as Alain's. No way would he have wanted Prost to set a quicker race lap. There was no reward, but that wouldn't have mattered.

Prost would have known that. And goading Ayrton into a mistake was his only chance that day. On lap 57, just his third in free air, Prost lapped in 1m 26.714s, which remained his quickest lap of the race.

When Senna got the message, he was already more than halfway round his 58th lap, which was 1m 27.339s. Next time round Ayrton went a full second quicker, 1m 26.321s, to comfortably beat Prost's time by almost four tenths.

That was 2.33sec slower than Senna's unbelievable 'out-of-body experience' pole position lap but, clearly, with around 30kg of fuel still on board and Goodyears that were almost 60 laps old, he was very much on it.

Ron Dennis then told Senna on the radio that Prost had backed off again, and Ayrton did likewise. It was seven laps later that Senna shunted. Had he simply lost concentration or, perhaps more plausibly, had he figured that it was time to make sure of that fastest lap?

Senna would have been sufficiently confident in his own superiority over Prost around Monaco to believe that a banzai lap 12 laps from the end would have been quicker than anything Alain might have come up with on the penultimate or last lap, even with the benefit of reduced fuel load. The calculations stack up. His near half-second margin a few laps earlier would have confirmed it to him.

↑ **His car in the Portier barrier, Senna left the scene quickly and returned, distraught, to his apartment, just a short walk away.**

📷 sutton-images.com

→ **Senna talks detail with McLaren's Steve Nichols.**

📷 sutton-images.com

So it was about the right time. Had he simply pushed too hard and taken a millimetre too much inside kerb at Portier?

For me, that's the most likely explanation. To concede as much, though, would have meant admitting that Prost had suckered him, which would have been unbearable. Better to simply say that he'd lost concentration? Which, technically, was still true.

These days, we get lap sector times and would know Senna's time between the start of the lap and Mirabeau, which would have provided a clue. Back then, we didn't. So I asked Steve Hallam, who worked with Senna at both Lotus and McLaren, if he'd ever had a conversation with him about it?

"Not directly," he says, "but we had a number of conversations after that time about how to manage a race. He would often say that when you get into a groove and a rhythm, and Monaco especially is a rhythm circuit, you're actually better doing what comes absolutely subconsciously and naturally than trying to do something unnatural, which is slow down.

"We had conversations about how to manage situations like that, post-1988, and he would sort of smile, knowingly. I wasn't at McLaren then but I know they were asking him to slow down. I think everybody learned from that experience. And not just with him but, going forward, how to get a driver to ease off without actually putting yourself more at risk."

Whatever, the consequences would have been crushingly clear to Senna. With the 9–6–4–3–2–1 championship points system in operation at the time, he should have left Monte Carlo with 18 points to Prost's 21, with two dominant victories after his Rio disqualification. The reality, though, was that Prost had 24 and Senna only 9.

A 15-point gap in a season where no other car was remotely close to the McLarens meant that Prost could afford to finish second to Ayrton for the next five races and still be joint top of the championship table.

Senna's Monte Carlo apartment wasn't far from Portier and that's where he went. McLaren team co-ordinator Jo Ramirez spoke to him first. Jo was in the tricky position of already being a friend to both Prost and Senna, having first met Alain in 1980 (at a Paul Ricard test when Alain was at McLaren first time around) and Ayrton in 1983 (at Macau while running the Theodore Racing F3 entries with Dick Bennetts). Recalling that Monaco night, Ramirez remembers. "I called the apartment and at first nobody answered. Then Isabelle, the lady who looked after the apartment, answered. I knew her well.

"I said, 'It's Jo, is Ayrton there?'

"She said, 'No, Signor Ayrton is not here.'

"I said I was sure he was there but she said that he

wasn't. So I told her that if he came, please call me. But nothing. So, at 9pm I called again and she answered again. I said, 'Look, I know he's there, please pass him the phone. Tell him it's not Ron or anyone else. It's me, Jo.'

"So in the end he takes the phone and he's still crying. 'I don't know what happened,' he said. 'I must be the stupidest idiot in the world! The wheel jumped out of my hands after I touched the inside.'

"When we'd finished speaking I told Ron that I'd spoken to him, and how bad he was, but that day he didn't show up again. When he did he was a little sheepish.

"He never really spoke about it. In future years, yes, I sometimes used to joke with him when we went to Monaco and say, 'Don't do an '88, will you?' But he didn't say a lot about it.

"When he made a mistake, which wasn't often, he used to get so upset with himself that nobody, not even Ron, could or would tell him off. He knew, himself. And he'd already be destroyed about it. He was the biggest perfectionist I've ever met. He didn't like to tolerate mistakes from the team but he tolerated his own even less.

"His post-accident emotion was pure anger with himself," Dennis confirms. "I have never seen or heard him more frustrated or angry. He knew that he had made a very fundamental error and couldn't cope with it at all. When he regained composure he was very negative about his performance, and apologetic."

29 MAY 1988

Mexican GP (Autodromo Hermanos Rodriguez)
McLaren-Honda MP4/4 • 2nd

Once again there was a seven-tenths gap between Senna and Prost on the Mexican grid, with Berger's Ferrari able to get within a few hundredths of the Frenchman.

But it was Prost who made the best start, with Piquet's second-row Lotus 100T briefly getting between the two McLarens. Early in the race Senna found that the Honda engine's pop-off valve was opening prematurely. Driving around some early understeer, he had worn his rear Goodyears and he was also on the limit with fuel consumption, although not as seriously as Berger's third-placed Ferrari.

Prost, meanwhile, had a visor tear-off become wedged in one of his McLaren's radiators and was alarmed by rising water temperature, but not enough to prevent him getting to the chequered flag 7sec in front of Senna, opening up an 18-point margin – worth two wins – over Ayrton in a championship chase that was obviously going to be the sole preserve of the McLaren pair.

12 JUNE 1988

Canadian GP (Montréal)
McLaren-Honda MP4/4 • 1st

Just a couple of tenths separated the McLarens on the
grid this time as Senna took his fifth pole position in as
many races for the team.

But Ayrton wasn't happy. Quite understandably,
he wanted to know why pole position was on the dirty
side of the track, the right-hand side, when the first
bend was a left-hander. He was told that the first
corner proper was a right-hander. He disputed it but
got nowhere. It was a scenario we would see again
– with much more serious consequences – at Suzuka
two years down the road...

Prost did indeed make the better getaway – from the
clean side – for the second successive race and took the
lead. But this was to be no Mexico. Senna shadowed him
all the way and when, on lap 19, Prost was delayed by
a backmarker, Ayrton was through.

That was the way it stayed and McLaren's only real
concern was fuel consumption, Montréal being the
trickiest track on the calendar fuel-wise. Worries that
the McLarens might run short of fuel intensified when
Senna and Prost started trying to outdo each other again

with lap times, Ayrton eventually taking fastest lap by
seven hundredths. In third place and poised to capitalise
was Thierry Boutsen's Benetton-Ford B188 – a normally
aspirated car that was allowed 65 more litres of fuel than
the turbo runners – but McLaren needn't have worried.
Senna and Prost took another 1–2 and the championship
score was now 39 to Alain and 24 to Ayrton.

19 JUNE 1988

United States GP (Detroit)
McLaren-Honda MP4/4 • 1st

Prost was unlikely to be able to do much about Senna in
Motown. Ayrton had won the two previous races at the
track and Prost had a pathological hatred of the place.
Ayrton took his sixth successive pole, 0.88sec quicker
than Gerhard Berger in the Ferrari. Prost was fourth,
1.41sec adrift of Senna – Monaco all over again.

Senna beat Berger into Turn 1 on the first lap and that
was the last anyone saw of him. However, Prost's dislike
of the Detroit track wasn't enough for him to allow anyone
else to beat his McLaren over the race distance – Alain
was the only other driver to complete 63 laps, even if it
did take him almost 40sec longer than Ayrton.

"WE MAKE HISTORY, YOU ONLY WRITE ABOUT IT..."

One of McLaren boss Ron Dennis's better-remembered lines came from the US Grand Prix in 1988. Some will know that he uttered a version of the above words, but not all will know the circumstances.

In Detroit, Senna failed to appear at the pole position press conference on Saturday. The US sports writers, more used to tennis players and golfers who appreciate the media's job and the benefits they get from the media, were unimpressed. After his race win, Senna did turn up, accompanied by Dennis, who started to defend his man.

"It's just not realistic to expect us to allow the drivers to be snatched away for more than half an hour at a time when we need their thought train to be concentrated totally on the technical debrief," Ron said. "We have found that it can take their mind off the job to the point where crucial pieces of technical information can be forgotten. This is all part of the effort to be consistently competitive and we feel unwilling to compromise in any area that may cause us to lose our sharp edge.

"We are trying to make history – you are only reporting it."

So there you had it. This was in the days before the sport's governing body made it a stipulation that drivers had to attend post-qualifying press conferences. Times change. The waiting world is more important, tech debriefs can wait. The racing media might well have retorted: we write about the artists, you only provide the tools...

Senna took pole at Detroit in 1988 and then missed the press conference, prompting Ron Dennis's condescending observation to the unimpressed media.

sutton-images.com

3 JULY 1988

French GP (Paul Ricard)
McLaren-Honda MP4/4 • 2nd

With the disliked North American tracks behind him, Prost was determined to reassert himself when the championship returned to Europe. Senna was in search of a record seventh consecutive pole but Alain managed to stop him, lapping 0.48sec quicker. Prost's car displayed an aggressive body language more reminiscent of his team-mate's.

"Alain was determined to stop Ayrton in France," recalls Jo Ramirez. "He had a really good set-up. I think the basic difference between the two of them was that Ayrton could drive a wheelbarrow fast but he wasn't as good as Alain at setting up the car. Ayrton would always change such little things – half a millimetre of ride height or half a pound more pressure in the left front – things that wouldn't make much difference.

"Alain was very happy with his car early in the second session, did a fantastic time and then just got out of the car. He said that if Ayrton or anybody else could do a

better lap than that, then they deserved pole. He put his jeans and T-shirt back on and went to watch the rest of practice from the pitwall. Ayrton was totally demoralised. You could see him getting wound up by it.

"Alain could always accept it when Ayrton was quicker, but not the other way around. As far as Ayrton was concerned, there had to be something wrong with the car."

Senna was fastest in the race morning warm-up but it was Prost who again led at the start, Alain able to open up a 3sec advantage as Ayrton dealt with the attentions of Berger's Ferrari.

Senna closed the gap, particularly when Alain was delayed lapping Oscar Larrauri's EuroBrun, but Prost kept hard on it. He knew that Senna was good in traffic and he knew that, with tyre stops planned, he needed a cushion. This was the first time since the heat of Brazil that the combination of ambient temperature and track surface would demand a change of rubber.

With just over 30 of the race's 80 laps down, Senna pitted for tyres just as Prost approached a gaggle of backmarkers. When Prost stopped a couple of laps later there was an issue with a sticking wheel and he rejoined

⬇ **Paul Ricard '88 – one of the few occasions when Prost got the better of Senna.**

📷 sutton-images.com

the fray behind Senna. Ayrton couldn't shake off Alain, however, and he had a gearbox problem too.

"About 10 laps before my stop the gear lever began to feel spongy, just like at Imola," Senna explained. "I started to miss the odd gear but whereas at Imola the problem stabilised, here it got worse. I couldn't use the engine to help slow the car under braking and without it the car became unstable."

Senna started to lock his fronts under braking and, with 20 laps to go, they came up to lap Piquet's Lotus which, itself, was about to lap Alex Caffi's Dallara and Pierluigi Martini's Minardi.

Prost was well aware that he had a reputation for being cautious in traffic while Senna was ruthless. This time, though, it was the other way round. Senna's gearbox worries weren't helping but when he showed circumspection coming through the fast Signes sweeper, Prost took it flat and launched the McLaren down the inside for the following Beausset corner, boxing Senna behind the Minardi.

Senna was later critical of Martini for not moving more decisively out of the way but he acknowledged that it was a good move by Prost. Alain now led by four victories to three and 54 points to 39.

10 JULY 1988

British GP (Silverstone)
McLaren-Honda MP4/4 • 1st

Silverstone was the first race of 1988 in which McLaren didn't take pole. In fact, the team didn't get a car on the front row. The front row for the British GP was Ferrari red with Gerhard Berger (1m 10.133s) on pole and Michele Alboreto (1m 10.332s) alongside, while Senna (1m 10.616s) and Prost (1m 10.736s) had to be content with third and fourth.

For the first time it wasn't plain sailing for McLaren. The MP4/4s had revised sidepods that had been the product of wind tunnel development but the pre-Silverstone tyre test had been washed out by rain and the revised cars didn't feel great on the opening day. Prost complained of understeer at Copse and Becketts, and oversteer through Stowe and Club – not ideal! For the remainder of the weekend, therefore, McLaren reverted to standard specification.

On race day, though, Prost had bigger problems – the first all-wet British GP for 27 years. Some thought that would give Ferrari, usually in trouble with fuel

⇑ **While Prost refused to drive blind into spray and withdrew, Senna scored a significant win at a soaking Silverstone.**

📷 sutton-images.com

157

DID SILVERSTONE TIP THE BALANCE?

The British GP was the race at which Senna got himself properly back in the championship fight, making a full nine-point gain on Prost to turn around the reversals suffered when he non-scored in Rio (after disqualification) and Monaco (after his lapse at Portier).

For giving up in the rain, Alain

→ **Prost was always a nail-biter and a thinker. He believed that driving blind into balls of spray at 200mph owed more to stupidity than bravery. He was comfortable with his decision to withdraw at Silverstone.**

📷 sutton-images.com

was slaughtered by sections of the media, most notably at home in France.

Prost's decision had its roots in the events of six years earlier, at Hockenheim in 1982, when Didier Pironi was horribly injured in an accident that ended his career. Pironi in his Ferrari pulled out to overtake Derek Daly's Williams but, unsighted by a ball of

spray, he hadn't seen Prost's Renault in front of him. The Ferrari became airborne over the back of Prost's car and Alain, obviously one of the first to arrive at the accident scene, saw the results. When Piquet arrived a little later, he was physically sick in his crash helmet.

The belief that Prost wasn't quick in the wet is a fallacy. His smooth, economical style meant that he was actually very fast on a wet surface – on his own. But he had long thought it madness to drive blind into balls of spray at 200mph. Pironi's accident merely underlined that belief.

Prost went straight back to the paddock and had a heart-to-heart with Renault team boss Gérard Larrousse. Briefly, he even contemplated retiring on the spot. He carried on, of course, but did say that in similar conditions to those he'd just witnessed, he'd make his own decisions and the team would have to live with them. Larrousse accepted that.

At Silverstone, Prost said: "When you are flat-out on the straight you see nothing at all. Nothing! I'm not worried about driving on a slippery track surface. That's all part of the business we're in. But when you're driving blind, that's not motor racing in my book.

"I think motor racing should be run in the dry. Look at the Open golf last week. They cancelled the third day because the weather was so bad. And in America they don't race Indycars in the rain. At the end of the day it's my judgment and my life. If people don't accept my view it's their problem, not mine. I can live with that."

consumption, a sporting chance to continue their qualifying form, but Berger disagreed. No chance versus the McLarens, wet or dry, he reckoned.

He was right, but it didn't stop him leading the first 13 laps, before Senna outsmarted him into the Woodcote chicane as they came up to lap – Prost!

Alain was having a nightmare. He was using a carbon clutch for the first time in the wet and bogged down at the start, being passed on all sides. He completed the first lap in 11th place, with Satoru Nakajima ahead and Eddie Cheever behind – both more than decent in the wet. He then lost places to Riccardo Patrese's Williams and Stefano Modena's EuroBrun! Then Alex Caffi's Dallara came by. Prost wasn't enamoured with his car's handling, his heart wasn't in it, and after 24 of the 65 laps he pulled off and parked.

With hindsight, Prost's actions could be said to have cost him the championship, but Alain would disagree. In the circumstances, there were no points to be had and in his own head he'd made the right decision, which is what mattered (see facing page). But it was the chance Senna had been waiting for. The season's tally was now four wins apiece and the score was Prost on 54 points and Senna on 48.

24 JULY 1988

German GP (Hockenheim)
McLaren-Honda MP4/4 • 1st

After a pre-race test at Hockenheim the McLarens appeared with the revised sidepods and internal turbo ducting that had been removed at Silverstone, and there was no sign of the handling problems that had afflicted the cars there.

Senna took his seventh pole in nine races with Prost predictably completing an all-McLaren front row. Once again, however, the race started in wet conditions. Senna took the lead and was never headed. But this was the same circuit that had convinced Prost of the folly of racing blind into spray. At Hockenheim the spray can be as bad as it gets, the tall pines of the forest encouraging moisture to hang in the air.

Prost, putting his feelings aside, fought his way into second place. He couldn't afford another non-score. But there was nothing he could do about Senna. With nine laps to go Alain put a wheel on a chicane kerb and spun. It didn't stop him finishing second but Senna took the flag 14sec in front. Ayrton was now 5–4 ahead in victories and just three points behind Alain in the championship.

↑ Perhaps not as much as it loved Nigel Mansell... but a British racing crowd always appreciated Ayrton's genius and commitment.
📷 sutton-images.com

3-07 GRAND PRIX DE BELGIQUE MOTOS
30 31-07 24H FRANCORCHAMPS
13 14-08 24H DE LIEGE MOTOS
28-08 GRAND PRIX DE BELGIQUE F.I
18-09 «1.000 KM DE SPA»
Marlboro
Marlboro
POWERED by HONDA
Marlboro
Shell
GOODYEAR
BOSS
Senna

7 AUGUST 1988

Hungarian GP (Hungaroring)
McLaren-Honda MP4/4 • 1st

The non-turbo drivers were hopeful that the tight, twisty Hungaroring would give them an opportunity to take the fight to the McLarens and, in qualifying at least, it looked that way. Finally the 1988 season had a battle worthy of the name.

Senna it was who eventually took his eighth pole of the year, but it was tight. Ayrton (1m 27.635s) was joined on the front row by Mansell's Williams (1m 27.743s), with Thierry Boutsen's Benetton (1m 27.970s) and Ivan Capelli's March (1m 28.350s) on the second row. The distinctive March-Judd 881 had for some time been doing things that hinted at the talents of a certain design chief called Adrian Newey...

Alessandro Nannini's Benetton (1m 28.493s) and Riccardo Patrese's Williams (1m 28.569s) were also within a second of Senna's pole, but you had to go all the way back to seventh before you found Prost (1m 28.778s).

Senna resisted Mansell's challenge into the first corner and led every lap of the 76. But he didn't have things all his own way. Prost, ninth at the end of lap 1, took second place from Boutsen's Benetton on lap 47 and had been conserving fuel while in traffic. But he soon upped the pace and eased onto Senna's tail. On lap 49 Senna came up to lap Gabriele Tarquini's Coloni at the same time as the Italian was trying to pass Philippe Alliot's Lola. Prost made it four abreast as they flew down the main straight!

Senna was forced to give him room or have a collision but Alain was on the dirty part of the track and slid wide in Turn 1, allowing Senna back through. Prost never tried again, troubled by a vibration in the left front wheel for the remainder of the race. Ayrton now led 6–4 on wins and, for the first time, had caught Alain on points. Both men had 66, with six races remaining.

28 AUGUST 1988

Belgian GP (Spa-Francorchamps)
McLaren-Honda MP4/4 • 1st

The McLarens dominated the front row again, but the gap between Senna and Prost, at 0.41sec, wasn't as big as might have been anticipated.

Before the race began Senna and Prost agreed that there would be no heroics at Turn 1, the tight La Source hairpin, and it was Prost who made it there first as Senna got too much wheelspin.

Prost's lead didn't last long. Senna, much quicker

⬆ **Estoril '88 was where bad feeling between Prost and Senna began.**

📷 sutton-images.com

through Eau Rouge with a full tank of fuel, was alongside and past by the time they reached the top of the hill and Les Combes. That would be the last anyone saw of him, Ayrton beating Alain by more than half a minute. It was now seven race wins to Prost's four and Senna was ahead on points for the first time, 75 to 72.

11 SEPTEMBER 1988

Italian GP (Monza)
McLaren-Honda MP4/4 • 10th (accident)

With his 10th pole position of the year, three tenths ahead of Prost, Senna set a new record, eclipsing the nine achieved by Ronnie Peterson, Niki Lauda (twice) and Nelson Piquet. It was 10 years since Peterson died at the same circuit and friends of Ronnie's were on hand to present Ayrton with a silver plate to mark his achievement. On the second successive high-speed circuit, the Ferraris were once again McLaren's closest rivals.

Sometimes things are written in the stars. Enzo Ferrari had died on 14 August, aged 90, and this was the first time that F1 cars had run at his beloved Monza since. Gerhard Berger and Michele Alboreto scored an emotional Ferrari 1–2 in front of the *tifosi*, while neither McLaren scored points (see facing page).

25 SEPTEMBER 1988

Portuguese GP (Estoril)
McLaren-Honda MP4/4 • 6th

Ayrton was quickest on the opening day, but next day, early in the second session, Prost – in a new chassis for this race – ran smaller turbos on his car and claimed pole, only his second of the year. As at Paul Ricard, scene of his first pole, Prost stopped early, changed into civvies and hung around on the pitwall, turning up the psychological heat on Ayrton.

At the start, Senna made the better getaway but the race was red-flagged because Derek Warwick (Arrows) stalled on the grid and was collected by Andrea de Cesaris (Rial), with Satoru Nakajima (Lotus) and Luis Sala (Minardi) also involved.

At the restart, Senna again got away better from the clean side of the grid but Prost crowded him towards the edge of the track. Senna kept coming and grabbed the lead into Turn 1. At the end of the lap, though, Prost got a better exit from the final corner and was tucked under Senna's rear wing as they blasted down the main straight. As Prost pulled out of the slipstream, Senna swerved right and almost put him into the pit wall. Alain refused to be intimidated and kept coming, but was less than impressed. Later, after Alain

AYRTON TRIPS UP AND ENDS THE WHITEWASH

When, pre-season, McLaren turned up late at Imola and stunned the F1 paddock with the MP4/4's pace, Ron Dennis returned to Woking and told the troops that they could win every race in 1988 with the car and drivers they had. And by the time they arrived at Monza for round 12, they had indeed won every race so far. And had it not been for an incident with Williams stand-in Jean-Louis Schlesser, they would have won all 16 of the season's races...

It was perhaps strange that the Frenchman, a day shy of his 40th birthday, was in the Williams at all. Nigel Mansell had chicken pox and was missing his second successive race. Martin Brundle stood in at Spa and was the team's choice for Monza, but Martin – the Williams test driver – was chasing the sports car world championship and Jaguar boss Tom Walkinshaw wouldn't release him.

"Spa had gone very well," Brundle remembers. "I finished seventh, I was quickest in the rain and I think it all went a bit too well. Tom wanted to keep me in the Jaguar and wouldn't give me permission to drive at Monza, and in fact persuaded me it would be a bad idea. Tom said, 'The car won't be quick there with a Judd engine.' So they put Schlesser in and it cost McLaren their clean sweep!"

American Al Unser Jr had tested a Williams and would have been an interesting choice, but he was committed to racing in the US, and Ferrari didn't want to release Roberto Moreno from a testing contract. And so Schlesser it was. The nephew of Jo Schlesser, killed

in the French GP at Rouen 20 years earlier, Jean-Louis had failed to qualify a RAM March for the French GP at Paul Ricard in 1983, and so Monza was his first F1 start. He lined up 22nd on the 26-car grid, a little over 2sec behind Riccardo Patrese, who started 10th in the sister Williams FW12.

Senna was coming up to lap Schlesser for the second time on the penultimate lap. Having led by more than a quarter of a minute from the Ferraris, Ayrton was now less than 5sec in front as he backed off to ensure that he wouldn't run short of fuel. He wasn't under undue pressure when he caught the Williams approaching the first chicane.

Schlesser, staying wide to leave the McLaren room, locked up on the dirt and Ayrton thought he was about to skate straight on into the gravel trap. Senna went inside the Williams and reached the apex of the left-hand part of the chicane without problem. Schlesser, however, managed to keep the Williams

out of the gravel and bounced his car over the inside kerb for the second part of the chicane. Senna, making an error of judgment, turned the McLaren into the second segment of the chicane and snagged the left front wheel of the Williams with his right rear. The McLaren looped into a spin, beached itself on the kerb and was out of the race.

Prost, meanwhile, had suffered an almost unheard of mechanical problem, retiring after 34 laps with a sick engine. McLaren's 100 per cent record had gone.

Senna was livid. He should have doubled Prost's wins total and taken a potentially decisive 12-point advantage in the championship with four rounds to go. But, instead, the gap between them was still just three points...

⬇ **Jean-Louis Schlesser's one-off run for Williams at Monza tripped up Senna at the first chicane and spoiled McLaren's clean sweep in 1988.**

📷 sutton-images.com

had taken his fifth win and Ayrton had finished a lowly sixth, they had words.

It had been a strange race for Senna. Prost had been able to run quick enough to win without problem, but Ayrton had been troubled by fuel read-outs that suggested he was going to struggle to make the finish.

Estoril: hostilities begin

Until Portugal, the Senna/Prost confrontation had been tense but under control. Prost had known that Senna would be quick, but probably not quite so stunningly quick.

Heading to Estoril, the situation was starting to look grim for Prost. Ayrton had seven wins to Alain's four, even if he was only three points ahead. And, such was the scoring system in operation that year, with only the best 11 results to count, Prost desperately needed wins.

Alain looked to be in better shape in Portugal and Senna's intimidation of him at the end of the first lap, as he tried to hang onto his lead, hinted a little at desperation. It was the first sign of nastiness.

"If Ayrton wants the championship that much, he can have it," Prost said later. "That was unacceptable."

By winning on a day when a troubled Senna could do no better than sixth, Prost put himself back into the lead of the championship, by five points, but the odds still favoured Senna. Prost had now registered five wins and six second places – 11 high scores – so each further win would improve his total by just three points and second places wouldn't help at all. Meanwhile, from 13 races (including Portugal), Senna had seven wins and two seconds, plus a single point for sixth at Estoril. His point-scoring potential over the last three rounds was much greater.

2 OCTOBER 1988

Spanish GP (Jerez)
McLaren-Honda MP4/4 • 4th

Senna took his 11th pole position of the year, just 0.07sec quicker than Prost, but Alain made the better start to lead, with Mansell's Williams getting between the two of them.

For the second successive race, Senna saw negative fuel consumption readings from very early on. On lap 39 of the 72 he was relegated to fourth place by Ivan Capelli's March and his tyre stop dropped him to seventh, out of the points, before he repassed Gerhard Berger's Ferrari, Mauricio Gugelmin's March and Riccardo Patrese's Williams to finish fourth. But it was a distant fourth, some 47sec behind Prost.

And yet, having taken the flag, Senna's car immediately ran out of fuel, at Turn 1. It had been that close. Senna was bewildered.

But his three points were crucial, as Prost had improved his score by the same margin and Senna remained only five points behind. If Ayrton won either of the two remaining races – Suzuka or Adelaide – he would be World Champion.

30 OCTOBER 1988

Japanese GP (Suzuka)
McLaren-Honda MP4/4 • 1st (WORLD CHAMPION)

The maths was simple. If Senna won, he was World Champion. If he didn't, it would go to the final round in Adelaide. There seemed little chance of anyone spoiling the McLaren/Senna/Prost party in Japan. Suzuka was Honda's test track, where McLaren-Honda test driver Emanuele Pirro had already logged 8,000 miles of testing during the year.

Given the ructions over perceived engine equality and the exchange of letters between FISA president Jean-Marie Balestre and Honda president Tadashi Kume (see facing page), it was less than ideal when Senna finished the first session of practice 1.6sec quicker than Prost...

Alain was out of sorts. With an upset stomach and still suffering the effects of jetlag, he only slept one hour the night before the opening day's action. Saturday was better – he'd had some sleep and his stomach felt better – and he was happier with the car, having taken over Senna's race chassis when Ayrton elected to stay with the spare for the rest of the weekend.

Immediately Prost was a second quicker than he had been on Friday and soon joined Senna on the front row. He even thought he might beat Ayrton to pole but on his only clear lap he hooked fourth gear instead of second as he accelerated out of the final chicane and sprinted for the line. Senna had his 12th pole of the year but there was only 0.32sec between them, and but for Prost's error the gap would have been less.

Race day brought changeable conditions and as start time approached there was drizzle, but it wasn't heavy enough for anyone to start on other than slicks. The start brought disaster for Senna: as the lights blinked green the pole position McLaren stalled and, with Ayrton frantically waving his arms in the air, he was fortunate not to be collected as the rest of the grid swarmed around him.

Senna blamed both himself and a sharp clutch but was fortunate that the Suzuka grid is slightly downhill, allowing him to eventually bump-start the engine and get away.

WAS HONDA PLAYING GAMES WITH ENGINES?

Senna's inexplicably poor form relative to Prost at Estoril and Jerez had sent the conspiracy theorists into overdrive. Ayrton had been cruising towards the title and then suddenly the performance was missing and he was in trouble with fuel consumption. What was going on?

One popular theory was that the Japanese Honda bosses wanted the title settled in their native land and that Ayrton might just have been slowed up a little to ensure that happened...

The French took it a stage further. Senna was Honda's favoured son, they said, and those stunning early-season gaps between the pair in qualifying – often seven tenths and sometimes more than a second in Senna's favour – proved it. How could anyone be that much quicker than Prost in the same car? But look what then happened in France, where Honda would gain more publicity if Alain set the pace: Prost took his first pole of the year and for the first time was able to outdrive Senna in the race. Suspicious.

It all prompted a rather unnecessary intervention from FISA president Jean-Marie Balestre who, like Prost of course, was French. Very probably, it was triggered by a quote from Osamu Goto, Honda's chief engineer, in the wake of the Spanish GP. Goto said: "Honda is now ready to give both drivers an equal chance of winning."

The word 'now' was probably just unfortunate English usage but some took it to mean that the Japanese hadn't done so thus far! Balestre then delivered an ultimatum, which he asked to be sent out by the Brazilian motorsport federation to its journalists.

"I will do everything to obtain guarantees from both Honda and McLaren that Prost and Senna are treated equally during the final two grands prix," Balestre said. "FISA will do everything possible to guarantee objectivity. The ultimate interests of those two manufacturers are parallel to those of motorsport in general, and we wouldn't want to tarnish its image with any irregularity. But in such a case, serious sanctions would be taken.

"It isn't that I've had any cause for doubt: just that, this year, we have found ourselves faced with particular circumstances with the domination of one team."

Balestre was never diplomatic when he could be bombastic, but Honda didn't receive the letter well.

Honda president Tadashi Kume responded: "I believe that motorsport should be conducted in the spirit of fair play and safety, in order to obtain the interest and emotional involvement of spectators and people concerned. The Honda Motor Co sees fairness as the highest requirement of its philosophy for conducting business, and sets this quality as an ideology in its corporate dealings.

"For the last two races, Honda will continue to supply identical engines which will allow drivers to give supreme demonstrations of their skills, as we have always done in line with our basic ideology."

Mr Kume then signed off by thanking Balestre for "consistently performing your important role as President of the FISA". Somewhat conspicuous by its absence was the word 'well'...

⬇ Osamu Goto's words got lost in translation en route to FISA president Jean-Marie Balestre.

📷 sutton-images.com

Prost led across the line at the end of the opening lap. Senna was eighth. Between them were Gerhard Berger (Ferrari), Ivan Capelli (March), Michele Alboreto (Ferrari), the Benettons of Thierry Boutsen and Alessandro Nannini, and Riccardo Patrese's Williams. Senna had been helped by contact between Warwick and Mansell that saw both trailing back to the pits.

Senna passed Patrese and Nannini on lap 2, Boutsen next time round and Alboreto the lap after that. Berger he despatched on lap 11, to put himself into the top three. Capelli's March, meanwhile, had passed the Ferrari five laps earlier and was now giving Prost a hard time in the drizzly conditions, quicker than the McLaren in the tight corners but outpowered on the straights.

When Aguri Suzuki, having his first grand prix, spun his Lola at the chicane and delayed Prost, who then missed a gear, Capelli actually led the race for a few yards before Prost reasserted himself into Turn 1. Sadly for Capelli, the March stopped on lap 20 with an electrical problem, which elevated Senna to second.

It had to be a win for Ayrton to clinch the title and he was 11sec behind Prost. On a dry track that deficit would have been difficult to claw back, but the Gods were with him. The drizzle was increasing: not enough to warrant a stop for wets (after which the rain might have stopped) but enough to make the surface very slippery on slicks. In these conditions, of course, Senna was peerless.

Senna got Prost's lead down to two seconds and as they headed into the chicane for the 27th time of 51, they caught Andrea de Cesaris. Through the chicane Prost lost time behind the Rial and, suffering the same sporadic gear-selection problems that had afflicted his qualifying effort, he missed a gear on the way out.

Senna needed no second invitation and sliced inside as they headed into Turn 1 for the 28th time. Once in front Ayrton, as usual, picked up time in traffic and with 15 laps to go had a 5sec margin over Prost. As the race entered its final 10 laps Prost gave it all he had and the gap came down from 5sec to 1.5sec within five laps. But then the rain started again. Senna, well aware that more than 75 per cent of the distance had been covered and thus full points would be awarded, pointed to the sky, as Prost had done four years earlier in Monaco...

This time, though, the race ran its course and when the new World Champion crossed the line, jubilant, he was 13sec clear of Prost. Senna wailed like a banshee in ecstatic celebration.

"Until today I always said my best drive was Estoril in '85 – my first win," Senna said later. "But not any more. This was my best." His eighth win in a single year – half the races – was a new record.

13 NOVEMBER 1988

Australian GP (Adelaide)
McLaren-Honda MP4/4 • 2nd

This was to be the last race of F1's turbo era – for the time being – and both Senna and Prost wanted to win it. Ayrton took pole with a lap 0.14sec quicker than Alain. But once more it was Alain who made the better start.

Berger, meanwhile, was fed up with fuel consumption runs and simply whacked up the boost and passed both McLarens. He knew he wouldn't make it to the end, but didn't care, just wanting to enjoy himself! In fact, he didn't have to wait long before he tangled with René Arnoux and ended his race, putting Senna back into second place.

If the McLaren MP4/4 had a weak point it was gear selection, and Senna was soon struggling. He eventually stripped second gear, much used in Adelaide, and did well to use boost settings and enrich fuel mixture to disguise the problem from Piquet, who backed off, allowing Senna to get the consumption back on track before the end and ensure McLaren's 10th 1–2 finish in 16 races.

⬇ Ayrton's Australian fans hail his first world title but were a bit optimistic about Adelaide... Ayrton stripped second gear and finished runner-up.

📷 sutton-images.com

A NEW ERA AYRTON SENNA '88 WORLD CHAMPION
SAN MARINO 1·5·88 BRITAIN 10·7·88 BELGIUM 28·8·88
CANADA 12·6·88 GERMANY 24·7·88 JAPAN 30·10·88
DETROIT 19·6·88 HUNGARY 7·8·88 ADELAIDE? 13·11·88

1989

ACRIMONY AT McLAREN

The 1989 season saw the end of the turbo era in F1 and a return to naturally aspirated engines. But, for McLaren's rivals, there was no reason to suspect that the team's stranglehold on F1 would be broken.

Ominously, when Senna and Prost tested at Imola with Honda's 3.5-litre V10, they set times beaten on the previous year's San Marino GP grid only by the McLaren-Honda turbos. Once again, it looked as if Ayrton and Alain would be each other's main foes...

← The underlying tension between Ayrton and Alain Prost that remained almost under control in 1988 exploded into open warfare in '89.

📷 sutton-images.com

FIRST IMPRESSIONS: MARTIN WHITMARSH

"The first time I met Ayrton was in 1989, when I was totally new to F1. We'd built a new car, he shook it down, and wrote it off on lap 12.

"He left Silverstone, drove to Heathrow and presumably his flight wasn't ready, so he drove to our old factory, came in and the first time I met him he walked into my office and apologised for writing off the car!

"For me, it was… blimey, Ayrton Senna's just walked in. And he's apologising to me! It was all a bit stunning…

"Ayrton being Ayrton, many, many people claim to have been super-close to him, some of whom – when I worked with him from 1989 to '93 – I never saw near him! So I prefer to err on the side of 'I didn't really know him', because I find that all a bit sickening…

"I didn't really know him. He was a tremendously charismatic individual but he was very private. The things people at McLaren remember are Donington '93 and the Brazil race two weeks before, which was our 100th win. He won five races that year and we were genuinely 50 horsepower off a works Renault at the time with a customer Cosworth.

"To be honest, he had family, he had this huge intensity about him, but he didn't have much else. He hadn't developed into a more rounded, balanced individual. I really don't think he had. It was sad. He used to fly helicopters and do lots of solo things, but then at the end of it he had a house at Quinta do Lago, a really nice house, and during the European season Adriane [Galisteu] and he used to go there. She was sweet and didn't have a malicious bone in her body, but there were problems between her and family, who I never really engaged with until more recently.

"In my personal opinion he had this slightly sad loneliness about him. He had this intensity and you sensed that wherever he was in the world he'd wake up thinking 'how am I going to get that competitive advantage over Alain Prost' or whoever. He was always absolutely courteous though."

← Whitmarsh: "Ayrton had this slightly sad loneliness about him."

📷 sutton-images.com

26 MARCH 1989

Brazilian GP (Jacarepagua)
McLaren-Honda MP4/5 • 11th

In a race that saw Johnny Herbert make his F1 debut some seven months after a potentially career-ending F3000 shunt at Brands Hatch, and Riccardo Patrese start a then record-breaking 177th GP, it was situation unchanged at the front. New champion Senna took a comfortable pole for McLaren-Honda, qualifying the new V10-engined MP4/5 0.87sec clear of Patrese's Renault-powered Williams FW12C. Next up were Berger's Ferrari, Boutsen's Williams, Prost's McLaren and Mansell's Ferrari.

Senna's hopes of winning at home lasted only as far as the first corner where, after a poor start, he found himself sandwiched between Patrese and Berger. In the resulting contact Berger spun and Senna clipped the right rear wheel of the Williams, losing his nosecone. After a slow return to the pits and the fitment of a new nose section, Ayrton rejoined, but the best he could manage was 11th place at the flag, two laps down. Meanwhile, clutch problems for Prost meant that he couldn't make a scheduled tyre stop, allowing Nigel Mansell to win his first race for Ferrari, aboard John Barnard's semi-automatic 640 which, hitherto, had suffered a number of reliability issues.

23 APRIL 1989

San Marino GP (Imola)
McLaren-Honda MP4/5 • 1st

If the rest of the field was encouraged by Mansell's Rio win, the optimism was short-lived as McLaren steamrollered the front row at Imola. Senna took pole in 1m 26.010s and Prost was second on 1m 26.235s, with Mansell's Ferrari their closest rival on 1m 27.652s...

In the circumstances, you might wonder at the need for an internal agreement between Ayrton and Alain concerning the start. The agreement was that whoever got ahead through the first corner (Tamburello) wouldn't be forced to go defensive and protect the inside of the following Tosa corner, compromising exit speed.

First time, no problem. Senna converted his pole, led through Tosa and went away from Alain by almost a second a lap for the first three laps. Prost himself was 5sec clear of Mansell by this stage. It was that easy.

But then Berger had a front-wing problem and went straight on at the flat-out Tamburello. The Ferrari suffered a heavy impact that pushed a right-side radiator into

the front of the fuel cell pontoon. The car burst into flames but, thankfully, with Berger momentarily unconscious, fire marshals arrived rapidly and put out the blaze. The race was red-flagged and restarted, the two parts to be aggregated.

This time, Prost made the better start. And so it was with some dismay, he said, that he reached the braking area for Tosa and found Ayrton on his inside, taking the lead. It was the start of an internal rift at McLaren that would never be repaired. They finished 1–2, lapping the entire field, Senna 40sec in front. But on the podium Prost's face was grim, there was no handshake, and Alain left straight away...

In view of what would occur later in the year at Suzuka, it is hugely ironic that Prost spun in the closing stages, missed out the chicane, rejoined on the straight, finished second and collected his six points – with no hint of a penalty. When Senna did the same at Suzuka, he was disqualified. The championship hinged on these two events.

⬇ Imola '89, first
start: Senna leads
into Tosa.

📷 sutton-images.com

IMOLA '89: HAD SENNA REALLY TRANSGRESSED?

McLaren team co-ordinator Jo Ramirez described the circumstances of the breakdown in the relationship between Senna and Prost at Imola in 1989 as follows:

"They decided that they were not going to race between the start and Tosa corner. The idea came initially from Ayrton and it was sensible. Whoever got the better start would maintain first place until Tosa and then, after that, the race would begin. Ayrton made the better start and went ahead. Then came Berger's big accident at Tamburello and the race was stopped.

"They talked again before the restart and made the same agreement. But this time Alain had the better start, went into Tosa, looked in his mirrors and saw Ayrton behind. Then, just as he was turning in, there was Ayrton. He had to move over to avoid hitting him and just couldn't believe it. Alain said that if he knew they had been racing he'd have put himself in the middle of the track and not left enough room.

"Alain was unbelievably upset. It ruined his race. Ayrton won easily and Alain just couldn't concentrate. He spun towards the end, which was almost unheard of for him.

"Alain refused to go to the Imola press conference. I told him he should go and he just said, 'No way. I'm so upset. Whatever I say in there, I'm going to regret.' He wouldn't talk to anyone, and that included Ayrton.

"Ron [Dennis] and Ayrton had a long conversation. Ron blamed him but in a very light way. In a sense he had to do that. Ron knew better than anyone that Ayrton was under contract for 1990, and Alain wasn't..."

Both drivers were due at the Pembrey circuit in Wales the following week. It may have seemed an odd venue for the two best drivers in the world, but it was tight and twisty, and regarded as a decent place to work on set-up for upcoming Monte Carlo. A visit to Wales hadn't been on the agenda for Ron Dennis but, in view of the apparent meltdown, he went to Pembrey to mediate. In Malcolm Folley's book *Senna versus Prost,* Alain described the meeting:

"Ron started to talk. He asked Ayrton, 'Is it true you had an agreement?' Ayrton said, 'Yes.' Ron then said, 'Why did you not honour it?' Ayrton said, 'It's not me – it's Alain who changed the agreement.' This was absolutely unbelievable. Ayrton offered all kinds of excuses. He said that the agreement was for the first start, not the second. Ron wasn't taken in by this.

"Then we had a good 20 minutes, maybe a half-hour discussion. I was hardly talking except to say this wasn't good for the spirit of the team, that it was starting to break up. Then Ayrton started to cry. Started to cry... That is the truth. It's difficult to understand why. Again, because he is different. He had lied. When he said to me, 'You broke the agreement', he was convinced he was right. I said, 'Ayrton, you were there.' Maybe he cried because he realised he was wrong and had lost his honour."

For Senna, they were tears of anger and frustration. He was the pole man,

had led the first start comfortably and second time around, after Alain got away better, he had come out of Tamburello quicker and right on Prost's gearbox. He'd got alongside well before the quick right leading into Tosa, was a car length up on the inside by the time they reached the braking point, Prost never had the opportunity to defend, Alain's exit from Tosa wasn't compromised and nearest rival Patrese wasn't close enough to challenge. So what was the fuss about?

Footage of the incident doesn't tally with Ramirez's account. Senna wasn't behind Prost going into Tosa, he was ahead. Prost didn't have to move to avoid Senna. And Alain couldn't have placed himself in the middle of the track on the entry to Tosa because Ayrton was already there. Senna's move was cleanly done well before the braking area for Tosa.

The key point is what was meant by 'the start'. Was it the entry to Tamburello or did it include the section of straight before Tosa? That is what Senna was talking about when he accused Prost of changing the agreement.

As far as Ayrton was concerned, to sit behind Alain would only have delayed the inevitable. If Prost was serious about being 'robbed', he might have had the good grace to finish closer than 40 seconds behind! But now, thanks to a totally disproportionate reaction and skilful politicking, Senna was the bad guy at a race he dominated from Friday to Sunday and the world was too stupid to either understand or care. The squabble was a much better story than the fact.

7 MAY 1989

Monaco GP (Monte Carlo)
McLaren-Honda MP4/5 • 1st

Ron Dennis's efforts to sort out his feuding superstars were not helped when Prost made his feelings towards Senna known in the French daily sports paper, *L'Equipe*.

Forgetting the psychological battle, on the track it was again no contest. A year after his 'religious experience' qualifying lap, Senna produced another stunning pole position. At a time when Prost could manage 'only' 1m 23.456s, itself almost a second quicker than third-placed Thierry Boutsen, Senna lapped in 1m 22.308s!

This time in the race there was no Berger to get between the McLarens at Turn 1, the Austrian still recovering from injuries sustained during his fortunate escape at Imola. Senna led from the start and made a decisive break when they hit traffic for the first time. As in 1988 it was another crushing performance by Senna, but right to the end this time!

Senna took the chequered flag 52sec clear of Prost as, once again, they lapped the entire field. Martin Brundle starred by qualifying a Brabham fourth, but it was left to team-mate Stefano Modena to join the McLaren men on the podium. In the championship, Ayrton and Alain had 18 points apiece.

28 MAY 1989

Mexican GP (Autodromo Hermanos Rodriguez)
McLaren-Honda MP4/5 • 1st

Senna was again decisively the quicker of the two McLaren drivers, beating Prost to pole by 0.9sec as they locked out the front row. It was a landmark pole for Ayrton too, equalling the record – at the time – of 33 achieved by Jim Clark.

With scorching temperatures, tyre choice was a critical factor. While Senna went for the harder Goodyear B compound on the left-hand side, Prost opted for the softer Cs all round. If it was normally 'the professor' who was sublime at this type of thing, it was Senna who got it right this time and sped off to take a hat-trick of wins.

Prost was soon in trouble with his left front tyre and the error of his rubber choice was compounded at his pit stop when, instead of new Bs all round, the team fitted just a new left front. Ultimately it meant that Prost also finished behind Patrese, Alboreto and Nannini. Ayrton now had a seven-point advantage in the defence of his title.

4 JUNE 1989

United States GP (Phoenix)
McLaren-Honda MP4/5 • Retired, 44 laps, electronics

America's new Phoenix race, which greeted F1 with brutally high temperatures, saw Senna continue his qualifying domination by a rude amount – 1.4sec over Prost! – and set a record 34th career pole.

Senna seemed to have the race bought and paid for, leading for the first 33 laps before suddenly starting to suffer from a misfire. The team changed the electronic box and the battery and Senna resumed for another 12 laps before the problem returned. Post-race inspection found nothing and it was thought that driver-to-pit radio transmissions had interfered with engine management sensors.

Prost duly picked up the pieces to score his first win of the year and, having been nowhere near Senna for pace at any race, now led the championship by two points.

16 JUNE 1989

Canadian GP (Montréal)
McLaren-Honda MP4/5 • 7th

Montréal would have been Senna's ninth consecutive F1 pole – but it wasn't to be. On his opening day qualifying run he found third gear jumping out and Prost was a few hundredths quicker. The weather then rendered improvement impossible on the second day.

With rain falling on race morning, most of the cars went to the grid on wet tyres and a wet race was declared. On the opening lap Senna passed Prost with such speed that Alain thought he must have a puncture. Nothing was found when the Frenchman pitted but, when he rejoined, the left front suspension pick-up point pulled out of the monocoque.

Senna stopped for a set of slicks after four laps and rejoined fifth. Just as he'd fought his way onto the tail of Patrese's leading Williams, still on wets, the rain returned. After pitting again to return to wet rubber, Senna resumed almost 55sec down. But Ayrton was now easily the quickest man on the track.

Patrese stopped for another set of wets after 35 laps and handed the lead to Derek Warwick, who kept it for just four laps before his Arrows was caught and passed by the flying McLaren. So with 30 laps to go, Senna was back in front. It looked like a simple cruise to the flag but for the second successive race he lost a certain nine points through unreliability. This time, unthinkably, it was a Honda engine failure!

← Senna scored his first Monaco win in a McLaren and made amends for his error the previous year.
sutton-images.com

→ Later in the
year McLaren
unexpectedly found
itself defending
Senna's retirement
in France, among
many other
irrelevancies...

📷 sutton-images.com

9 JULY 1989

French GP (Paul Ricard)
McLaren-Honda MP4/5 • Retired, 0 laps, transmission

For the second successive season Prost got the better of Senna in qualifying at Paul Ricard to take his first 'genuine' pole of 1989, the margin between them just 0.02sec. Alain dominated paddock gossip with his press conference on Friday morning to announce that he wouldn't be driving for McLaren in 1990.

Senna got the better start but, behind, Mauricio Gugelmin's March triggered a multiple accident that brought out the red flag and meant a restart. Taking it, Senna's car broke its transmission and Ayrton was out on the spot.

"I was about at the point where I change from first to second gear when the car just stopped accelerating," Senna explained. "Then, when I got back to the paddock, I was called up to the stewards and asked why I pulled off the circuit on the left rather than the right. For some reason they seemed to think I was closer to the right, which I wasn't. Anybody could see that on the television. Eventually they said, 'OK, we accept your explanation.' But I was really mad with all that. It was complete nonsense." It was nonsense, and nonsense that would be revisited a few months later...

Senna's mechanical problem gave Prost a comfortable win and an 11-point advantage in the championship.

16 JULY 1989

British GP (Silverstone) • McLaren-Honda MP4/5
Retired, 11 laps, gearbox/spin

At Silverstone McLaren debuted a transverse gearbox after many miles of testing. But there was trouble in qualifying when telltale wisps of smoke signalled problems with the engine oil tank that were found to be caused by a manufacturing fault. The team's practice programme was restricted but this didn't prevent Senna and Prost claiming the front row, with Mansell's Ferrari within half a second.

Senna was physical in his rebuttal of Prost's first-corner challenge but it wasn't long before he started to have problems with gear selection. Determined to resist the challenge of Prost and Mansell, however, he pressed on, holding the lever in as he did so. Prost noticed Senna lose control a couple of times before finally surrendering the back end terminally at Becketts, his afternoon ending in the gravel trap. Once again, Prost picked up the pieces and another maximum score. Alain now led Ayrton by 20 points.

30 JULY 1989

German GP (Hockenheim)
McLaren-Honda MP4/5 • 1st

While paddock speculation suggested that Prost would partner Mansell at Ferrari in 1990, the Honda-powered McLarens used their power to maximum effect at the flat-out Hockenheim and easily claimed the front row once again, with Ayrton almost a full second quicker than Alain.

In the race Gerhard Berger offered token resistance by making the best start from row 2 and leading into Turn 1, but both McLarens pulled effortlessly past further round the lap. Senna led for 19 laps until he made his tyre stop, where a problem occurred at the right rear.

Senna rejoined 5sec behind Prost and gradually set about whittling down the gap. With 10 of the 45 laps to go it was only 2sec. Having followed Senna earlier in the race, Prost knew how difficult it would be for his rival to handle turbulent air and in fact it looked as if Alain would hang on until, two laps from home, the McLaren wouldn't engage sixth gear on the run down to the Stadium section. At last, a bit of luck for Senna, who swept past to win his fourth race of the year.

13 AUGUST 1989

Hungarian GP (Hungaroring)
McLaren-Honda MP4/5 • 2nd

The McLaren wasn't the class of the field at the tight Hungaroring. That accolade went to Williams, for whom Riccardo Patrese took pole position. Senna needed to take the MP4/5 by the scruff of the neck to put it on the front row alongside the Italian, with Prost down in fifth place.

The race went down in history as one of Nigel Mansell's most memorable. Patrese was able to hold off Senna for the first 52 laps, by which time Mansell, who had sacrificed qualifying to concentrate on race performance, had managed to work the Ferrari through from 12th to third.

Patrese, having collected some debris from Nakajima's Lotus, suffered a holed radiator and retired after a great effort. Senna calmly passed him into Turn 1 but had Mansell looming large in his mirrors.

With 20 laps to go they caught Stefan Johansson's Onyx, which had just emerged from the pits with a gearbox problem. The Swede failed to engage a gear out of Turn 4 and Senna almost tripped over him, momentarily having to back off. Mansell needed no second invitation to sweep by and win.

With a vibration from the front end and Prost back in fourth place, Ayrton accepted second place and collected the six points. The championship score was now Alain 56, Ayrton 42.

27 AUGUST 1989

Belgian GP (Spa-Francorchamps)
McLaren-Honda MP4/5 • 1st

The mighty Spa gave Senna a 37th career pole and McLaren its 50th as Ayrton lapped 0.6sec quicker than Prost. An updated version of the Honda RA109E V10 engine was introduced at Spa to address the MP4/5's Achilles Heel – lack of drivability at low revs, with abrupt throttle response – and the drivers judged the car better, but not perfect. But at Spa, of course, the revs don't drop too much, La Source apart!

Spa in the rain is much feared and there was a delayed start when Brabham drivers Martin Brundle and Stefano Modena both crashed their BT58s on the formation lap. When the starting lights eventually went green it was Senna who led Prost through La Source and down to Eau

Rouge. Ayrton seemed to be able to draw clear at will and it was left to Prost to fend off the attentions of Nigel Mansell's Ferrari.

Senna duly served up another wet-weather masterclass to take his fifth win of the year and close to within nine points of Prost.

10 SEPTEMBER 1989

Italian GP (Monza) • McLaren-Honda MP4/5
Retired, 44 laps, engine

With just five races to go and Prost leading the championship by 62 points to 51, despite Senna's superiority pretty much everywhere, Monza was crucial. Predictably enough it was strained, and tensions were heightened when it was revealed that Prost had put his name to a Ferrari contract on the Wednesday before the race. He would indeed partner Nigel Mansell in 1990.

Mansell's Hungarian win had owed much to Nigel's opportunism but Ferrari was still reckoned to be closing the performance gap to McLaren-Honda. The first appearance of its modified V12 at Monza was expected to bring it even closer. And that's the way it looked. But then Senna produced one of his spellbinding qualifying laps.

Ayrton's 1m 23.720s was over a second quicker than Berger's Ferrari best, the Austrian having beaten Mansell by just 0.005sec. Prost, meanwhile, was fourth, his 1m 25.510s adrift of Senna by 1.79sec!

Such a margin at Monte Carlo is one thing, partially explained away by Senna's total commitment and risk-taking versus Prost's degree of reserve. But Alain was perplexed at how he could amass such a deficit around a lap of Monza. Maybe Ayrton was a bit more committed on the brakes at the chicanes, but, 1.79sec...

Inevitably there were murmurings about preferential treatment, with Alain no doubt feeling that, with the ink still damp on his Ferrari contract, the timing was suspicious...

Senna converted his pole position and drove effortlessly away from Berger, with Mansell running third, ahead of Prost. The McLaren was undoubtedly the quicker car but by the time Alain had despatched the Ferraris, Senna was 20sec up the road.

Senna had the race in his pocket but a flashing oil light was a concern. Sure enough, with eight laps to go his Honda V10 let go spectacularly on the run down to Parabolica, Ayrton spinning on his own oil. Prost, again, picked up the pieces.

Senna was stunned. The championship score was now 71 points to 51 in Prost's favour. Phoenix, Montréal, Silverstone and now Monza – Senna had led all four convincingly before mechanical problems intervened. That would have been an extra 36 points. And Prost, Senna knew, had inherited the win in three of those four races, meaning that the real points swing was 45. And that's before you even consider the startline transmission failure at Ricard, which Alain also won. Senna knew that he should be 25 points ahead with his title almost defended, not 20 behind. It would be a tall order from there, and he knew it.

Prost, though, wasn't looking particularly happy either. Famously, on the podium he dropped his trophy to the *tifosi* below, enraging Ron Dennis. And Alain, in his post-race press conference, said that despite the 20-point lead, he wasn't confident and not happy with his treatment from Honda. That 1.79sec, no doubt...

Senna led convincingly at Monza but a blown engine with eight laps to go was hugely costly to his title defence.
sutton-images.com

PROST'S PUBLIC McLAREN DIVORCE AND 'CUPGATE'

"It became obvious quite soon after Imola that Alain wouldn't be staying with McLaren in 1990," says team co-ordinator Jo Ramirez. "As well as the trouble with Ayrton, I think he reckoned that McLaren weren't going to have the top car all the time, and that he needed a better car than Ayrton's if he was going to beat him. I think he realised that he couldn't do it in the same car.

"Monza was the last time that Prost drove a McLaren in Italy. There was the crowd, the fever and, of course, their knowledge that Alain had signed for Ferrari. He was the hero coming home. Every time he left the pitlane they cheered. Ayrton's car broke in the race, Alain won, and as he waited to come down off the podium all the *tifosi* were shouting 'Cup! Cup!'

"I could see him deliberating about what to do and in the end he dropped it down to them. I've never seen anything like it. That cup – within three seconds there was nothing left of it. Somebody took the top, someone else took one handle. The thing was just torn to pieces.

"Ron had the constructors' cup and as Alain came down the steps, Ron showed it to him and then threw it down at his feet. Hard. Really slammed it down. Ron was so upset, I couldn't believe it. Alain turned to me and said, 'Oh shit! What do I do now?'

"Anyone could see from the trophy

← From the Monza podium, race-winner Prost, who had just signed for Ferrari for 1990, faced this sea of flag-waving Ferrari fans and gave in to their demands that he surrender the winner's trophy to them, enraging Ron Dennis.

sutton-images.com

→ Happier times for Ron Dennis during Prost's six seasons with McLaren – Ron regarded the trophy incident at Monza as an open show of disrespect to both McLaren and himself.

📷 sutton-images.com

room at the factory how carefully all our cups were kept and polished. It even says in the drivers' contracts that the trophies belong to the team. If they want a copy, I arrange for one and they pay for it. Ron took what Alain did very personally; an open show of disrespect towards the team and himself. I tried to persuade him that Alain didn't mean it like that. He was going to an Italian team, they were all shouting for the cup and he had no choice. I felt the same way as Ron about the team, its history and things like that, but I knew Alain didn't mean it.

"I had a replica cup made and always wanted an opportunity for Alain to give it to Ron. Eventually, at the end of 1995, when it was announced that Alain was coming back to us as a consultant, I wrapped the replica cup up before the McLaren Christmas dinner. As I introduced Alain to everyone who didn't know him, he stepped up and told Ron he had something for him..."

That, of course, was six years later. In the immediate aftermath there was a bigger problem. That 1.79sec gap in qualifying had prompted Prost to publicly raise doubts about fair treatment at the hands of Honda. The Japanese didn't like it.

Before the next race at Estoril there appeared a statement from Honda Marlboro McLaren, signed by Dennis, F1 PR manager Yoshinobu Noguchi and, no doubt under duress, Prost himself. It read:

"As a result of the consequences of press statements and incidents at the Italian GP, Alain Prost, Honda and McLaren have had extensive

discussions and wish, via this joint statement, to put on record their intentions for creating the best possible working environment for the driver and team for the remainder of the season. Honda and McLaren have again reassured Alain, to his satisfaction, of their commitment to equality and will continue this policy regardless of Alain's move to another team for the 1990 season.

"Alain deeply regrets the adverse publicity and the resulting embarrassment that have been caused by his actions. Honda and McLaren have accepted that these resulted from Alain's perception of his treatment by the team and were not made with malicious intent. He has agreed that in future any doubts that he has on this subject will be discussed with the relevant engineers prior to comments being made to the press.

The team also expresses its disdain and dissatisfaction over inaccurate, unqualified and damaging statements made by third parties

subsequent to Monza. Honda and McLaren wish to emphasise that their partnership is founded not only on their desire to strive for technical excellence and continuous success but, more importantly, on achieving these objectives with the values of fairness and honesty."

This, quite clearly, was nothing more than PR puff. The final paragraph was supposed to be a rebuke to FISA president Jean-Marie Balestre who, undeterred by the rumpus he'd caused a year earlier with his letter to Honda demanding equal treatment, had done the same again with comments post-Monza.

McLaren, however, had failed to sufficiently spell that out. The majority of the world's motor racing press interpreted 'third parties' as Nigel Mansell and Keke Rosberg, both of whom had been saying that, based on their own experiences at Williams-Honda, they could sympathise with Prost's reservations about even-handedness.

24 SEPTEMBER 1989

Portuguese GP (Estoril)
McLaren-Honda MP4/5 • Retired, 48 laps, accident

Once again, Senna took pole position at Estoril with a lap 0.6sec clear of Berger's Ferrari and Prost another 0.15sec adrift. If that was all straightforward, the race was anything but...

Senna had a quick spin in the race morning warm-up in which he'd been quickest, but with the Ferraris close. Berger also made a better start than the pole man and, worryingly for Senna, started to leave the McLaren by almost a second a lap. Making matters worse, Senna had Mansell's Ferrari right on his gearbox and Nigel made it a Ferrari 1–2 as he went inside the McLaren into Turn 1 on lap 8. When the two Ferraris caught backmarkers, Senna and Prost weren't far behind and it looked as if the tyre stops would be all-important. They were, but not in quite the way imagined...

Berger's stop was a good one. Senna's wasn't. And Mansell overshot the Ferrari pit completely and came to a stop at Benetton. Amid confusion as the Ferrari mechanics ran to the car, Nigel selected reverse and got himself back into position. But reversing in the pitlane is prohibited and he was to be black-flagged.

For one glorious lap Pierluigi Martini led the Portuguese GP for Minardi, before Berger took over again, about 4sec in front of the delayed Senna, with Mansell charging. The black flag, along with Mansell's number 27, was displayed at the start/finish line, but three times Nigel ignored it. He claimed that he didn't see it because he was so close behind Senna's McLaren.

Senna clearly hadn't seen it either, or he wouldn't have bothered defending second place. These two had 'previous', of course, and Ron Dennis got on the radio and told Senna to ignore Mansell. But Ayrton didn't hear the message and asked for Dennis to repeat it. Ron didn't get a chance. Moments later Mansell and Senna collided at Turn 1.

This time, Mansell started his move much later than when he'd passed Ayrton on lap 8. The Ferrari wasn't alongside as they reached the turn-in point and Senna took his line. The McLaren's right rear wheel hit the Ferrari's left front, damaging the suspension of both cars, which were out of the race.

Mansell, sheepishly, ran straight back to the pits. Senna, livid, tried to comprehend the fact that he'd scored no points again, while Prost picked up another six in this, his 150th F1 start. With just the 11 best results to count towards the championship, Alain only increased his total by four but his championship lead over Senna

↓ Costly – Senna and Mansell in the Portuguese gravel after their controversial tangle.

📷 sutton-images.com

was now out to 24 points. Ayrton had just six scores – five wins and a second – and so pretty much needed to win the three remaining races, in Spain, Japan and Australia.

Spanish GP (Jerez)
McLaren-Honda MP4/5 • 1st

As the teams decamped to Jerez there was controversy as FISA suspended Mansell for repeatedly ignoring the black flag in Portugal the previous weekend. Nigel threatened to quit if the governing body didn't rescind its decision, which, fittingly considering the location, acted as red rag to bull and got Nigel precisely nowhere.

Senna was thus playing with fire when, in practice, he drove through waved yellow flags at the scene of a big accident to Gregor Foitek, then through a red flag displayed at the start/finish line. In light of what had just happened to Mansell and the 'topicality', Ayrton was fortunate to cop just a $20,000 fine.

Another pole position duly fell his way, the 40th, but any tiny shreds of bonhomie left in Prost's

relationship with the team disappeared when Senna was allocated the spare car because he was behind in the championship, despite it being Alain's turn to have it. The Frenchman, unhappy with the balance of his race car, qualified third, behind Berger's Ferrari.

Needing to win, Senna did just that, with ease. First into Turn 1, the McLaren was never seen again, taking the flag 27sec ahead of Berger with Prost almost a minute in arrears. Prost's third place improved his championship score by just the one point, but it was significant. With 76 points to Senna's 60, it meant that a win and a second in Japan and Australia were not enough for Ayrton – he needed to win both to retain his title.

Japanese GP (Suzuka)
McLaren-Honda MP4/5 • Disqualified

The way the championship was balanced, calling it was difficult. Prost had the points on the board but could only improve his score by winning and the Ferraris couldn't be relied upon to outperform Senna at either Suzuka or the final race in Adelaide. Senna couldn't afford a slip-up and

↑ Senna scored a dominant win in Spain but still needed to win in Japan and Australia to retain his title.

📷 sutton-images.com

to retain his title he had to win both of the last races. Undeniably, he would start both as strong favourite, so Prost, somehow, had to beat him in one or the other – and that was a big ask.

The scale of Prost's task became wholly apparent after another of Senna's totally mesmerising qualifying laps gave him pole with a 1.73sec margin over Alain. Unlike Monza, there was no murmuring about the engines here. Senna had looked that quick!

Prost knew he wasn't going to outqualify Ayrton at Suzuka of all places, but also knew that he had to get onto the front row to stand any chance of beating Senna off the line. Thankfully for Alain, at such a power track the Ferraris weren't the kind of nuisance they were at circuits like Hungaroring or Estoril, and he managed the task comfortably.

The drivers were made aware in the briefing that there would be a shorter-than-usual gap between red and green at the start to prevent the sloping Suzuka grid wreaking havoc with clutches, but Senna still seemed to be caught napping. Into Turn 1, Prost led.

Alain, figuring that he might have to overtake during the course of the afternoon, was running less wing than Ayrton, and, initially, started to pull away. But it was likely, over the race distance, that Senna's set-up would be kinder to the tyres and he would be in better shape later on.

That's exactly how it played out. Prost's tyre stop, 21 laps into the 53, was a good one; Senna's three laps later, less so. When they were back up to racing speed with 30 laps to run, Prost led by around 5sec, but Senna was now in attack mode and gradually whittled away the gap.

Ayrton's fastest lap, 38th time round, was half a second quicker than the best Prost was able to respond with five laps later. Inexorably Senna closed in, but getting by wasn't going to be easy. With Prost's car carrying slightly more straightline speed but Senna's better on the brakes with the stability of more wing, the chicane looked to be the only place to mount an attack. On lap 43, Senna made his move, Prost saw him coming and turned in very, very early. If they collided, remember, Prost was champion...

Inevitably, contact was made and the McLarens came to an entangled halt in the middle of the track. Prost immediately popped his belts and climbed out, later claiming that it was a big mistake not to realise that he could have continued...

Senna, meanwhile, was first pulled back and then pushed down the escape road, during which he managed to restart the car. The rules prohibited driving against the flow of traffic and so Ayrton rejoined by weaving through the blocks in the escape road exit.

With both Ferraris victim to mechanical dramas, Alessandro Nannini's Benetton was the closest challenger to the McLarens when they collided, but a minute behind, so Senna still led across the line for the first time at the end of lap 47. When his front wing, damaged in the contact with Prost, eventually parted company with the rest of the car, Senna pitted for a replacement and charged back into the race just over 5sec behind Nannini with four laps to go.

The McLaren quickly caught the Benetton and Senna went by at the scene of his tangle with Prost to lead the final two laps and take the chequered flag, his championship defence still seemingly intact. But when the three drivers came out to mount the podium, they were Nannini and the Williams drivers, Patrese and Boutsen. Senna had been excluded for missing out part of the track when he rejoined.

McLaren immediately appealed the exclusion with a hearing scheduled for the following Friday.

What of Prost and Senna? Prost offered a handshake, saying he was sorry it had ended that way. Senna ignored him.

"I was absolutely certain that I would win the race or have an accident like this," Prost said. "Of course I realised that Senna absolutely wanted to win, but his problem is that he can neither accept the possibility of not winning, nor that somebody will resist one of his overtaking manoeuvres.

"Many times over the last couple of years I have opened the door to him. If I hadn't done, then we would have crashed like today. But before the race here, I said that I wasn't going to leave the door open any longer. And that happened.

"I must admit that Ayrton is an extremely good driver, almost unbelievably quick. He is extremely motivated but, in my view, he is driving too hard. To be honest, from a personal viewpoint, it has become absolutely impossible to work with him."

Shortly after the race, Senna put out a statement revealing his own views.

"That was the only place I could overtake," he said. "And somebody who should not have been there just closed the door and that was that. The results as they stand provisionally do not reflect the truth of the race in either the sporting sense or in the sense of the regulations. I see the results as temporary.

"It's a pity that we had to appeal in abnormal situations like this. We must fight with all our available resources. Now the matter is out of our hands. What I have done is done, and is correct. From now this matter will be in the hands of lawyers, people who understand the theoretical side. As for the practical side, it was obvious that I won on the track."

SUZUKA SCANDAL: FISA MOVES THE GOALPOSTS

It was fairly obvious what had happened, was it not? Prost knew that if he took Senna out, he was champion. Helicopter evidence shows him turning in very early to the chicane and initiating the required contact.

"I think everyone knew it was Alain's fault but they were fighting for the World Championship at the penultimate race," remembers Jo Ramirez. "He knew that Ayrton was quicker and he had to protect his position.

"Alain had always said, when they were team-mates and sometimes before, that if Ayrton was quicker he would always open the door. But now the championship was at stake he wasn't going to. And he didn't just shut the door, he slammed it!

"That was absolutely the lowest moment for the team. We entirely dominated the meeting and came home with nothing. It was disgusting. We felt bitterly disappointed. Cheated. Ayrton won the race, he was the best man there and he should have got it. Ron said he would fight for it in the courts if he had to.

"Alain made the worst mistake of his life that day. We were at the airport on the Monday, waiting for the plane, and I said: 'You know, there was absolutely nothing wrong with your car. Nothing. Not a scratch – air in all four tyres, the front wing was all there.

"He said, 'I know. It was such a big impact that the steering wheel came out of my hand and when I looked down, one wheel was off at an angle. What I didn't realise was that the other one was at the same angle too!'

"Ayrton had to come in to change his nose and so all Alain had to do was keep going and win the race. Ayrton would have been second and Alain would have been champion. He'll remember that all his life, I tell you..."

Well, maybe, except that in the heat of the moment Prost would have had no way of knowing that Senna's front wing was about to detach itself on the following lap. Prost's intention, clearly, was that neither of them would emerge from the chicane. It was simply that such intimidatory driving was so alien to his instincts that he didn't do it well enough!

But the stage was so well set that what would happen next was all too obvious, surely? Senna would be rightly reinstated five days later and we'd have a dramatic winner-take-all championship finale in Adelaide. We could hardly wait. In subsequent years that's undoubtedly what would have happened, but not in the reign of FISA president Jean-Marie Balestre, a Frenchman remember...

When Senna, Ron Dennis, Honda personnel and their legal delegation, advised by one Jean-François Prat, arrived at the FISA HQ in Paris's Place de la Concorde, they had prepared what they believed was a good case to counter Senna's disqualification for breaching Article 56 of the sporting regulations by resuming the race via the escape road rather than the circuit.

Undeterred by the slightly surreal circumstances of having to prepare a case against his own driver – albeit one who had just signed for Ferrari – Dennis was armed with helicopter footage that proved beyond doubt that the contact was caused by Prost turning in earlier than usual.

McLaren argued that in steering down the escape road rather than into the chicane while being pushed, Senna was behaving responsibly in ensuring that course marshals weren't unnecessarily endangered. Then, having managed to restart his engine, Ayrton has no choice but to rejoin via the escape road because Article 54 of the regulations stated: 'Drivers are strictly forbidden to drive their car in the opposite direction to the race under pain of immediate exclusion.'

The team also argued that the need to hold the podium ceremony had placed unacceptable pressure on the stewards to arrive at a decision, 'a breach of conventional procedure' in which all the relevant facts and regulations need to be properly studied.

Dennis had also compiled footage of a number of previous instances of drivers missing out chicanes and rejoining the circuit without incurring a penalty, most notably Prost at the controversial Imola race that very same year, when Alain scored six points!

Any fair-minded judicial panel ruling with equanimity would have been hard pressed to do other than find in Senna's favour and reinstate him. That, however, is not what this was. McLaren was astonished to discover that in the four days between the end of the race and the appeal hearing, FISA had prepared its own document regarding the decisions of the Japanese stewards, raising all manner of additional allegations against Ayrton and opining that the Suzuka disqualification should be supplemented by a fine and suspended ban!

↑ Prost watching
as Senna pits for
a new nose
📷 sutton-images.com

Senna states his case – then hangs himself

There was little doubt that the Suzuka stewards made
a fundamental error in excluding Senna for missing out
the chicane – there were so many examples of similar
behaviour that attracted no penalty and it was equally
clear that Senna gained no advantage. Hence the need
for the governing body's shifting of goalposts before the
appeal hearing.

Nigel Roebuck wrote in his popular 'Fifth Column' in
Autosport: "To my mind as soon as he (Senna) received
the second push start (in the escape road) he was out of
the game, and quite why that wasn't cited by the stewards
as grounds for his disqualification is beyond me."

It was a line peddled by many others at the time but,
as Nigel admitted, it was only an opinion and, in fact, it
was easy to appreciate why the second push was no
reasonable justification for exclusion. First, the rules
didn't specify the acceptability of one push, two pushes
or a hundred pushes. And more importantly, would it have
been sensible to have an abandoned car left in the escape
road after a braking area that cars approach at around
180mph?

It's fair to say that in 1989 Senna's relationship with large
swathes of the British F1 press was lukewarm at best.
Much of that could be traced back to their affrontedness at
his refusal to permit Derek Warwick's recruitment to Lotus

some three years earlier. And, where Prost was generally
approachable, Ayrton wasn't.

Autosport, however, did publish an interview that Senna
conducted with Japanese journalists post-Suzuka, provided
by Kunihiko Akai, and it bears review in its entirety:

Q: *How do you feel about the McLaren appeal now?*
A: *We have to try and regain the victory and carry on the
fight in Australia. I haven't lost yet. Whatever happens
in Paris I believe I should have won the championship
a lot earlier already. But we had some failures, so the
championship is in a difficult position. As far as I am
concerned, I used the experience from last year as a driver,
and I did a much better job this year than a year ago.*

Q: *It's obvious you do not feel that you have broken
any rule. What defence will you be offering to the
suggestion that you took an illegal short cut?*
A: *What happened to me, my behaviour, is normal.
Whenever a driver makes a mistake, he goes off the circuit
and rejoins later without penalty, even if he cuts a chicane.
It happened this year in Spa, with Mansell; he lost the car
under braking at the chicane, he went off the circuit, cut
the chicane and rejoined at the next corner. No problem.
And there is nothing wrong with it, because you cannot turn
around and come back against the direction of the circuit,*

because that is a dangerous manoeuvre and it's against the rules. It has happened in many cases, not just these two; there are 10 or 20 cases.

Q: Did you present this argument to the Suzuka stewards?
A: Of course. Unfortunately the stewards had convinced themselves that I should have turned right immediately (into the chicane). But, as I pointed out, if I had tried to do that I would have put the car in a dangerous place. At that moment I didn't have the engine running. I had to put the car in a safe place. That's what the rules say and that's what I did. In the process of doing it I rejoined the circuit. Then they said, 'Oh, but you should have turned around and come back to the place where you left the circuit.' I could not do that though: I would be against the circuit. I would be facing cars coming into the chicane, and if they missed the chicane they would have hit me head-on. That again is dangerous and against the rules.

Q: *You mean they had no intention of giving you a fair hearing?*
A: Exactly. It was disgraceful, for me, for my team, because it was clear to us that the disqualification was already established by the people concerned before I even arrived there.

Q: *Why do you say 'disgraceful'?*
A: The stewards of the meeting said to me, first of all, 'Why did you cause an accident?' Cause an accident? We (Prost and I) were fighting close, that's racing, and that happens. I didn't make any polemics by saying that he closed the door and caused the accident. Then they said I used the pit lane to overtake. I said that the pit lane, under the rules, is part of the racing circuit. And where I went wasn't the pit lane, it's the entrance of the pit lane. And at Suzuka that is well used, even when you're not fighting. When you come under braking there, it's on the line of the braking, so you use it consistently.

I overtook many cars there, not only in this race but in last year's race. I just said, 'OK, that's not a good argument.'

Then they said I was push-started, but I pointed out that the rules say you may be push-started. 'Ah, OK,' they said, 'but you should have turned to the right.' I said: 'No, I could not turn to the right, the car would not turn, I didn't have the engine running, it would have been a dangerous manoeuvre and I would have been infringing the regulations.'

So then they said, 'Oh, but when you got the engine started you should have turned around and gone back to the place you left.' So I replied: 'I would have been going against the direction of the circuit. The rules say you cannot do it.' So they have no argument. They told me to leave the room, and when they asked me back it was to say I was disqualified. It is disgraceful.

Q: *You have become noted for your good starts yet at Suzuka you got beaten away by Prost?*
A: I made a bad start, my own mistake. It's not been so easy this year with the normally aspirated engine. With so much power at the bottom end, you can get a lot of wheelspin very easily.

Q: *So there was no special mistake?*
A: No, I didn't miss a gear. I just had too much wheelspin in first gear. It's a little bit dirtier on the inside of the circuit, which gave me wheelspin.

Q: *So, from that moment you had to adapt yourself to being in second place behind Prost. What was your plan?*
A: Prost pushed very hard, at the beginning especially. In my estimation he was pushing so hard that there was a danger of compromising the tyre and car performance. Over a full grand prix distance, the physical and mental stress would have been perhaps too great also. So I tried to go as quick as I could, without compromising the car because if we had both not finished it would not matter for him. So it was a big tactical fight, not just technical. Then my pit stop was a bit slower than his, maybe one second, due to a problem with a front wheel. In this situation, one second means a lot. Then from half distance onwards I started to catch. I was always catching on a clear circuit. Then sometimes in traffic he would go away, and vice versa. I had to be positive and strong in my mind, very strong. So I completely applied my mind to driving fast, consistent, and aiming for victory. When I caught him I realised then that he had more speed than me: out of the corners, under acceleration.

Q: *Was it the wing settings?*
A: I had a little bit more on the rear, but that was more a balance set-up than downforce. The wing represented maybe 2kph on the straight. It was under acceleration where I was losing. I think maybe I had some electronic difficulties, so I lost a bit of performance. So Alain had a better performance. But it's not possible to establish. I lost power during the race, it was definitely less than it was in qualifying, for whatever reason.

I saw clearly that the only passing place was the chicane, because it's the only heavy braking place. I could have an advantage because I have a technique of using the engine to slow down, as well as using the brakes. Then the right moment came. I was close to him on the straight, close behind him in the slipstream. To stay close, I had to do the quick corner before the chicane right behind him, which was very dangerous for me. Because I was in his slipstream, my wings lost downforce.

Q: *You did 100 per cent at 130R?*

A: *Yeah, completely committed... but dangerous because I had turbulence from his car and I lost aerodynamic downforce. But I still did it, and then I came with the speed and momentum to take him under braking. He was in the middle of the circuit so I came to the inside and outbraked him completely, and we were almost side-by-side and there was no more room. And then he turned in. There I was, half a wheel behind him, and he just turned in. There was no space left.*

Q: *Prost had warned you he would not open the door. Do you think he hit you on purpose?*

A: *What he did was unbelievable, normally. But you could understand because he could only gain, he had nothing to lose. He had to make sure that I would not go through because if I had passed him, it was finished for him. I was faster than him and I would have gone away. So what he did was just to turn the steering wheel and let the cars engage, to make sure we both stopped.*

Q: *What were your feelings at that moment?*

A: *I was upset, but what could I do? The cars were in a dangerous place. We were almost in the chicane. I stayed in the car to move out of a dangerous place. The marshals tried to move the cars but they couldn't do it without pushing the cars back to disengage the wheels. In the process of pushing the car straight I even disconnected my radio, I thought it was finished.*

But in the process of pushing straight I realised that maybe I could restart. So I put the ignition on and tried a bump start and the engine restarted. I was already halfway down the escape road, so I rejoined the circuit. I had to do one complete lap with no wing, and the car was loose. I even went off the track once. When I came to the pits the team did a really fantastic job changing the nose.

When I went back out I didn't even know what position I was in. Fortunately though, they had connected my radio again at the stop. They told me I was 6sec behind Nannini. I looked at my onboard computer to see how many laps left and just went for it. And I caught him very quickly. But again, out of the slow corners, he went away, the same as Prost. But I had much more top speed than him.

So I think about it and I say, 'OK, I use my top speed on the straight to catch up, do the quick corner again and pass him under braking at the chicane. And that's what I did: I overtook him under braking.

It was the same situation as Prost and everything went normal. Because if he had closed the door, like the other did, there was no way it would have worked, because I was already inside. So everything went well, I took the lead and we won the race.

Q: *As a religious person, is there anything to learn from what happened at Suzuka?*

A: *When you have a hard time you suddenly have doubts. But His reasons, on many occasions, are only His reasons. Only He knows why this should happen, even if it seems like a bad thing. Our understanding is so short, so small compared to His, that on many occasions we cannot understand. That is where faith is the beginning of everything. I finally found that in my life that is what gives me the strength to go through the nice times and the difficult times.*

This year, on many occasions when I was winning a race, everything going fine, suddenly 'Boom!' and something goes wrong. I am sure that in different years I would have got out of the car mad, completely upset, and been very critical. I did the opposite this year. I was disappointed of course, but I had equilibrium and I was at peace. I was able to accept it in a constructive way. I have rationalised it and I accept it. It is something that will count positively sometime in my future.

Senna's position was thus clearly explained and logical. In any equitable situation it would have resulted in his Suzuka win being reinstated. But that wasn't the process in operation. When the FIA International Court of Appeal confirmed the decision of the Suzuka stewards and gave Senna a six-month suspended ban and fined him $100,000, Ayrton could check himself no longer.

"What we have in Formula 1, what we had in Suzuka, reflects the present political situation in motorsport," he said. "People who have credibility must use that credibility to build something positive, instead of destroying people and putting them down.

"It [the appeal procedure] is totally wrong in principle. There is no doubt it is very unfair. But that's what they can do at the moment and what we have to put up with. What we have seen is a true manipulation of the World Championship."

It was a theme Ayrton repeated in a press conference at home in Brazil after the season-closing Adelaide GP, accusing Jean-Marie Balestre himself of being party to it, "whether out of patriotism, friendship or for other reasons I prefer not to mention."

Putting aside the rights and wrongs of the Suzuka situation, it was those words that resulted in Senna being summoned to Paris and guaranteed a winter-long stand-off with the FISA president that had Senna seriously considering packing it all in.

McLaren boss Ron Dennis was threatening civil court action against FISA to establish fair play.

"This, as far as McLaren is concerned, is not going to be tucked under the carpet," Dennis confirmed. "What

took place is wrong, it was done for the wrong reasons. We are going to fight.

"Somewhere along the line these decisions that are taken, the way that they are taken, the methods by which they are taken, must come to a stop. We think it has gone far enough."

Balestre wasn't about to let Dennis have the final word...

"I do not understand the open furore of certain members of the McLaren team against both myself and FISA," he stormed. "The accusations by some Brazilian press men that I have manipulated the Japanese GP stewards and the Court of Appeal are defamatory and damaging.

"No force, no political or legal power in the world outside the FIA can change this decision. For those who will be at war, I am sorry to say that there will be a few heads, even prestigious ones, that will risk a fall..."

Dennis had been warned. Take it further and you risk your team's future participation in the World Championship. For Ron, it wouldn't be the last time he encountered such a threat...

As things transpired, unfortunately – and no doubt to the relief of the governing body – Senna's failure to win the season-closing Adelaide GP rendered all further action pointless.

Australian GP (Adelaide)
McLaren-Honda MP4/5 • Retired, 13 laps, accident

Amid all the acrimony, the F1 circus arrived in Adelaide for the season finale. There was more trouble to come, this time over the decision to start the race in what most drivers agreed were appalling conditions.

Senna had taken his customary pole position with 0.74sec in hand over Prost, and there was another strong performance from Pierluigi Martini, who would start the Minardi third.

On race day, however, after a dry morning warm-up session, the rain arrived and showed no signs of letting up. A half-hour acclimatisation session was allowed. The main issue was standing water on the Brabham Straight, which featured a number of dips and undulations. Mansell was spooked when he spun his Ferrari in a straight line on a puddle he didn't see.

"You can't believe how bad it was," he said. "The aquaplaning is worse than I've ever known. I was a complete passenger. And that was on the straight! I don't think it's on to start a race in conditions like this."

Many of his colleagues agreed, but not all. Men like Tyrrell driver Stefano Modena said that they would never

Senna's tearful appearance at the Adelaide press conference betrayed his burning sense of injustice over FISA's handling of Suzuka.

sutton-images.com

get another drive in their lives if they didn't climb into their cars at the appointed hour. And, of course, if McLaren and Senna were going to take further action in an attempt to overturn the FISA nonsense, Ayrton needed the Australian GP to go ahead, and he needed to win it.

For Prost, of course, this was the unacceptable side of F1. Yes, he could drive fast on a wet track. No, he didn't fancy doing 180mph into blinding spray with visibility of around two metres, thanks very much. Those images of Didier Pironi at Hockenheim seven years earlier still loomed large in the mind.

"I cannot understand the sense in people going out there in conditions like that," Alain said. "I'm very upset. You've only got one life. The track is absolutely undrivable. We've never seen aquaplaning like it."

Alain, predictably, did the first lap, pulled into the pits and climbed out. Privately, even Senna knew the conditions were bad, and later said of Prost's decision: "He did the right thing. There was nothing to be gained by racing – he wasn't going to win the race and he couldn't add anything to his championship score if he did, so in the circumstances it was the right decision."

Recent history had shown that in conditions like that, nobody other than Senna was going to win the race. Ayrton's superiority was unbelievable. He was 8sec clear of Martini at the end of the opening lap! After 10 laps he led Thierry Boutsen's Williams by more than half a minute.

On lap 14 though, the 1989 World Championship was finally, indisputably Prost's, rendering irrelevant anything that might or might not take place in a court room.

Iconic TV images from a rearward-facing camera mounted on Brundle's Brabham showed Senna's McLaren arriving at an entirely different kind of speed and ploughing straight into the back of Martin's car, removing the McLaren's left front wheel. The potential for that kind of thing was exactly why Prost had already changed back into civvies.

"I was lapping Piquet, who was over on the right, and just felt an impact," Senna said. "I was in fifth, just about to change up to sixth and I never saw Brundle. I was just driving into spray."

Then came a line suggesting that Ayrton had become so self-absorbed with everything that had gone on at Suzuka and beyond that he didn't fully appreciate that there was existence outside his own orbit.

"After I was out," he added, "I can't understand why they didn't stop the race. Nothing could happen any more which would affect the championship and it would have been better to stop it rather than continue to risk everyone out there."

The inference that it had been acceptable to risk everyone so long as Ayrton stood to achieve some benefit caused more than the odd raised eyebrow!

PUTTING AYRTON'S CASE
A PERSONAL RECOLLECTION

You know that feeling you get when confronted with a thumping great injustice? That's the way it was for me after Senna's disqualification from the Japanese GP at Suzuka. I'd been on the staff of *Autosport* for five years and was responsible for international news. As such, I was in the audience at the Heathrow Penta when Ron Dennis flew back from the Far East to present the World Champion's case before flying back out for the season finale in Adelaide.

Having listened, then seen the FIA uphold the disqualification, fine Senna and impose a suspended ban on him, I wrote the following 'Dodgy Business' column in *Autosport*:

So Prost is champion but he has never beaten Senna in a straight fight all year. Makes a bit of a mockery of the whole thing, that. Add in the happenings in Paris last week and Ayrton must feel like telling everyone precisely where to stick it.

Senna, in my humble opinion, has also suffered a raw deal from the press for a very long time now. Hardly has an opportunity to have a dig been missed.

His problem, it would seem, stems from his failure to allow Derek Warwick to join Lotus back in 1986. For weeks the ramblings went on. It was defenceless, Peter Warr was weak to allow it to happen. Who does Senna think he is? On and on.

Senna himself had been blocked from joining Brabham by Piquet in 1984. It's called politics and is part of everyday life. By the time of the Warwick incident Senna saw himself as the best in the world and he had many offers. If he was to stay with Lotus it would be on his terms. He wasn't frightened of Warwick, merely thought that Lotus couldn't do a good job for Derek, a recognised top liner at the time, without jeopardising his own chances. Fair enough. If your standing allows you to dictate terms then you are a fool not to take advantage of it.

Warr's position was equally simple. As manager of the team, his main priority was to hang on to its biggest asset.

The way that Senna was portrayed as villain of the piece in Britain, the place where he'd done the bulk of his racing remember, probably did much to nurture his current lack of time for the press in general.

Jingoism is something I've encountered quite a few times in my brief journalistic career. People come and ask why you don't go out of your way to promote British drivers. When you tell them it's not your job, they look at you as if you have two heads. It's something that annoys me intensely. I couldn't give a damn where somebody's mother was when she gave birth, or what nationality she is. My job is to report on a person's performance in a motor race.

I will always remember Senna ploughing into the wall in the European F3 round at Silverstone in '83. A huge roar went up from the Woodcote grandstands. Up until that event, Ayrton had led all but two laps of the nine British F3 races to that point. An amazing feat. At that stage he'd done nothing to antagonise anyone. Except win all those races...

Brundle beat him for the first time that afternoon. If you're going to be balanced about it, you have to admit that Senna then made mistakes. He crashed four times in the second half of the season, three times making contact with Brundle. He received a fine and endorsement at Oulton Park.

Here was the first hint that he was suspect under

↑ Ron Dennis flew
straight back to the
UK post-Japan to
fight Senna's corner.
📷 sutton-images.com

pressure. Second places, despite a sizeable lead in the championship, were unacceptable to him.

The problem is that the man believes himself to be the best there is, and thus had difficulty reconciling the fact that Brundle was beating him. Why was Brundle beating him if he was the best?

Dick Bennetts, boss of West Surrey Racing, which ran Senna, recalls: "We later found out that Eddie Jordan (running Brundle) had got hold of a different specification Toyota engine from Novamotor, the only one in existence, with less friction on the cam pulley. I figure he had a couple of horsepower more and it was enough to tilt the balance. We had to run less wing to stay with Martin on the straights but that cost us in the corners. Those sort of things are crucial in F3. At the time, though, we couldn't figure out why."

What of Senna's personality in those days? Bennetts again: "He was strong-willed, utterly dedicated and hard. He knew exactly what he wanted. But he was also down-to-earth and a great guy to work with.

"I put him up with a friend of mine in Walton. There was a crowd of us, about 10, and we'd have barbecues and so forth. He was great fun and it was only when there was a bigger gathering, maybe 40 or so, that he'd retreat into himself and be quiet. Shy really. But you don't have to be a talker to be a racing driver."

No, you don't, but it certainly helps. Recently I asked a Formula 1 insider why everyone eagerly eats up every word Prost says, while they all love to hate Senna?

"Simple," he replied, "Alain is a pleasant and co-operative fellow whereas Ayrton is sullen and difficult."

I have great admiration for Prost, but find this whiter-than-white portrayal of the ultimate professional vis-à-vis the evil, impetuous Senna very irksome. Memories are short. I remember Prost heading the championship by some margin in '83 but feeling threatened by the advances made by Piquet and Brabham-BMW. He made a mess of Tarzan at Zandvoort and punted Nelson off. The following year he spun out at Osterreichring, although admittedly with extenuating circumstances, and ended up losing the championship to team-mate Lauda by half a point.

The difference is that Prost knows how to conduct himself. After the Piquet incident he stood up and admitted that he was at fault. Apologised. A little humility goes a very long way. It's a lesson Senna would do very well to learn. Jackie Stewart has oft been quoted saying that you win grands prix by eliminating as many of the factors that are trying to stop you. Eliminating animosity among your peers can only help.

Senna, though, has always had a problem in this respect. Most racing drivers have fragile egos. Blown-off racing drivers are especially sensitive. And blown-off racing drivers formerly thought to be the best are akin to eggshells. Interesting to note the names that have complained the loudest about Senna: Rosberg, Lauda, Piquet, Mansell and Prost. Hmmm...

Ayrton, however, seldom bothers to put his case and, I venture, isn't very often asked. Why? Because he hasn't got time for the press, remember.

As a result of that, we don't know a lot about him. He's aloof, isn't he? He's arrogant, he reads a bible, he's dangerous, he's worryingly obsessive, he's wrapped up in himself, he has no sense of humour.

"He called me up after winning the Spanish GP," recalls Dick Bennetts. "I congratulated him but he just grunted, didn't want to talk about that. He wanted to know why my former driver [Eddie Irvine] was wearing a similar helmet design to him. He thought it was amusing. Then he wanted to know why Allan McNish had stalled at one of the F3 races. He always knows what's happening, always was sharp."

Senna, admittedly, is no ambassador for the sport but has, this year, been very professional. Never once has he rubbished anyone, although four mechanical failures have likely cost him wins. By rights, the championship should have been his long since.

Prost, meanwhile, the ultimate professional remember, has whinged publicly about his team, his engine, and his team-mate, as well as failing to once overcome Ayrton on the track. A deserving champion? That's up to you, but I know what I think.

And then we came to Japan. I attended a McLaren press conference last week on the subject of Ayrton's appeal (against the Suzuka disqualification). I went to the

Heathrow Penta knowing that I was about to be sold one side of a story. I was determined to forget that and remain objective. I came away angry.

Helicopter footage of the incident (not seen by the race stewards but by the appeal court) convinced me that Prost did indeed turn in very early. It was also patently obvious to me that the decision to disqualify Senna was taken without proper opportunity to consider the evidence. It amused me that nobody even thought to call into question Prost's driving. He's the nice guy, isn't he...

Still, no point going over old ground. What riled me was that when McLaren got to Paris, the goalposts had been shifted to Monza (last year's Schlesser incident), and Rio, and Ricard, and Estoril, and Jerez. Venues of recent dangerous driving by Senna, said FISA.

Monza? Stupid maybe, dangerous, no. Rio, yes, there's a case. Ricard is ludicrous (Senna broke the transmission on the line and he had no drive), Estoril eminently debatable and Jerez already accounted for (a reprimand for ignoring flag signals).

The appeal, as we know, was dismissed. Rules on the Japan incident are clear as mud, but among video evidence, showing precedents where drivers have gone unpenalised for missing chicanes, lay the ultimate irony. San Marino this year: car spins and misses chicane, rejoins circuit on the straight, driver goes on to finish second and score six points. Who? Prost!

Before writing this, I tried to understand why I wanted to argue the Senna angle. I don't even know the guy. A cynic immediately told me that such was probably a very good reason...

Joking apart, it's probably for the same reason that I wasn't heartbroken in '86 when Mansell's tyre blew in Adelaide while Britain wept into its cornflake bowls. I didn't want that for Nigel but did consider that Prost had done the best job over the year, so didn't get a huge sense of injustice. This year, he hasn't. It galls me to think that people will look back over the records and see that in the same cars at McLaren, Senna and Prost won a title apiece. To me, they're not in the same league.

Marc Surer, spectating with a colleague at Hockenheim, said of Senna: "Watching that guy gives me goose bumps. He's the only one who does that, and having been out there and done it myself, I don't really understand why."

The FIA Formula 1 World Championship is for racing drivers, not PR men.

> "Most racing drivers have fragile egos. Blown-off racing drivers are especially sensitive. And blown-off racing drivers previously thought to be the best are akin to eggshells."

The piece appeared in the 9 November edition of *Autosport*, the same magazine that reported the season-closing Australian GP, held in appalling conditions in Adelaide. I received an avalanche of support for the views expressed, and among many letters one of the most appreciative was from former F1 entrant Rob Walker.

THE LEGACY OF THE McLAREN YEARS

At the time, the rivalry between Prost and Senna in 1988/89 was spoken of in hushed tones. Books have been written about it. It was compared to some of the greatest stand-offs in sporting history – like Ali/Frazier and Borg/McEnroe.

The reality, though, was somewhat different. If Senna's ambition had been to destroy Prost rather than merely beat him, he more or less achieved his wish, even if, to Ayrton's great annoyance, the record books show that they emerged with a title apiece from their two seasons together at McLaren.

During that time Senna won 14 of the 32 races (15 if you count the Suzuka travesty) to Alain's 11. But had it not been for that unprecedented four-race run of McLaren unreliability in mid-1989, those numbers would have been an entirely more representative 18 wins to eight. Yes, Prost scored more points, but that was solely down to Senna suffering a disproportionate share of unreliability that, Ron Dennis said, was nothing to do with Ayrton.

Senna took 27 pole positions to Prost's four, and outqualified him 28–4 by an average of 0.67sec. One of the greatest rivalries in sport? Most of the time, it wasn't even close.

Does the perceived closeness of the Senna/Prost rivalry really stand scrutiny?
📷 sutton-images.com

INCENSED SENNA
PONDERS QUITTING

When Senna crashed out of the Adelaide GP while trying to lap Martin Brundle, there was none of the angst that might have been anticipated.

"I'm going home to Brazil to decide what to do," Ayrton said, enigmatically.

Ron Dennis expounded years later: "The post-Suzuka period following the collision with Alain and what took place after it, the unfairness of it, deeply affected Ayrton. In fact, he retired, and it took a great deal of effort on my part to convince him to come back and race.

"That's the sort of person he was. If he found himself feeling that circumstances were unjust – and it wasn't always things that affected him, it could have been other drivers or just motor racing – then he would be deeply influenced.

"But this time it was about him. The lobbying by Jean-Marie Balestre and the process that took place immediately after the Suzuka race, and in subsequent years, was grossly unfair. Ayrton had won the race and, OK, it wouldn't have given him the championship as things turned out, but how did being so up and down emotionally affect his performance in the last race in Adelaide?"

It's an interesting point. On a wet track Senna's superiority was always even more marked than in the dry, as he'd proven in peerless performances such as Monaco '84, Estoril '85 and Suzuka '88.

From pole position it should have been a relative formality for Ayrton to win in Adelaide, as much as it ever could be amid the dangers of aquaplaning and blinding spray.

Clearly, half a minute ahead after 10 laps, nobody was going to get near him. But when Senna hit Brundle he was still driving like a man possessed, lapping drivers like Martin and Nelson Piquet just 14 laps into a 70-lap race on a track with a lap time in the wet of 1m 40s plus! It was as if he was trying to win the race by five laps when five seconds would have sufficed.

"He was crazy there," recalls Brundle. "His team was begging him to slow down and you couldn't see a thing. I'd spun going down the straight the previous lap, in top gear, and was just floating on the water. I mean, I was running seventh, and he was lapping me, 14 laps in! He was just angry. And driving angrily."

Was Senna trying to embarrass Balestre and FISA as deeply as possible? His sense of injustice, after all, was more than justified. He'd attempted to pass Prost and Nannini at Suzuka in a manner that had been done many times before and would be done many times afterwards, without ever being labelled 'dangerous'.

The double standards and ineptitude displayed by the governing body were scandalous. As Gerhard Berger said in Adelaide: "FISA punishes Senna because they say he's dangerous and then they let us race in weather that is a hundred times more dangerous than any driver ever could be..."

The Suzuka stewards' case against Senna was flaky in the extreme, each point easily shot down – as previously described – with the rule book on Ayrton's side. The case against Senna was so weak that it had no chance of standing up to the scrutiny of a Court of Appeal, in front of lawyers, and so FISA had little choice but to alter the charge sheet.

In many jurisdictions a person's prior record is inadmissible in the proving of guilt and can only be brought into play when passing sentence once guilt is established. FISA, though, dredged up for the Court of Appeal's consideration half a dozen instances of alleged dangerous driving that were totally irrelevant to events at Suzuka.

During this task, they displayed yet more ineptitude.

"The events which have occurred in the last few months during several grands prix," said FISA, "prove that even if A. Senna is a talented driver, he is also a driver who endangers the safety of other drivers.

> ## Ron Dennis: "The unfairness of it deeply affected Ayrton. In fact, he retired, and it took a great deal of effort on my part to convince him to come back and race."

"The FISA regrets that with the whole world watching, the F1 World Champion has once again abandoned the sporting field to venture into legal territory."

On the contrary, it was FISA that had done so.

The governing body's report ahead of the appeal court pompously added that FISA found itself obliged to reiterate a certain number of serious errors committed by Senna. Specifically, these were the incidents in the 1988 Italian GP (the collision with Schlesser), the 1989 Brazilian GP (collision with Berger), the 1989 French GP (dangerous change of direction at the start, cutting across the track from right to left), the 1989 Portuguese GP (shared responsibility for the collision with Mansell) and the 1989 Spanish GP (failure to respect the red flag giving the order to 'stop the race').

All of this, in the main, was fabrication. The Italian GP incident with Schlesser may have been ill-advised but certainly wasn't dangerous. Even Berger agreed that the Brazilian GP was a racing incident. The French GP accusation was farcical – Senna had broken the differential off the line, had no drive, was already on the left and simply pulling off the track. In the Portuguese GP, after Senna and Mansell had already negotiated a Benetton on the straight, Ayrton himself was taken out by a late move into Turn 1 from Mansell, who was nowhere near alongside when they reached the turn-in point and in any case shouldn't even have been on the circuit because he had already been black-flagged for reversing in the pits! In the Spanish GP Senna was guilty

"The case against Senna was so weak that it had no chance of standing up to the scrutiny of a Court of Appeal... and so FISA had little choice but to alter the charge sheet."

but the incident had already been dealt with by a fine, and FISA couldn't even get the circumstances right as the incident followed an accident to Gregor Foitek that had occurred in practice, not the race...

It was shockingly amateurish. If FISA had wanted to have a legitimate go at Senna they might have thought to include Estoril in 1988 when he was brutally aggressive with Prost on the main straight. The document had all the hallmarks of being knocked together in half an hour by someone with little or no understanding of F1, and it also begged a question. If Senna had committed all these transgressions, why had no previous action been taken?

As well as that, Ron Dennis stated that the original stewards' decision issued at Suzuka (decision number 17) was reproduced as decision number 16 in the appeal court and that a new decision number 17 was produced (with the same 14.55pm time) that was unsigned by himself. That was, he said, "a direct contravention of article 156 of the FIA regulations which states that instructions and communications to competitors will be distributed to competitors, who must give a written receipt. We had no prior knowledge of document 17."

In fact there was nothing controversial in document 17 but Dennis believed that it was illustrative of the inconsistency prevalent throughout the whole affair.

"You know," said one sports journalist, "last year at the Seoul Olympics I watched the boxer Roy Jones Jr win every round on his way to the Light Middleweight final. He did the same thing in the final, landing 86 scoring punches to Korean opponent Park Si-Hun's 32. He was also awarded the outstanding boxer of the games accolade. But the administrators were Korean and they gave the gold medal to their own man. It was the worst decision I've seen in sport. But this smells just as bad..."

In the interests of balance it should be reiterated that FISA's Suzuka disgrace didn't directly cost Senna his world title. As Ayrton himself admitted, he was behind Prost with six laps to go in Japan because he'd made a poor start from pole. And even withstanding Ayrton's explanation that he'd risked 130R flat-out despite the turbulence from Prost's car and resulting reduction in front downforce, Senna launched his outbraking attempt into the chicane from quite a long way back.

Yes, Prost turned in early and made sure of the contact. But he was always going to. No competitive racing driver opens the door to a slightly desperate late attack at a slow corner with the world title at stake.

If the roles had been reversed, Senna would have done precisely the same – but for the fact that he'd have been 20 seconds up the road. What Prost did was very little different to what Michael Schumacher attempted to do to Jacques Villeneuve at Jerez eight years later.

Schumacher, of course, was vilified, with nobody even questioning Villeneuve's move, his right front locked and the Williams about to run wide when contact happened. Nobody called Jacques dangerous, disqualified him or fabricated a list of phoney offences he'd supposedly committed over the previous year. Villeneuve's move was as unlikely to come off as Senna's. But it did. He was as fortunate as Senna to be able to continue, but it would have been as daft to label him dangerous, at a slow corner, as it was Senna.

Perception is often more about reputation than fact. Prost had a whiter-than-white reputation. Senna and Schumacher didn't. Sometimes your past catches up with you. What Michael didn't have, of course, was a German boss of the governing federation anxious to further his cause...

↑ **Was Suzuka '89 a sporting travesty on the same scale as the 1988 Seoul Olympics 'home' decision that cost boxing legend Roy Jones Jr a gold medal?**
📷 Getty Images

← **Senna's run-in with the authorities in 1989 made him seriously consider climbing out and walking away for good.**
📷 sutton-images.com

"The document had all the hallmarks of being knocked together in half an hour… and it also begged a question. If Senna had committed all these transgressions, why had no previous action been taken?"

1990

WIN AT
ALL COSTS

With the 1989 season concluding in such acrimonious circumstances and the two-year internal McLaren 'war' at an end with Alain Prost's move to Ferrari, Gerhard Berger was the new man with the invidious task of being Ayrton Senna's team-mate. Initial testing showed Berger to have a fundamental issue fitting his lanky frame into McLaren's MP4/5B. It was a situation that would improve, but only slightly, as the season wore on.

Senna's initial problem was whether he was going to be allowed to fit into the McLaren at all. The team had finished the 1989 season with the avowed determination to take on the governing body over its disqualification from the Japanese GP and the manner in which the subsequent Court of Appeal was conducted.

Post-Adelaide, Senna had returned home to Brazil, where he held a press conference accusing FISA and its president, Jean-Marie Balestre, of manipulating the outcome of the World Championship in Prost's favour.

Senna then had to return to Europe to face the music before the World Motor Sport Council in Paris where, in the words of Balestre, he "adopted an arrogant and defiant manner, displaying continued gestures of impatience". With good reason, you may think...

The WMSC decided to refuse Senna's application

← **With Prost taking his World Champion's No 1 with him to Ferrari, Ayrton and Alain again battled out the 1990 championship in equally acrimonious circumstances.**

📷 sutton-images.com

↑ **The 1989 fine paid by McLaren, Senna checks out his Superlicence paperwork.**

📷 sutton-images.com

for an F1 Superlicence unless he withdrew his allegations, as a result of breaching Articles 28 and 59 of the International Sporting Code.

Predictably, there was silence from Brazil. The deadline for entering the 1990 championship also passed without payment of a $100,000 fine imposed on Senna, and Balestre insisted that he would turn down any entry until he had an apology.

Ultimately, McLaren paid the fine and FISA confirmed two McLarens, 'one to be driven by Gerhard Berger and the second by a driver who as yet remains to be named'. At the same time, the governing body pointedly reminded everyone that the deadline for a Superlicence application was February 15...

When there was still no reaction from Senna's beach abode in Brazil's Angra dos Reis, FISA issued a definitive list of 1990 entrants with a pair of McLarens to be driven by Gerhard Berger and Jonathan Palmer. An hour later, Senna's name was added, with FISA

simultaneously publishing a statement from Senna, which read:

"During the meeting of the FISA World Council which took place on December 7, 1989, I listened to statements and testimonies from various people, and from these statements one must conclude that they provide proof that no pressure group or the President of the FISA influenced the decisions regarding the results of the 1989 FIA Formula 1 World Championship."

Balestre wished Senna all the best for the forthcoming season, but not before Senna had revealed that his statement had been the result of lengthy negotiations and that McLaren had paid his fine. Which, just for good measure, Balestre pointed out was illegal, as the Sporting Code pointed out that such penalty fell on the driver himself. The spat rumbled on but Senna would at least be on the grid, Prost now looking across at him from a Ferrari cockpit.

11 MARCH 1990

11 MARCH 1990

United States GP (Phoenix)
McLaren-Honda MP4/5B • 1st

Gerhard Berger started his first race for McLaren from pole position (1m 28.884s) with Ayrton Senna fifth (1m 29.431s)!

But before anyone got too excited, it was no indicator of things to come – quite the reverse in fact. Senna had engine problems on Friday, a misfire developing into something more serious-sounding. A new power unit was required. When the Saturday session was rained out, Ayrton found himself off the front row for the first time since Silverstone 1988.

Race day was a different story. Senna topped the race morning warm-up and sized up a grid that had a distinctly unfamiliar look. Behind Berger, Pierluigi Martini had put a Minardi on the front row (!), with the second row comprising Andrea de Cesaris's Dallara and Jean Alesi's Tyrrell.

At the green, Alesi made a ballistic start to lead, with Senna up to fourth by the end of the first lap and Martini back to fifth. Ayrton passed de Cesaris on lap 4 and took second place on lap 9 when Berger slid into a tyre barrier.

As his fuel load lightened, Senna gradually hauled in Alesi's leading Tyrrell and passed it on the inside of the first turn on lap 34 of the 72. He ran a bit wide on exit, though, and Alesi came back alongside and braved it out into Turn 2 to retake the lead.

Next time round, Senna repeated the move decisively, and proceeded to win by 8sec from Alesi, whose performance was praised by Senna.

"I was impressed by the way he was driving," Ayrton said. "He was clean but very determined. It was just the kind of racing I like." This was a thinly veiled message for Monsieur Prost: Alain qualified seventh on his Ferrari debut and got up to fourth before retiring with an engine failure.

Senna started his 1990 campaign with a victory in Phoenix.
sutton-images.com

25 MARCH 1990

Brazilian GP (Interlagos)
McLaren-Honda MP4/5B • 3rd

For his home grand prix, which he had still never won, Senna duly took pole position 0.61sec quicker than new team-mate Berger. A general agreement among the drivers had decreed that pole position should be on the right even though the first corner was a left-hander. This was because the advantage of starting from the rubbered racing line was thought to be greater than having the inside line for Turn 1. Remember this, because it was to become of stronger significance later in the year...

Senna led from the start, with first Berger and then Thierry Boutsen's Williams giving chase. With his tyre stop completed without problem, Ayrton seemed to be in complete control. But then, on lap 41, he came up to lap his former Lotus team-mate Satoru Nakajima, who promptly moved out of the way but got on the marbles and found himself swiping Senna's nose at the next

⬇ **Gerhard Berger replaced Alain Prost as Senna's McLaren team-mate in 1990.**

📷 sutton-images.com

corner. Ayrton had to pit and rejoined half a minute behind Berger and the dreaded Prost, whose Ferrari was now leading Senna's home GP.

The new nose on the McLaren didn't appear to be as efficient as the previous one and a disgruntled Senna finished third while Prost duly took the win.

Balestre's incendiary gesture

Given the politics that had gone on over the winter between the FISA president and Brazil's favourite son, it was less than subtle of Jean-Marie Balestre to turn up at Interlagos and start blowing kisses to the crowd.

And less than dignified, in a country bedeviled by rampant inflation, to say: "This is our World Championship, the World Championship of the FIA... We have the same problem with the World Rally Championship in Corsica and maybe the Corsicans are a bit hotter than the Brazilians. They not only throw tomatoes, they throw real bombs. But at the moment the Brazilians cannot afford to buy tomatoes."

How to win friends and influence people...

San Marino GP (Imola) • McLaren-Honda MP4/5B
Retired, 3 laps, wheel/spin

Pole position at Imola once again fell to Senna, just over half a second clear of Berger as McLaren monopolised the front row.

Ayrton's race, however, was to last just three laps. Leading, Senna suddenly found that he couldn't slow the car on the approach to Rivazza and went into the sand trap on the exit, his right rear tyre flat. A small stone had become trapped in a recess of the brake caliper and had machined a groove in the rim, causing loss of tyre pressure as the wheel simultaneously failed and broke the brake disc.

Monaco GP (Monte Carlo)
McLaren-Honda MP4/5B • 1st

Was Ayrton losing his touch? He took pole position but allowed Prost within half a second of him around the streets of Monte Carlo! Ayrton's time was 1m 21.314s in the McLaren, Prost's 1m 21.776s in the Ferrari. Perhaps a better reference was the man in the same car. This time it was Gerhard Berger's turn to ponder how he had managed to drop 1.37sec to Senna in 2.06 miles. Prost could have told him all about that...

Senna duly converted pole and led, but there was mayhem behind. Alesi, with great opportunism, mugged Prost into Mirabeau to claim second. When Prost found the piece of road he wanted occupied by his young countryman's Tyrrell and couldn't turn in, Gerhard Berger tried to take his McLaren inside Prost as well, but misjudged the move and clobbered the Ferrari, bringing out a red flag.

There was more all-French comedy as a disgruntled Prost sounded off about Alesi to Jean-Marie Balestre ahead of the restart – he changed his mind when he saw footage of what happened – and the FISA president admonished a bemused Alesi who, until that point, had looked up to Prost as a hero.

According to Alesi, Prost had been daydreaming on the way into Mirabeau. At the restart Alain made sure he wasn't and fended off the unfortunate Alesi until the Ferrari electronics failed after 30 laps.

Alesi, once second, was more than 20sec behind Senna but Ayrton felt his engine losing power and reduced revs for the duration, pacing himself to finish just over a second clear of the Tyrrell at the flag. "It was

enough," Ayrton said, and you wondered again why he hadn't adopted that same approach in Adelaide six months previously...

↑ **A third Monte Carlo win for Ayrton.**
📷 sutton-images.com

Canadian GP (Montréal)
McLaren-Honda MP4/5B • 1st

The Montréal pole battle was much closer, Senna beating Berger to the top spot by just seven hundredths. Work had been done to make the tall Austrian more comfortable in his MP4/5B, by making the seating position more upright in order to lower his legs in the cockpit and prevent his knees coming into contact with the instrument panel whenever he moved his feet on the pedals.

It didn't, however, prevent some dodgy clutch control from Berger off the grid. Gerhard was on the move before the green came on, earning himself a one-minute penalty.

Senna's 23rd victory was achieved on a wet but drying track with wet tyres needed for the opening stint and then a set of slicks bolted on after 12 laps for the remainder of the 70. Senna duly waved Berger by so that Gerhard could get on with reducing his penalty deficit as much as possible. It was a good effort too, Berger moving ahead

of Prost's Ferrari and into fourth place on adjusted time on the very last lap. On the road, he was 45sec clear of his race-winning team-mate, which proves just how little Senna was extended in beating Nelson Piquet's Benetton by 10sec, while Mansell was on the podium for the first time that year.

24 JUNE 1990

Mexican GP (Autodromo Hermanos Rodriguez)
McLaren-Honda MP4/5B • 20th (puncture)

Senna celebrated his 100th GP start in Mexico. And it was quite astonishing that he was shooting for his 47th pole, especially when one considers that in his debut year with Toleman he had no chance of pole.

Team-mate Berger denied him, however, the Austrian's MP4/5B much more at home over the track's notorious bumps than Senna's chassis. Gerhard was comfortably 0.45sec quicker, the pair split by Riccardo Patrese's Williams.

But Ayrton made the better start and began to eke

out an advantage. Gerhard caned his softer-compound Goodyears trying to stay with his team-mate and it all looked straightforward for Senna until later in the race.

Prost, unable to make the Goodyear qualifiers work on the Ferrari, endured a troubled qualifying session and even spun on his way to qualifying 13th. On race day, though, he was on the move and up into second place ahead of team-mate Mansell with 13 laps to go. He was 12sec behind Senna, a hopeless situation at that stage of the race but for the fact that Senna was starting to have tyre trouble.

In fact, Ayrton had a slow puncture in the right rear but, owing to miscommunication with the pit wall, he was told to stay out. With eight laps to go Prost had the Ferrari in front as Senna's tyre gave out and the car suffered terminal damage as he tried to get it back to the pits.

Prost scored his second Ferrari win, while Mansell made it a Maranello 1–2 as he and Berger brought the closing laps to life. Berger had barged past Mansell at Turn 1 with two laps remaining, locking up and giving the Ferrari a hefty clout as he did so. Mansell, deeply unimpressed, wasn't about to let it rest and, unbelievably,

GETTING TO THE BOTTOM OF THINGS...

"From the moment that Ayrton and I had tossed a coin to settle our contractual issue," recalls Ron Dennis, "fiscal competition reared its head in many ways.

"In Mexico we were sat waiting for the meal to come and there was this whole range of hot sauces with crackers that you dipped in. This stuff varied in severity and dialogue had taken place with the waiter about which was the hottest.

"Everyone tried a bit and it was genuinely eye-watering stuff. Ayrton said, 'I can't take any of that. I'm from Brazil and I like spicy things but I can't eat that.' So I said that I could eat the whole bowl for $1,000 and he took the bet. He hesitated a bit because he was concerned about being deliberately ensnared but to his credit he didn't back out.

"I thought, "Well, it's not going to kill me... clearly it's going to burn but if I eat it very, very quickly, before the chemicals start to work in my mouth, it will be inside me and I will be $1,000 better off.' So I picked up a spoon and ate it literally as fast as I could, much to his surprise.

"I suffered the initial aftershock, comfortably balanced by the money. I was drinking water and after half an hour I'd managed to completely neutralise the chemical effect and by the time I'd had a couple of glasses of wine I thought it was the easiest thousand dollars I'd ever earned... only to find out, after a few hours, that not only did it have an ingoing chemical effect, but also an outgoing chemical effect...

"I was in some trouble and didn't get a lot of sleep... Ayrton would have loved the idea of me having to go into the bathroom to unscrew the showerhead, which was on a flexi cable, and administer liquid coolant!

"As with many of the things that took place, whether it involved Ayrton, me, Gerhard or my wife, Lisa, the worst thing that you could do was admit that you'd been got. You went to great lengths to conceal anything that happened. So, next morning, everyone's waiting and wanting to know how it went, and I just acted as if nothing had happened. But I didn't feel great...

"Probably the best one with Ayrton the victim came after we'd been in Australia hatching plans as to what we could do to really inflict pain on each other.

"Gerhard stole Ayrton's passport and, without him knowing, we surgically removed his picture and cut out of a very dubious magazine an equivalent size of male genitalia and carefully put it in with sellotape, so that at a glance you didn't realise that anything had taken place other than there wasn't a face where there was supposed to be a face.

"Ayrton was going back to Brazil and I think had got special clearance out of Australia, so hadn't needed his passport. Whatever the route was, he had to go through Argentina, which was the first time anyone looked at his passport. They weren't amused and he spent 24 hours there because they wouldn't allow him to pass through without his passport being rectified. But he never admitted it for months...'

⬇ Don't tell him, Lisa, but I don't feel so good...

📷 sutton-images.com

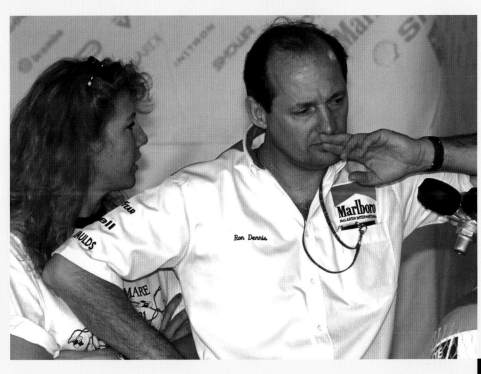

DID SENNA PROMPT NIGEL'S 'RETIREMENT'?

As the Mansell faithful filed sadly out of Silverstone, their hopes of another heroic British GP win dashed by Nigel's gearbox problems, little did they know that back in the paddock their favourite son was announcing his retirement!

Privately, Mansell had been talking about it for a couple of races. Ferrari was anxious for him to re-sign for 1991 but Nigel was deeply frustrated by a series of mechanical problems that had left him without a win at the season's mid-point, while Prost could boast four. And, politically, he'd been outmanoeuvred at Ferrari.

"I'm bound to wonder why these problems don't happen to the other guy," Mansell lamented after his Silverstone non-finish.

Something else was eating him. Nigel had agreed, in return for a pay rise, to Prost having joint number one status at Ferrari when Alain left McLaren the previous year. But now what he craved was that undisputed lead driver status with a winning team.

In the background Mansell had been talking to Frank Williams about a return to the team. When, ahead of Silverstone, Nigel indicated that he was ready to sign for 1991, Frank said he needed more time. It was then that Mansell realised that Williams had hopes of luring Senna from McLaren. Ayrton was out of contract at the end of the year. Ron Dennis wanted a minimum two-year new deal but Ayrton just the one and, at the time, negotiations were between a rock and a hard place.

Mansell's double frustration drove the retirement announcement. When he said that his decision was irrevocable because he couldn't put his family through everything again, many believed him. But almost as many didn't. And they were right. When Senna and Dennis sorted themselves out, Mansell's Williams deal would be back on again, for serious money. But Nigel didn't like being second choice...

← **Hey, know what? Frank wanted me before you...**
📷 sutton-images.com

→ **Senna celebrated his 100th Formula 1 start in Mexico.**
📷 sutton-images.com

drove around the outside of the McLaren at the daunting, banked Peraltada final turn. It was a good job Berger lifted, otherwise both would probably have come down in Guatemala!

Six races in, the championship position was: Senna, 31 points; Berger and Prost, 23; Alesi, Mansell and Piquet, 13.

8 JULY 1990

French GP (Paul Ricard)
McLaren-Honda MP4/5B • 3rd

For the second successive race Berger got the better of Senna in qualifying, this time by just three hundredths as Mansell pipped both McLarens to pole, his first since Mexico '87, at team-mate Prost's home race.

Berger beat Mansell into Turn 1 and Ayrton passed Nigel second time round, the McLarens running 1–2 for the first 27 of the 80 laps before Gerhard made a tyre stop. It wasn't a quick one but Senna's, two laps later, was worse, his car stationary for more than a quarter of a minute as the team grappled with a rear wheel nut. When he rejoined, Senna was eighth. The predicted fireworks didn't materialise and third was the best he could do.

The star of the race was Ivan Capelli, whose Leyton House car led for 45 laps before fuel starvation problems allowed Prost to nail him with three laps to go, but the Italian still made it to the line second, 3sec ahead of Senna's McLaren. Prost and Senna now had three 1990 wins apiece and the championship table was starting to take on a more familiar look. Senna led with 35 points, with Prost on 32.

15 JULY 1990

British GP (Silverstone)
McLaren-Honda MP4/5B • 3rd

For the second successive race Mansell grabbed pole position but Senna, alongside him on the front row, beat the Ferrari away. Mansell's was the better-handling car, though, and after tracking Ayrton for 12 laps Nigel dived past at Bridge Corner, to the home crowd's delight.

Senna, trying to stay with the Ferrari, then took too much inside kerb at Copse and had a lurid spin, allowing Berger, Boutsen and Prost through as Ayrton gathered it together. He then pitted to get rid of a badly flat-spotted set of tyres. Prost, having started fifth, had the other Ferrari up into second place just before half distance and, to the consternation of the crowd, was soon eating into Mansell's lead. Nigel had gearbox problems and was

powerless to stop Alain getting ahead with just over 20 laps to go. Mansell's challenge finally expired along with his gearbox after 55 laps.

That put Senna back into fourth place, which became a podium place when team-mate Berger fell victim to a throttle problem with four laps to go. Ominously for Senna, though, a hat-trick of wins had taken Prost to the top of the championship for the first time that year, with 41 points to Ayrton's 39. With Berger their nearest challenger some 14 points adrift, it looked like being a contest between the pair of them once again.

29 JULY 1990

German GP (Hockenheim)
McLaren-Honda MP4/5B • 1st

On the high-speed Hockenheim the powerful V10 Honda was the thing to have and the McLarens of Senna and Berger claimed the front row with the Ferraris on row 2, Ayrton taking pole a quarter of a second clear of Gerhard.

Most chose Goodyear's C-compound tyres for the race but Benetton's selection of the harder B-compound rubber suggested that the team was intending to run through the 45 laps non-stop. That's the way it played out. Piquet's Benetton was out with an engine failure at half distance, however, and Sandro Nannini was left to champion the cause.

Senna and Berger led the early laps but when Ayrton stopped for a new set of rubber after 17 laps, he rejoined just behind Nannini, who set the race's fastest lap shortly afterwards. This was going to be no walk in the park for Senna and he had to wait until just 10 laps before the end, when Nannini was in traffic, to use the better acceleration of the Honda out of Hockenheim's chicane to go by and claim his 24th grand prix win. With Prost a distant fourth in the only Ferrari to finish, Senna retook the championship lead with 48 points to Alain's 44. They now had four wins apiece.

12 AUGUST 1990

Hungarian GP (Hungaroring)
McLaren-Honda MP4/5B • 2nd

As expected, the tight Hungaroring didn't play to the strengths of the McLaren-Honda and it was the Williams pair of Riccardo Patrese and Thierry Boutsen who headed the grid, a couple of tenths quicker than Berger and Senna.

Senna made a poor start and completed lap 1 back in sixth place behind Boutsen, Berger, Patrese, Mansell

and Alesi. It took until lap 21 before he managed to go inside Alesi's Tyrrell at Turn 1. The McLaren felt like it was bottoming out and Senna, who'd also flat-spotted a tyre, headed for the pits. It seemed he'd had an issue similar to the Imola one, with a stone machining his wheel and causing loss of tyre pressure, but this time he got new wheels and tyres in good time.

Senna used them to good effect. After Alesi and Prost retired, he was up to third with 20 laps to go and catching leader Boutsen and Nannini. On lap 64 Senna tried to pass the Italian at the chicane but Sandro refused to give way. The pair tangled and the Benetton was pitched into the air and out of the race. Senna managed to continue and spent the rest of the race hounding his friend Boutsen, who never left a gap. With Prost non-scoring, Senna now led the championship by 10 points.

25 AUGUST 1990

Belgian GP (Spa-Francorchamps)
McLaren-Honda MP4/5B • 1st

Back on a circuit where they could stretch their legs, the McLaren-Honda MP4/5Bs took the front row with Senna on pole, half a second clear of Berger.

After protracted negotiations with Ron Dennis and a big offer from Frank Williams, Senna had finally inked a new McLaren deal for 1991/92 reckoned to be worth $15 million a year. He then went out and proved his worth by leading every lap en route to a 25th grand prix win, equaling Jim Clark's tally.

As at Hockenheim he faced a threat from a non-stopping Nannini, but emerged from his pitstop just ahead of the Benetton and went away. Prost briefly reduced the gap but Senna had everything in hand and took the flag 4sec ahead of the Ferrari to open up a 13-point margin over Alain in the championship with five races to go.

9 SEPTEMBER 1990

Italian GP (Monza)
McLaren-Honda MP4/5B • 1st

As ever, the *tifosi* were desperate to see a Ferrari victory at home and, as in 1989, when Prost was a McLaren driver but with a signed Maranello contract, they were vociferous in their support of Alain.

Senna, however, used the Honda horses to beat Prost to pole by four tenths and, for the second race in succession, was never headed. His choice of Goodyear's B-compound tyre proved perfect and Senna

PAYING HOMAGE TO JIM CLARK

Senna's fifth win of the season at Spa brought him to 25 grand prix wins, level with Niki Lauda and Jim Clark, one ahead of Juan Manuel Fangio and behind only Jackie Stewart and Alain Prost at that time.

Next to Fangio, Clark was the driver Senna most admired. Six months later, Senna went to stay with Prof Sid Watkins at the F1 medic's house in Coldstream, Berwickshire, so that he could pay a secret visit to the Jim Clark Room in nearby Duns. Ayrton respectfully signed the visitors' book before borrowing a slide to use in a talk at Clark's old school, Loretto, where Ayrton addressed the pupils.

He did so in response to a letter from Matthew Watkins, the Prof's elder stepson, who was also a pupil there. Later, in a reception at the deputy headmaster's home, Senna fell into deep conversation with the Bishop of Truro, who was due to conduct the Sunday morning school chapel service the following day.

In his book, *Life at the Limit*, Watkins said: "Later that night he returned to Portugal, leaving the students and staff pondering this extraordinary man and reassessing their ideas about racing drivers. On Sunday the Bishop of Truro began his sermon with the confession that he had been spiritually and verbally outclassed as a preacher by Ayrton Senna."

⬇ **Prof Sid Watkins, Formula 1's medical chief, took Ayrton to the Jim Clark Room in Scotland.**
📷 sutton-images.com

ran untroubled to his 26th win while Prost blistered a set of the harder A-compound tyres while trapped behind Berger's McLaren for the first 20 laps. It all added up to a disappointing day for the Ferrari fans and a 16-point championship lead for Senna with four rounds to go.

23 SEPTEMBER 1990

Portuguese GP (Estoril)
McLaren-Honda MP4/5B • 2nd

A Ferrari proved to be the car to have at Estoril and it was Nigel Mansell who pipped Prost to the pole by 0.04sec, with Senna failing by just 0.01sec to dislodge the Frenchman from the front row. With Berger fourth quickest, the McLaren pair occupied row 2.

As Mansell's love affair with Maranello was now well and truly over, Senna had no need to worry about his start position. Off the line Nigel chopped across in front of Alain – the pair touched and Prost was almost forced into the pit wall – and left a large hole for the McLarens to surge through from the second row. So at the end of the opening lap Senna led Berger, Mansell was third and a disgruntled Prost down in fifth, behind Piquet's Benetton.

It took Prost 14 laps to negotiate Nelson but he set fastest lap the moment he did and the race shaped up into an entertaining McLaren/Ferrari battle. Once the tyre stops were completed Senna led from Mansell, Berger, Nannini's non-stopping Benetton, and Prost. Alain was soon past the Benetton and within 7sec of the lead. Senna, perhaps unusually for him, was more concerned with out-scoring Prost than with winning the race. Mindful of Mansell's clash with him at Estoril a year earlier, Ayrton put up little resistance as Nigel swept by to take the lead into Turn 1 with just 20 laps to go.

Prost managed to go by Berger on lap 59 and so, with 12 laps to go, the world awaited the results as Alain tried to separate Ayrton from second place. But he didn't get the chance. An accident to Alex Caffi left the young Italian trapped in his Arrows by his legs and brought out the red flag, with a result declared after 61 laps.

It was Mansell's first win of a dismal year at Ferrari and there was no way that he had been prepared to defer to Prost's championship aspirations. It was also timely for Nigel, given that his retirement decision now seemed to be in abeyance, with Senna confirmed again at McLaren, and big-money talks could reopen with Williams.

On the podium Mansell and Senna seemed to constitute a mutual admiration society – deeply ironic after the events of a year earlier – while Prost's face was glum, for he was now 18 points behind Senna in the championship with three rounds remaining.

30 SEPTEMBER 1990

Spanish GP (Jerez) • McLaren-Honda MP4/5B
Retired, 53 laps, holed radiator

As the championship protagonists filled the front row, Senna claimed his 50th pole position, 0.44sec ahead of Prost's Ferrari.

Ayrton's pole lap was mesmerising and all the more incredible in view of the fact that, just prior to it, his head was full of images of a severely injured Martin Donnelly. The Irishman had suffered a violent qualifying accident and Senna, concerned, had attended the scene.

Donnelly later recalled: "Obviously I didn't know he was there but Ayrton had stood watching as Sid Watkins got me stabilised, because I'd swallowed my tongue. Sid stuck two tubes up my nose and then down my throat to clear the airways, cut the strap off my helmet, removed it and got some intravenous drips into me.

"Then qualifying resumed and Ayrton did that stunning fastest-ever lap of Jerez. What sort of man can do that? What sort of a man can watch someone fighting for his life then go back, pull down the visor and put together a lap like that? He has to be someone who, as well as the caring and human side, is also totally ruthless and dedicated."

Come the race, the Ferrari looked the better car on full tanks. Although Prost couldn't find a way past Senna's McLaren on the track, he took the lead at the tyre stops and was only briefly headed for a couple of laps by Piquet, who was planning to run through without a tyre stop but was destined to retire in any case.

Senna's race was over 20 laps before the end when a radiator bracket from Yannick Dalmas's AGS holed the McLaren's radiator and forced Ayrton to switch off as the Honda engine lost all water. The Senna/Prost championship gap was back down to nine points and Suzuka was next...

21 OCTOBER 1990

Japanese GP (Suzuka) • McLaren-Honda MP4/5B
Retired, 0 laps, accident (WORLD CHAMPION)

On the Wednesday before the Japanese GP, Senna asked the race organisers to move the Suzuka pole from the right-hand side of the grid for the first corner, a right-hander, to the left, where there was more grip on the racing line. The change wouldn't have been revolutionary and would only have mirrored what took place at Interlagos earlier in the year. Prost agreed, although he was no doubt aware that Senna was more likely to claim the Suzuka pole than he was.

The race morning drivers' briefing and its affect on Senna was publicly seen years later in the movie *Senna*.

"Morning," said FIA race director Roland Bruynseraede, greeting the drivers. "The number of laps from the green light to the chequered flag will be 53. Dangerous behaviour and/or dangerous manoeuvres will be investigated immediately and may lead to suspension of the licence for one or more F1 World Championship events." So, behave yourselves, boys. In other words – no repeat of last year...

"Any questions?" he asked.

Nelson Piquet stuck up a hand and said: "There was a big fuck-up last year with Ayrton. Why do we have to repeat the same thing? The safest thing is that if you miss the chicane, the stewards [marshals] stop you [in the escape road]. When there is no traffic, they let you go [rejoin via the end of the escape road]. If you have to turn around and go backwards against the other cars – that's dangerous."

In other words, let's do exactly what Ayrton had done the previous year and had been disqualified for, costing him his World Championship...

"Does everyone feel that way?" asked McLaren boss Ron Dennis.

"Yes," they all agreed, and so Bruynseraede confirmed that that was what would happen.

Senna immediately made for the exit, saying: "I can't stand this. It's a joke. After what happened last year it's a joke, this situation. We've just proved here, I said nothing, and you see somebody raising the point and everybody agreeing. Last year was really bad. I'm sorry..." And with that, he walked through the door and out of the meeting.

And it got worse. It was announced that drivers who crossed the dotted line delineating the entrance to the pit lane, which was just before the first right-hand segment of the chicane, would be penalised. Which in reality precluded overtaking moves of the kind that Senna had attempted on Prost the previous year and effectively pulled off to pass Nannini.

Considering that the chicane was the only feasible overtaking spot on the circuit for closely matched cars – and even then very difficult – the governing body had effectively turned Suzuka into Monte Carlo in terms of making a passing move stick.

Then came confirmation that the repeated request to switch pole to the clean side of the grid had been denied.

McLaren boss Ron Dennis, under the impression that the switch had been approved, said: "Pole position was Ayrton's and then suddenly pole position was mysteriously moved to the dirty side of the circuit, which he felt was unjust."

Senna went much further than that.

↑ **Mansell again proved Senna's nemesis in Portugal.**
📷 sutton-images.com

"That decision," he said, "was influenced by Balestre. I know that. I was fucked many times by the system. I told myself, today, no way. Today has to be my way. I don't care what happens. It has to be my way."

That was Senna's mindset as he took up his pole on the slippery side of the circuit. He'd also seen that, as in Jerez, Prost's Ferrari had been quicker than him – by three tenths – in the race morning warm-up on full tanks. Mansell, in the other Ferrari, had been quicker still.

There was every possibility, therefore, that the Ferrari was the better race car. And now passing at the chicane wasn't allowed, even if you could stay within striking distance. And Prost, he knew, was likely to make the better start off the rubbered side of the grid.

Quite possibly, therefore, the first corner was the closest Senna was going to get to Prost all afternoon and, if such was the reality, the championship would go down to the final race in Adelaide, where anything could happen.

Prost, as Senna predicted, did indeed make the better start from the grippier side of the track and was clearly ahead as they reached the turn-in point. The solution was simple. As Prost went on the brakes Ayrton kept coming, up the inside, and wiped Alain out at the first corner, taking both cars off into the gravel trap on the outside of Turn 1. He wasn't about to be screwed by the system again. He was World Champion for the second time.

4 NOVEMBER 1990

Australian GP (Adelaide)
McLaren-Honda MP4/5B • Retired, 61 laps, accident

The curtain came down on 1990 in Adelaide with Senna on pole by more than half a second from Berger, with the Ferraris on row 2, Mansell a hundredth quicker than Prost in Nigel's final race for Maranello.

Senna and Berger led away but Mansell was soon up to second place when Gerhard accidentally knocked the ignition off as he attempted to alter the fuel mixture settings! Nigel then shadowed Senna as the pair set a cracking pace that nobody else could match. It was a good contest until just after half distance, when Mansell disappeared down the first chicane escape road and lost a quarter of a minute.

It should then have been a formality for Senna but, 19 laps from home, he spun the McLaren into a tyre barrier when second gear failed to engage. "I was on the limit with the brakes and had put most of the balance onto the rear wheels to save the fronts," Senna explained. His departure left Nelson Piquet to take a second successive win for Benetton just 3sec in front of the recovering Mansell.

Another controversial year was at an end.

← A Senna/Prost Suzuka contretemps settled the World Championship for the second successive season in 1990.
📷 sutton-images.com

⬇ This time as they walked back, it was Senna who was champion.
📷 sutton-images.com

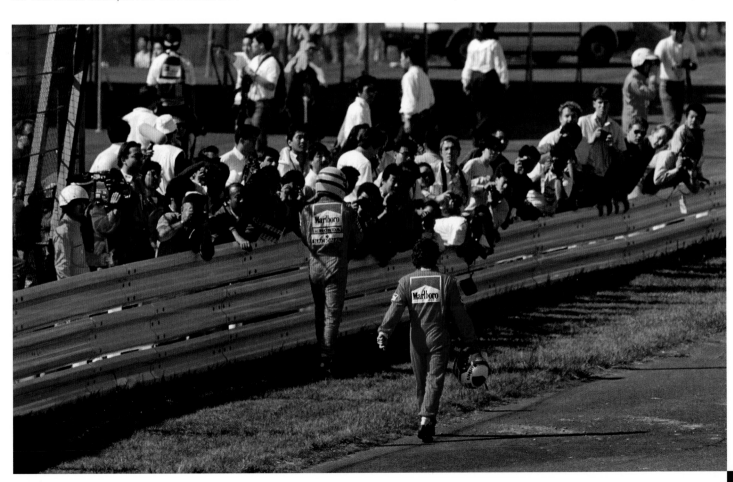

SUZUKA 1990: THE AFTERMATH

The way the 1990 World Championship ended was entirely predictable. Senna, the best driver of 1989 by a country mile, had been royally had over and lost his world title in shockingly unfair circumstances. He could see a similar situation shaping up again and put a stop to it. It was that simple.

While not many could justify the use of a Formula 1 car as a weapon at close to 150mph and there was much hand-wringing, particularly among the Prost disciples, Senna didn't appear to have a problem with it. If you didn't want to put yourself in a highly charged, emotional, competitive environment where you might become involved in someone else's issue, then don't sign on as a racing driver. Go and work in a bank. He didn't say as much, but he might have done.

If the system wouldn't deliver justice, he'd deliver his own. Prost had done it to him the year before and now he'd got even. Yes, the chicane might have been safer than Turn 1 but he may never have been close enough. End of story.

Senna obviously couldn't admit, there and then, that he'd deliberately rammed Prost off the road, but he did admit as much in an outburst at Suzuka a year later, when it was known that Max Mosley was replacing Balestre as FISA president.

Surprisingly perhaps, it was the end of the story for that day and that season. The race wasn't restarted and, despite Bruynseraede's warning, no action was taken against Senna. But it was an empty way to conclude a season, leaving the teams, the mechanics and F1 fans around the world feeling short-changed.

"I have to say, I was praying for a restart," said McLaren's Jo Ramirez. "I thought it was bad. It was as bad as the year before. Ayrton walked back to the pits and there was some talk that they were going to stop the race. He went mad about that. Inside, though, I was hoping for a restart. The public was cheated. OK if it happens near the end, but not on the first lap."

Ramirez denies that his sentiment was down to the fact that he was still a Prost fan at heart. "No, no," he says, "The Ferrari was good but we could have beaten Alain, I'm sure. I just wanted us to do it on the track..."

What was Ron Dennis's opinion of his driver's actions?

"We all have weaknesses and I think Ayrton might well have read the section in his own particular guide manual (the Bible) which talked about an eye for an eye and a tooth for a tooth. He was basically, I think, following the path of balance and trying to find a way to justify behaviour that he wasn't particularly comfortable with but which he felt was a way of balancing the books.

"I wasn't supportive of it but I enjoyed the benefit of it, so in truth you find yourself thinking about things. Was that a just outcome? Was that the way it should be? But the conversation that took place, not at that moment nor on that day, wasn't inconsistent with our common view that we do not win at all costs. I do not think that Ayrton was particularly proud of that particular judgment.

← **The Ferrari faithful made their feelings known.**

sutton-images.com

It wasn't one of his finest moments and I think that, in the end, even he couldn't justify it on the basis of the outcome because with his approach he would have preferred to win the World Championship a different way."

From Senna's body language when he returned to the pits, it was self-evident that there was significant inner turmoil at what he had just done. He wasn't, for example, celebrating his second World Championship with the same degree of ecstasy that accompanied his first. Dennis quickly realised that he had work to do.

"What you do in those circumstances is immediately evaluate the repercussions that could spring from it and you professionally guide him in a way to avoid it becoming an issue. You are basically having to support the situation in order that you don't become embroiled in post-event politics."

Did Ron mean that he told Senna what to say?

"Would I do something like that?" he smiled.

Dennis could see that Senna, stewing for 12 months over the injustice of Suzuka '89, and stewing further about another perceived injustice over pole position and now placed in a difficult situation, was potentially a loose cannon in front of the world's media. If he admitted that Prost had it coming and said as much, Senna and McLaren were in trouble. Another disqualification loomed.

But Senna managed to bite his tongue and do something that he struggled with but that in the circumstances was his only option. He lied. He had to present the incident as a racing accident.

"Prost took a chance going into the first corner when he couldn't afford to," Senna said. "He knew that I was going to come down the inside and he closed the door."

In fact, the door was never remotely open because Alain had been so far in front from his undeserved starting advantage.

Prost hit back: "If everyone wants to drive in this way, then the sport is finished. Senna is completely opposite in character

to what he wants people to believe. He is the opposite of honest. Motor racing is sport, not war. This man has no value. I forget him..."

The claim by Senna and Dennis that the organisers' failure to site pole on the left had been a causal factor in the accident was, some felt, stretching the bounds of credibility. And for those with a casual interest and no knowledge of the finer nuances, it was easy to agree. If Senna was on pole position then surely he should have been able to pass Prost and beat him over the 53 laps, should he not?

Well, let's see. The Ferrari had made progress throughout the year and showed every indication of being the superior car in race trim, as at the previous round. "From the technical viewpoint I believe we won the World Championship," Prost confirmed.

The Ferraris had been comfortably faster than the McLarens in the morning warm-up, with Mansell almost a full second quicker than Berger. And Senna was well aware that a driver of Prost's quality was quite capable of driving 53 laps of Suzuka without making a significant error. To win the race, therefore, it was fundamental that Ayrton led and tasked Alain with passing him.

↑ **No prizes for guessing where Stirling Moss's sympathy lay.**
📷 sutton-images.com

And that became even more important when, pre-race, it was made evident that a driver wasn't going to be able to pass at the chicane without incurring a penalty.

The start, therefore, took on massive significance. And Senna had been stitched up again. You don't spend two days busting a gut to take pole in order to start at a disadvantage. But that was the situation facing him. Few seemed to fully appreciate just how important the run down to that first corner actually was. Ron and Ayrton stretching the bounds of reason? Hardly...

Did it give Senna the right to take matters into his own hands? No. But should he have found himself in that position at all? No. It was more official bungling. If ever there was a justification for governing body action against dangerous driving, it was Suzuka in 1990. But nothing...

That the governing body took no action against Senna spoke volumes. They knew the truth. And after the unpalatable actions of the previous year, even Balestre knew that it would have been going too far.

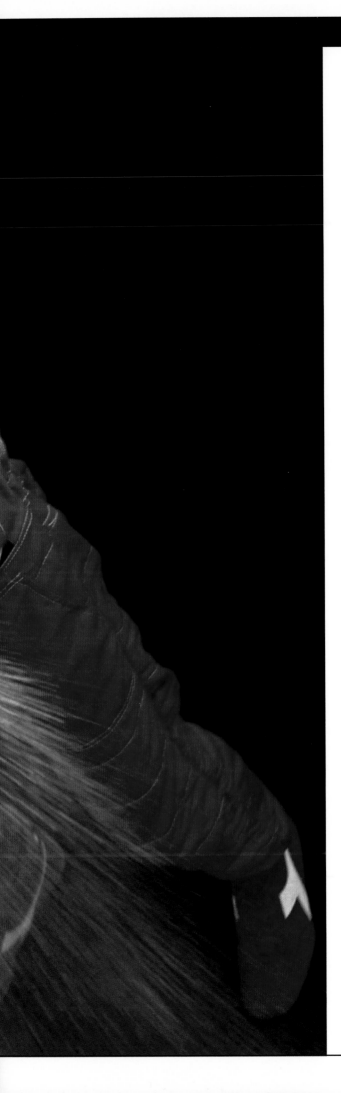

1991

THREE TIMES A CHAMPION

For 1991 Honda switched from its 72-degree V10 to a new 60-degree V12 and, initially, Senna had his doubts. It had become customary for Ayrton to spend his winter back in Brazil and that was his modus operandi once more, with Berger and test drivers Jonathan Palmer and Allan McNish doing most of the test work in Europe and Japan.

When Senna flew over to try the car in the final pre-season test at Estoril, he figured that despite the V12 delivering more power than the old V10, which was now being supplied to Tyrrell, insufficient development progress had been made.

Some thought that verdict a little rich from someone who had just dragged himself off the beach, but Senna had one eye on the pace of progress at Williams-Renault, which now had Nigel Mansell back as undisputed team leader alongside Riccardo Patrese.

Ferrari, meanwhile, had replaced Mansell with Jean Alesi and, despite impressive pre-season testing pace, was about to begin a decline. For the first time since 1980 Prost wouldn't win a grand prix and he would be fired after the Japanese GP for calling the Ferrari 'a red truck'.

← **Senna claimed the last of his five Spa-Francorchamps victories in 1991.**

📷 sutton-images.com

10 MARCH 1991

United States GP (Phoenix)
McLaren-Honda MP4/6 • 1st

It looked like a familiar story as 1991 kicked off with Senna
and Prost sharing the front row in Phoenix. Ayrton had more
than a second in hand over the Ferrari as the Williams-
Renault FW14s of Patrese and Mansell filled row 2.

Senna led every lap of the way to take a comfortable
16sec victory over Prost. Both Williams cars fell victim
to gearbox troubles, the team running a Ferrari-style
electro-hydraulic semi-automatic gearbox for the first time.
Early problems in that department masked the chassis/
aerodynamic progress the team had made following the
recruitment of Adrian Newey from Leyton House to join
Patrick Head.

24 MARCH 1991

Brazilian GP (Interlagos)
McLaren-Honda MP4/6 • 1st

For the eighth time of asking Ayrton Senna was trying to
win his home grand prix. Predictably enough he took pole
position with just over three-tenths in hand over Patrese's

Williams, while Mansell's sister car also separated Ayrton
from McLaren team-mate Berger.

Senna led away but soon found that he couldn't shake
Mansell until the Williams team leader gave him some
respite via a slow pit stop for new rubber, after which
Mansell found it hard to engage a gear. Senna, finding
the handling not to his liking as the race wore on, asked
for different tyre pressures on his next set of Goodyears
and emerged from the pits with a 7.5sec advantage
over Mansell.

When Nigel's challenge was extinguished by gearbox
trouble 12 laps from the end, it should have been relatively
straightforward for Senna to break that home jinx.
But Ayrton had problems of his own...

With half a dozen laps to go, Senna led by 20sec but
suddenly found he couldn't get fourth gear. Then third
went missing, then fifth, then third came back again.
With one lap to go, Patrese was just 3.5sec behind but
in trouble of his own with the Williams semi-auto.

Rain, which had started to fall lightly with 10 laps to go,
was now heavier, making areas of the track treacherous,
which probably played into Senna's hands as he found
sixth gear and left it there.

The effort of grappling with the gearbox and the
accompanying tension meant that Senna was now
suffering from cramp and shoulder spasms. Never in
his life had he been happier to see a chequered flag,

SENNA'S HOME WIN – DIVINE INTERVENTION?

More than once already in his career, Senna had talked about his religious beliefs and his successes being a gift from God. In 1988 there was that surreal qualifying lap at Monaco and then his first World Championship title at Suzuka, after which he felt "at peace", a weight lifted. And now his destiny – winning in front of his own people.

If Senna hadn't been quite so sensational a driver, so sublime in his skills, the notion of divine intervention might have left him open to ridicule, but the religious dimension did give Senna a vulnerability to those who wanted to make mischief. Prost, for example, had said during 1989 that Senna's apparent belief that he couldn't kill himself made him a danger to other drivers.

"Ayrton most definitely didn't feel that he was invincible," says Ron Dennis. "He knew very well the risks. My perception is that he was brought up in a family that was normal in its approach to religion, with the exception of his sister Viviane, who sought and found peace of mind in her own beliefs.

"She encouraged Ayrton to seek similar comfort from religion and he did follow a religious way of life, but not in an extreme way. He used the impartiality of the Bible as a sort of guidance to his own life. He wasn't obsessed, he wasn't deeply religious, but he read the Bible and, specifically, parts of the Bible that Viviane talked about. He had a mistrust of virtually all humans and it took a lot of time to understand him and be able to develop mutual trust and respect.

"He wouldn't tolerate fools and he would occasionally make mistakes in relationships with people – people who were polished in their approach to developing friendships. Inevitably they would let him down and he would switch off to those people. In the end I always felt that his group of friends, the people he trusted, was constantly diminishing."

➔ **Was there a little help from Him up there?**

📷 sutton-images.com

for more reasons than one. Finally, he had done it at home. Interlagos went wild. The radio messages were so ecstatic as to seem almost unhinged! As Ayrton stopped to collect a national flag, the McLaren, still stuck in sixth, had had enough and ground to a halt. Senna needed to be towed back to parc fermé where, totally exhausted, he was helped from the car.

Barely able to move his upper body and shoulders, Senna requested that father Milton hugged him 'gently' and didn't want anyone else to come near. On the podium, he struggled to lift the trophy over his head. The win, he said, was a gift from Him...

28 APRIL 1991

San Marino GP (Imola)
McLaren-Honda MP4/6 • 1st

If there was any doubt that Williams was making serious inroads into McLaren's F1 domination, Imola quashed them. Here was a power track and yet Ayrton Senna's V12-powered McLaren-Honda could only pip Riccardo Patrese's Williams-Renault FW14 to pole by 0.08sec.

In the race Patrese became the first person of the year to head the World Champion by leading for the first nine

laps before engine trouble intervened. Nigel Mansell, meanwhile, didn't manage a lap after a collision with Martin Brundle's Brabham prompted by yet more gearbox problems.

The Ferraris took care of themselves, with Prost spinning on the warm-up lap and Alesi sliding off at Tosa. That left the McLarens to totally dominate a soporific race, with JJ Lehto's Dallara-Judd, which had started 16th, finishing third!

12 MAY 1991

Monaco GP (Monte Carlo)
McLaren-Honda MP4/6 • 1st

With a hat-trick of wins already on the 1991 scoreboard and his personal brilliance magnified within the tight confines of Monte Carlo, anything other than another Senna win was almost unthinkable. And so it proved.

Ayrton inevitably claimed pole, his 56th, with a lap in 1m 20.344s but he wasn't totally out of sight, Italian Stefano Modena using Honda's V10 to lap within half a second and put a Tyrrell on the front row of the grid for the first time since Jody Scheckter with the six-wheeler 15 years earlier!

Race day gave Senna an untroubled 18sec win over Mansell's Williams, which could only qualify fifth after a suspension issue saw Nigel hit the barrier no fewer than three times during the practice days. With 10 points for a win (instead of nine) introduced for 1991, Senna had a maximum 40 points at the top of the championship table, from Prost (11), Berger (10) and Patrese, Piquet and Mansell (6).

2 JUNE 1991

Canadian GP (Montréal)
McLaren-Honda MP4/6 • Retired, 25 laps, electrics

Before the first race Senna had said that he wasn't convinced sufficient progress had been made by McLaren-Honda over the winter and, despite winning the first four races, he kept saying it.

In those races Williams had experienced various mechanical dramas but in Montréal it was McLaren's turn to hit trouble, with the truth of Ayrton's words starting to hit home when the team failed to get a car on the front row at a track perfectly suited to Honda horsepower. Ayrton put a piston through the side of the block on Friday, Patrese suffering a sizeable shunt on the

resulting oil, which stopped practice but ultimately didn't stop Riccardo taking pole as Williams monopolised the front row.

It was Mansell who dominated the race, however, leading every lap bar the final one, when he accidentally let the revs drop too low as he prematurely waved to the crowd down at the hairpin, letting the engine die. A gleeful Piquet, who was 40sec behind at the time, inherited the win while Senna posted a retirement. He left Montréal with plenty to think about, having been unable to run with the Williams pair before an alternator problem put him out.

16 JUNE 1991

Mexican GP (Autodromo Hermanos Rodriguez)
McLaren-Honda MP4/6 • 3rd

In Friday's qualifying session, Ayrton had the biggest accident of his F1 career to date. After a dominant Canadian showing, last lap notwithstanding, Williams-Renault was setting the pace again. Senna, trying to get among them in the final minutes of Friday qualifying, tried to take the daunting banked Peraltada corner in sixth gear. Realising he'd overdone it, he attempted to snick down to

⬇ As time went by in 1991, Senna's thoughts that McLaren and Honda had made insufficient progress were confirmed by Mansell and Williams.

📷 sutton-images.com

SENNA GIVES HIMSELF A FRIGHT IN MEXICO

Ayrton arrived in Mexico with ten stitches in a head wound following a lucky escape from a jet-ski accident in Brazil. But in Friday qualifying he was on his head again, after solid contact with the tyre barrier at Peraltada flipped the McLaren, and, needless to say, he didn't enjoy the experience of being upside-down in the gravel.

"He was having a good old moan and groan," Ron Dennis reveals. "He was complaining about a pain in one of his ears. He was pretty much unscathed but being a bit of a drama queen.

"When you see the car inverted in the gravel you fear the worst because the rollover bar can get buried and forces can be levied on the driver. He was pretty shaken up and a bit panicky in the medical centre.

"Sid could be humorously intolerant of the drivers' behaviour and wasn't particularly sympathetic. While Ayrton was moaning and groaning Sid almost laughingly hooked a piece of gravel, which had gone up inside the helmet, out of Ayrton's ear. It was sort of like someone had reattached part of his body because he thought this pain was never going to go away, but it was a stone in the ear.

"That was one of those moments when he experienced fear. He knew he wasn't invincible. Did he go through his career believing that nothing could ever happen to him and that he was protected? Definitely not. It wasn't how he was. He knew his limits, he knew the danger and he was always very balanced about the fact that he put himself in a risky position."

It wasn't the first time Senna had fallen foul of this corner and it wouldn't be the last...

⬇ **Trying too hard in Mexico, Senna rolled his MP4/6.**

📷 sutton-images.com

fifth mid-corner, unsettled the car, spun backwards into the tyre barrier and flipped.

"My fault," he admitted, "but with a semi-auto it wouldn't have been a problem."

Senna was now firmly on the case of both Honda and the team, saying openly that the McLaren MP4/6 chassis was no match for the Williams and that the V12 Honda wasn't delivering sufficient extra horsepower to compensate for its weight and fuel consumption penalties. Ayrton started the race third and finished there, some 17sec behind a Williams 1–2 in which Patrese shaded Mansell.

7 JULY 1991

French GP (Magny Cours)
McLaren-Honda MP4/6 • 3rd

For the seventh consecutive time, Riccardo Patrese outqualified Nigel Mansell to take pole position for Williams, with Prost's Ferrari joining the Italian on the front row at Alain's home race, held at Magny Cours for the first time. The track was the seventh venue for the French GP in the Formula 1 era, following Reims, Rouen, Clermont-Ferrand, Le Mans-Bugatti, Paul Ricard and Dijon.

Senna managed to set quickest time on Friday but had no answer to Williams the following day. In the race, Patrese suffered more Williams gearbox gremlins when the car selected neutral as he tried to change from first to second off the line. He was rapidly engulfed and could finish no better than a lapped fifth.

Mansell picked up the pieces, though, and took a long overdue first win of the year when he outfumbled early leader Prost in the new Ferrari 643 as the pair came up to lap Andrea de Cesaris's Jordan. Prost retook the lead at the tyre stops but Mansell hunted him down and repassed.

Ominously for Senna, once again he couldn't match the race pace of the lead battle and was more than half a minute behind the winning Williams when the flag fell.

14 JULY 1991

British GP (Silverstone)
McLaren-Honda MP4/6 • 4th (out of fuel)

Silverstone had undergone major redesign but it remained a power track. Irrespective of that, Senna and the McLaren-Honda struggled to get within seven tenths of the Williams-Renault FW14 of Nigel Mansell, who was typically fired up in front of his home crowd.

Nigel won for the second time in a week but team-mate Patrese was eliminated after a collision with Berger on the second lap. That should have left Senna heading for a comfortable second place but, on the last lap, the words he uttered in Canada proved right on the money.

The Honda V12's fuel consumption was indeed an issue and despite a confusing message from his dashboard read-out, which suggested that Ayrton had sufficient fuel left, the car ran dry on the final lap. Berger and Prost swept by and Senna was left with fourth place, stranded out on the track until memorably hitching a ride home on Mansell's winning car.

Mansell's margin, 42sec over Berger, confirmed to McLaren that they had a serious fight on their hands. Nigel was now a comfortable second in the championship with 33 points to Ayrton's 53. Those four wins on the trot at the start of the year seemed an awfully long time ago...

28 JULY 1991

German GP (Hockenheim)
McLaren-Honda MP4/6 • 7th (out of fuel)

Hockenheim speed-trap figures that had a Williams FW14 almost 10mph quicker than a McLaren MP4/6 reflected two things: the excellent aerodynamics of Adrian Newey's car and a lack of punch from the Honda V12 that Senna had spoken of the first time he drove it.

Despite a sizeable shunt during pre-race testing, Senna was as committed as ever and managed to put his McLaren on the front row alongside Mansell. There was no way he could live with the Williams in the race, though, Mansell disappearing up the road to win his third grand prix of the month.

Senna made a poor start and lost a place to Berger, soon finding himself occupied by Prost's attempts to relieve him of third place. On lap 17 Patrese showed Prost how it should be done when he went round the outside of the Ferrari into the first chicane and then outbraked Senna into the Stadium section. A good effort!

Both Senna and Prost took that as the cue to pit for fresh rubber and rejoined in the same order. Senna continued to drive a very wide car and when, on lap 38, Prost attempted to run round the outside of the McLaren into the first chicane, Senna left him with nowhere to go and Alain ended his afternoon in the escape road, unable to select reverse.

It was their first on-track spat since the events of Suzuka nine months earlier and Prost didn't mince his words.

"He did everything to stop me passing him," Alain said. "He weaved around and some of his braking was... how can I say? Unusual. That's the last time he does that to me. I have no problem being on the same track with him but I will push him off if he tries that again."

"I think we all know about Prost and his complaining," Senna retorted.

Senna had bigger things to worry about because the McLaren ran out of fuel on the last lap for the second successive race, allowing Berger and the Jordans of de Cesaris and Bertrand Gachot to claim the remaining points on offer behind Mansell, Patrese and Alesi. Fourth-placed Berger's McLaren then ran out of fuel on the slowdown lap. Honda had work to do.

11 AUGUST 1991

Hungarian GP (Hungaroring)
McLaren-Honda MP4/6 • 1st

On the face of it, Hungary could have been expected to bring another Williams success, but the team said that the FW14 wasn't best suited to slow corners. McLaren had also been busy with an exhaustive test at Silverstone and arrived with one of the MP4/6s fitted with a semi-automatic box, but when Senna damaged that chassis on Friday morning it was converted back to manual specification. Ayrton also benefited from efforts to pare down the MP4/6's weight as much as possible.

On his final qualifying run Senna produced one of those mesmeric qualifying laps, more than 1.2sec quicker than Patrese's best for Williams. Mansell had to be satisfied with row 2.

From the moment when Ayrton chopped across Patrese to protect the inside for Turn 1, the McLaren was never headed in the race. Senna didn't have things all his own way, though, and had to resist attacks from first Patrese, then Mansell, before crossing the line with a 5sec advantage to score his first win since Monaco three months earlier. But Mansell kept up the pressure with second place. The score was now Senna on 61 points and Mansell on 49, with six rounds to go.

Off the track, Prost had been sanctioned with a suspended one-race ban for his comments post-Hockenheim when, as well as having a go at Senna, he criticised the governing body for inconsistent driver penalties. FISA took the opportunity to call both drivers to discuss the German incident, after which Prost asked the officials to leave. The sport's two main men then indulged in a long conversation aimed at a rapprochement.

"Perhaps it won't work," Senna said, "but we both want to try."

↑ Mansell pushed
Senna hard at Spa
and passed him,
but a mechanical
problem was a hammer
blow to Nigel's
championship hopes.

📷 sutton-images.com

29 AUGUST 1991

Belgian GP (Spa-Francorchamps)
McLaren-Honda MP4/6 • 1st

Senna's win at Spa, his sixth of the season, was a hammer blow to the hopes of Mansell, who retired his Williams from the lead at half distance.

The engine and chassis lightening work recently done by McLaren allowed Senna to take a 58th career pole by a full second from Prost's Ferrari and Mansell's Williams, which were separated by just 0.007sec. Variable inlet trumpets had improved the Honda's mid-range punch.

In the race Mansell quickly dispensed with Prost and put Senna under huge pressure, although he couldn't find a way by. His problem was solved when Senna suffered a stuck wheel nut at his tyre stop after 15 laps, leaving Mansell to take control. Nigel looked well set for a maximum score until an electrical problem put him out.

That handed the lead to Jean Alesi's Ferrari, which, in turn, succumbed to an engine failure just as the young Frenchman seemed about to break his F1 duck.

Senna gratefully retook the lead and hung on despite a recurrence of the gearbox problems that had hampered him at Interlagos.

Missing first and second gears, Senna was in trouble at La Source and de Cesaris's Jordan closed to within 3sec before succumbing to a cooked engine three laps from the end. A threat from Patrese then dissolved when Riccardo suffered once again from the FW14's Achilles Heel, gearbox problems, which allowed Berger to complete a most fortuitous McLaren 1–2. Senna now had a 22-point lead over Mansell in the championship and the comfort of knowing that he could finish second to Mansell in every race for the remainder of the season and still retain his title. And, crucially, Williams was still suffering reliability lapses.

Elsewhere, Jordan driver Bertrand Gachot had been sentenced to 18 months in jail following an altercation with a taxi driver at London's Hyde Park Corner during which Gachot had defended himself with CS gas. The Belgian's unexpected incarceration allowed a certain Michael Schumacher to make his F1 debut and wow the F1 fraternity – de Cesaris in particular! – by qualifying seventh. We would hear more of him...

Italian GP (Monza)
McLaren-Honda MP4/6 • 2nd

Senna took yet another pole position, but by just 0.13sec from Mansell, and soon came under pressure from the Williams pair in the race. First it was Mansell, but then Nigel moved over to allow team-mate Patrese to attack the McLaren.

Patrese passed Senna at the Ascari chicane at half distance but spun on the very next lap, claiming that he'd got neutral when he asked for third gear. He resumed but was out half a lap later with clutch failure.

Mansell now attacked hard as Senna began to suffer vibrations and lock the brakes. He flat-spotted a tyre into the first chicane and was easy meat for Nigel, who went on to score a decisive win 15sec in front of Senna, who abandoned his non-stop plans to pit for a new set of rubber. The score was now Ayrton with 77, Nigel 59.

Portuguese GP (Estoril)
McLaren-Honda MP4/6 • 2nd

At Estoril both championship protagonists had to play second fiddle to their team-mates. Riccardo Patrese took a brilliant pole position when, fired up by an engine failure, he was finally allowed back out in Mansell's spare car with five minutes to go, resulting in a fabulous lap that was 0.22sec quicker than Berger's McLaren.

At the start of the race Mansell drove a hugely aggressive opening few corners, going round the outside of Senna at Turn 1, then chopping back across the McLaren's nose and going inside Berger at the following corner, putting himself behind Patrese to make it a Williams 1–2 at the conclusion of the first lap.

Mansell's Williams was clearly superior, but two years on from his Portuguese nightmare – when he was black-flagged for reversing in the pitlane and then took

⬇ **Senna started 1991 with four straight wins but by year's end the Williams FW14 was the class of the field.**

📷 sutton-images.com

out Senna – Nigel was in trouble again. This time it was a breakdown in communications during his tyre stop that saw the team release him without properly attaching his right rear wheel, which rolled away through the adjoining Tyrrell pit. Mansell came to a three-wheeled halt in the acceleration lane of the pits, where the team attached another wheel and sent him on his way. In doing so, however, they broke the rules, a fact that was promptly pointed out by the McLaren management in case race control were asleep. After an inexcusable 20-lap delay, Nigel was duly black-flagged, his title hopes effectively gone.

The result was a comfortable win for Patrese, 20sec clear of Senna, who was now on the brink of his third World Championship. Ayrton had a 24-point advantage and was expected to sew it up a week later in the first Spanish GP to be run at Circuit de Catalunya, just outside Barcelona.

29 SEPTEMBER 1991

Spanish GP (Catalunya)
McLaren-Honda MP4/6 • 5th

For the second successive race it was a member of the supporting cast who took pole, Berger's McLaren beating Mansell's Williams to the honour as Senna and Patrese shared row 2.

There was bad blood in what would turn out to be Jean-Marie Balestre's last drivers' briefing as FISA president. After Mansell's opening-lap aggression in Portugal, which Senna had somewhat richly complained about, Balestre said that Nigel was under observation – which caused Mansell to get to his feet and say that it was Senna who should be looked at. Ayrton replied with a volley of expletives before Piquet joined in and enquired whether someone needed to die before FISA finally took any action against a leading driver...

It was against that background that the world saw those iconic TV images of Senna and Mansell running down the main straight side-by-side at 190mph, jinking at each other, inches apart. It was lap 5 and a switch from wet tyres to dries beckoned, but that wasn't about to deter Nigel, who claimed the inside line for Turn 1 and second place, and went after Berger's leading McLaren. He took the lead when Gerhard made a tyre stop three laps later.

A cautious Williams tyre stop, understandable after the Portuguese debacle, put Mansell back behind the McLaren again but a rapid one by the McLaren crew saw Senna rejoin in the lead, just ahead of Berger. Ayrton promptly waved Gerhard by. He wasn't just being tactical. Against Goodyear's advice, he had fitted the harder B-compound tyres on the left-hand side and, given the new track's lack of grip, was struggling to get them up to temperature. That was instrumental in Senna

An iconic image: Ayrton and Nigel dispute territory in the first Spanish GP at Circuit de Catalunya.

sutton-images.com

231

losing the car out of the final turn on lap 13 and spinning, which let Mansell, Schumacher, Prost and Piquet by.

Mansell then forced his way past Berger to lead once more. Senna's wrong tyre selection saw him finish a distant fifth, behind Alesi, Patrese, Prost and Mansell, the victorious Williams more than a minute clear of the McLaren. Mansell thus trimmed the gap to 16 points. It wasn't over yet, and Suzuka was next...

20 OCTOBER 1991

Japanese GP (Suzuka)
McLaren-Honda MP4/6 • 2nd (WORLD CHAMPION)

The McLaren preoccupation at Suzuka was to keep Mansell off the pole and that was achieved when Berger, who got the better of Senna in qualifying for the third successive race, took the honour some 0.19sec quicker than Ayrton. Given the race tactics we would see from the team, however, Senna probably didn't try as hard as he might have done... Mansell's Williams was just thee hundredths slower.

Interestingly, considering the ructions of the previous year, this time pole position was indeed on the left, meaning that Senna, second, started from the slippery side once again. Gerhard duly converted his advantage and

Senna managed to fend off Mansell, who didn't make the best of getaways.

If Mansell failed to win, Senna would be champion – so the McLaren tactic was clear from the start. Berger sprinted away at the front, increasing his advantage by more than a second a lap, while Senna held Mansell at bay.

At the start of lap 10 Mansell got off-line on the way into Turn 1, ran wide and spun into the gravel, ending his title challenge there and then. Senna was World Champion for the third time.

Pre-race, Senna and Berger had an agreement that whoever got through Turn 1 ahead would win the race. Besides, Ayrton probably owed Gerhard one for his support throughout the year. So it was with some surprise that McLaren witnessed Senna speed up by a couple of seconds a lap, reel in Berger and overtake him. When Gerhard had a sticky wheel at his tyre stop, the gap grew to over 10sec.

Patrese, in more gearbox trouble, was no threat. Senna radioed in to check the result that the team expected and the message came back that Gerhard should win. Rather than do it discreetly, Senna slowed down out of the final turn and allowed Gerhard to go by just before they crossed the line to record his first win in a McLaren. It did seem ever so slightly patronising. Post-race, however, the media had rather more to talk about...

3 NOVEMBER 1991

Australian GP (Adelaide)
McLaren-Honda MP4/6 • 1st

The circus arrived in Adelaide for the final act of '91 without Alain Prost. Having already engineered the mid-season departure from Ferrari of sporting director Cesare Fiorio, Alain had opened his mouth once too often about Ferrari's lack of direction. On holiday in Queensland after Japan, Prost received the news that his contract had been terminated with immediate effect and that Gianni Morbidelli would replace him for Adelaide. With all the top seats already gone for 1992, Alain was suddenly looking at a sabbatical.

Although there was an end-of-term feeling, the constructors' championship was still to be settled, McLaren coming into the race with an 11-point advantage over Williams. Senna comfortably took pole from Berger, with Mansell and Patrese on the second row.

On Sunday, though, constant rain threatened a repeat of 1989, where the drivers had been critical of the decision to run the race. But once again the Adelaide race was started. Senna didn't think it should have been.

"It was impossible when we had these conditions two years ago," Ayrton said, "but this time it was even worse. It was just a matter of staying on the circuit."

This he managed to do, with a narrow lead over Mansell for the first 14 laps. But when Nigel lost it and slammed into the wall at the start of the 15th lap, with rain now pelting down and Senna gesticulating towards the sky, the red flag was finally displayed and the 1991 season was over, with the first half-points race since Ayrton had signalled his arrival in Monte Carlo seven years earlier.

The Adelaide GP, rain-afflicted for the second time in three years, was red-flagged after 14 laps, Senna winning the shortest race in F1 history.

sutton-images.com

SENNA VENTS HIS SPLEEN

T he catalyst was the deposing of 71-year-old Frenchman Jean-Marie Balestre as FISA president in favour of Max Mosley between the end of the European season at Catalunya and the Japanese GP at Suzuka.

When Senna secured his third world title at Suzuka and was confident that he could face no recriminations from Balestre, he chose the post-race press conference to say precisely what he thought about the previous two visits to Japan. He used some choice language, not aware, as McLaren's Martin Whitmarsh explained, that his rant was being picked up by the circuit PA and broadcast all round the circuit – a treat for any spectators who could understand English!

"I won this race in 1989 and was prevented from going onto the podium by Jean-Marie Balestre," Senna began. "I was robbed badly by the system and that I will never forget; 1989 was unforgivable and I still struggle to cope with that. They decided against me and that wasn't juctice, so what took place over the winter was shit.

"I never sent apologies to that guy," Senna went on. "They changed the press release. They changed the deal. They wanted to make a deal with us. I didn't want to. I was pushed by Ron and Honda and I agreed to some terms. After I agreed I signed the paper and sent it by fax. They completely changed the terms.

"Then, in 1990, before we started qualifying, Gerhard and I went to the officials and asked them to change the pole position because it was in the wrong place.

The officials said , 'Yes, no problem.' I got pole, and then what happened? Balestre gave an order that we don't change pole. We said that it had been agreed. They said, 'No, we don't think so.' This was really shit.

"I said to myself, 'OK, you try to work cleanly and do the job properly and then you get fucked by stupid people. All right, if tomorrow Prost beats me off the line, at the first corner I will go for it, and he better not turn in because he is not going to make it.' And it just happened.

"I wish it hadn't. We were both off and it was a shit end to the World Championship. It wasn't good for me and not good for F1. It was the result of wrong decisions and partiality from the people making them. I won the championship. So what? It was a bad example for everyone.

"If you get fucked every single time when you're trying to do your job cleanly and properly, by other people taking advantage of it, what should you do? Stand behind and say, 'Thank you, yes, thank you.' No, you should fight for what you think is right. And I really felt that I was fighting for something that was correct because I was fucked in the winter and I was fucked when I got pole.

"I tell you, if pole had been on the good side last year, nothing would have happened. I would have got a better start. It was the result of a bad decision. And we all know why, and the result was the first corner. I did contribute to it but it wasn't my responsibility."

← On the opposite side of the fence in the FISA/FOCA war, Max Mosley was now 'Establishment' and replaced Jean-Marie Balestre as FISA president.

📷 sutton-images.com

Some F1 commentators had a big problem with Senna's Suzuka outburst, feeling that it brought the sport into disrepute and devalued the third world title that he'd just won, although any logic surrounding the latter was hard to fathom.

Others were delighted. Senna might have toned down the expletives, they felt, but Balestre surely had that coming. Everybody knew Senna had taken Prost off in 1990, and Ayrton knew everybody knew, so let's finally admit as much. Wasn't he only getting even and preventing World Championship fraud for a second year?

Senna had struggled mightily with claiming it was a 'racing accident' a year earlier but would have faced disqualification if he'd done otherwise. Although he sometimes had a self-serving perspective of what was just and never had a problem convincing himself he was right, he did always struggle with untruth.

The rant, however, gave the new FISA president something of a problem. Here was the highest-profile driver in motor sport admitting that he'd clinched a World Championship by ramming his rival off the road. As the new Main Man, Max Mosley would look weak if he ignored it. But equally, Balestre's disgraceful handling of events at Suzuka in 1989 had been a strong card in Mosley's electioneering and he had come to power promising to be 'non-interventionist' as far as F1 was concerned. As amusing as that was in light of subsequent events, he'd only said as much a few weeks earlier...

The final outcome was a press release signed by Senna and issued by McLaren. It basically said that he hadn't deliberately shunted Prost off, just wanted the same piece of road, and that he really shouldn't have got so seriously stuck into dear old Jean-Marie. Merely for the record, it read:

"Following a frank discussion with the President of the FISA, Mr Max Mosley, I would like to make it clear that my remarks concerning the accident with Alain Prost in 1990 have been misinterpreted. What I said was that I had decided, in the event of both drivers going for the same piece of road, that I wouldn't be the one who gave way. All racing drivers do this occasionally.

"At no time did I deliberately collide with Alain, furthermore I now feel that my remarks concerning the former FISA president were inappropriate and the language used wasn't in good taste.

"I hope this matter is now closed and that we can enjoy an outstanding sporting contest in Australia without further controversy."

⬆ **With Jean-Marie Balestre out of the way, Senna said exactly what he thought...**
📷 sutton-images.com

⬇ **You've said enough, son... Dennis cuts short Senna's tirade.**
📷 sutton-images.com

1992
AYRTON EATS NIGEL'S DUST

The 1992 season developed into one of Senna's most difficult at McLaren. The active-ride Williams-Renault FW14B of Nigel Mansell was totally dominant, with an active McLaren not arriving until Monza. Add to that a heavy, thirsty new 75-degree Honda V12, which Senna wasn't convinced was initially as powerful as the previous year's 60-degree version, and he had his work cut out.

Ayrton would soon be trying actively to defect to Williams, but he was beaten to it by Prost, on sabbatical for a year after being sacked for rude comments about his Ferrari.

← In Hungary Senna scored the second of his three 1992 wins on the day that Mansell secured his World Championship with five rounds still to go.

📷 sutton-images.com

1 MARCH 1992

South African GP (Kyalami)
McLaren-Honda MP4/6B • 3rd

This was a very different Kyalami from the one that had last hosted a grand prix in 1985, when Nigel Mansell won. No sign of the old Crowthorne, Jukskei Sweep, Barbecue Bend or Leeukop – this was very much a 'modern' F1 circuit.

It didn't seem to matter to Mansell as he put the active Williams on pole, almost three-quarters of a second in front of Senna, and beat the defending champion by 35sec in the race, with Williams team-mate Riccardo Patrese 10sec in front of third-placed Ayrton.

"I think that if I am over half a minute behind Nigel, Williams has a good advantage," Senna said. Mansell was a bit sniffy about that, pointing out that Ayrton had won plenty of previous races by similarly big margins.

⬇ **As physio Josef Leberer straps him in, Senna's tanned face reflects the glum reality of the Williams FW14B's superiority...**

📷 sutton-images.com

22 MARCH 1992

Mexican GP (Autodromo Hermanos Rodriguez)
McLaren-Honda MP4/6B • Retired, 11 laps, transmission

With a race date three months earlier, to twin with Brazil, the Mexican GP also featured a circuit change as the 180-degree Peraltada had been modifed to become two 90-degree corners, prompted by Senna's flip there the previous year. The modifications, however, did little to iron out the inherent bumpiness of the place and the drivers found the track as challenging as ever – and it was an ideal place to have an active-ride Williams.

The McLaren MP4/6B – the team was still using the previous year's car – was left severely lacking, its stiffly sprung chassis so bad on the bumps that Berger spun three times and Senna crashed again at Peraltada. Ayrton was trapped in the car by a wishbone for 10 minutes and was in considerable pain.

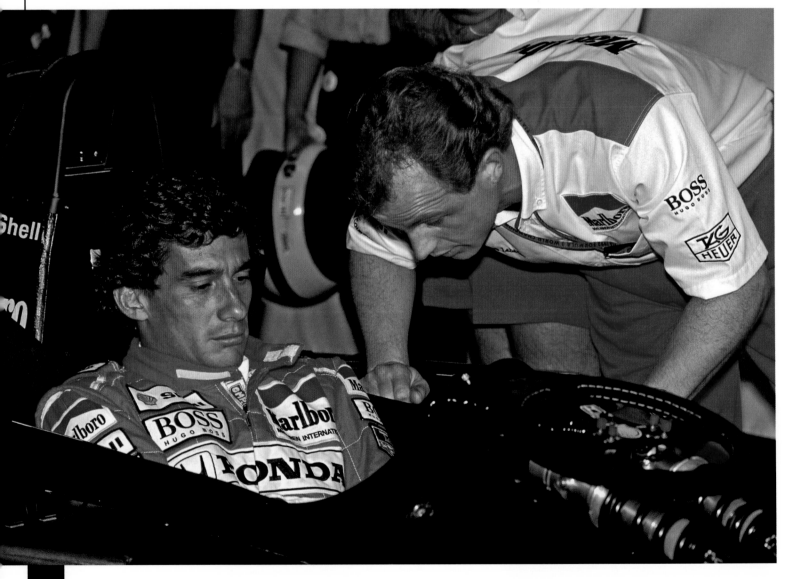

↑ **We're not in the ball game... Senna and Berger contemplate the pace of the Williams cars in 1992.**

📷 sutton-images.com

"He was so convinced he'd broken his legs," said Prof Sid Watkins, "that I cut open his overalls to demonstrate they were intact before we lifted him out of the car. He came out a bit dishevelled with his Y-fronts fully exposed and he didn't see the funny side until a bit later!"

For the first time in more than four years there wasn't a McLaren on the front two rows of the grid. The race produced the second successive Williams 1–2 with Senna out after 11 laps with transmission failure while running third.

5 APRIL 1992

Brazilian GP (Interlagos) • McLaren-Honda MP4/7A Retired, 17 laps, electrics

A coming-together between Mansell and Senna at the end of qualifying put the Williams into the wall at a tight left-hander in the infield section, but Nigel didn't blame Ayrton: "I thought he'd pulled over to let me through."

The incident didn't prevent Mansell from heading another all-Williams front row with a time 2.2sec faster than Senna's third-placed McLaren MP4/7A, making its first appearance at a race. Predictably enough the Williams cars were the only ones to complete the full 71 laps as Ayrton retired with electrical problems, but

not before he'd annoyed a certain Michael Schumacher, who finished third.

Senna had been in trouble from the start, his engine repeatedly misfiring and cutting out. Soon Ayrton had a train of cars behind him and was having to be very defensive in the tight infield. Sometimes the car refused to pick up and Senna eventually retired from his home race in the pits, making his feelings known with a bootful of revs before he got out of the car.

Amusingly, Schumacher hadn't been aware of Senna's difficulties and laid into Brazil's favourite son at the post-race press conference.

"I got the feeling he was playing with us," Michael said. "I'm not sure what the game was but it wasn't nice and for a three-times World Champion not necessary." Senna, when he found out, didn't much like that...

3 MAY 1992

Spanish GP (Catalunya) McLaren-Honda MP4/7A • 9th (62 laps, spin)

Nigel Mansell again claimed pole position, by exactly one full second from Schumacher, who started from the front row for the first time on the debut of the new Benetton B192. Senna headed row 2, 0.01sec behind Michael.

Ayrton didn't get a great start and trailed Mansell, Patrese, Alesi and Schumacher at the end of the first lap. He fought his way up to third but, after a battle with team-mate Berger, spun on lap 57 and then again – terminally – on lap 63, just two laps from the finish. After the opening four races Mansell had a maximum 40 points on the scoreboard, Ayrton just four.

17 MAY 1992

San Marino GP (Imola)
McLaren-Honda MP4/7A • 3rd

Here the animals went to the grid two-by-two: Williams shared the first row, McLaren the second, Benetton the third and Ferrari the fourth. But the times said it all. Mansell, on pole again, was 1.24sec quicker than Senna's third-placed McLaren. It used to be a given that a Honda engine was *de rigueur* at a power track such as Imola. But no longer. The thing to have was an active-ride Williams FW14B.

Mansell duly reeled off his fifth win on the trot, 10sec ahead of team-mate Patrese, with Senna finishing best of the rest, 40sec behind Riccardo and 4sec in front of old F3 foe Martin Brundle's Benetton.

31 MAY 1992

Monaco GP (Monte Carlo)
McLaren-Honda MP4/7A • 1st

Even Senna's Monte Carlo prowess made little difference and he couldn't stop another Williams front-row lock-out. Despite Ayrton qualifying 0.62sec clear of Berger in the other MP4/7A, Mansell was 1.1sec faster.

Senna made a determined bid to displace Patrese into the first corner and managed it, but he could do nothing about Mansell, who pulled away at a second a lap in the early stages. Ayrton knew that his only hope of equalling Graham Hill's record of five Monaco wins was for Mansell to have a problem, and it duly occurred with eight laps to go.

The Williams went sideways in the tunnel and Mansell, sensing he had a puncture, charged into the pits. The team's packing-up process had already started, however, and it was a slow stop, with his new tyres not properly pre-heated.

While Nigel was stationary, Senna's McLaren became the first car other than a Williams to lead a race all season. Mansell, however, was only 5sec adrift when he shot back out of the pits and determined to close down the gap.

Senna, his tyres going away, now had to resist the

much faster Williams on fresh rubber. This he calmly did, placing his car in the only realistic places Mansell could attack, and took the flag 0.21sec in front.

Canadian GP (Montréal) • McLaren-Honda MP4/7A
Retired, 37 laps, electrics

The Ile Notre-Dame circuit proved better suited to the McLaren-Honda and after a strong first qualifying session and a wet second one, Senna was able to stop the run of Williams pole positions and claim the 61st of his career.

Mansell didn't waste any time making a point. "I think that proves what I have been saying for a long time, namely that the Honda engine is ahead on power." Senna retorted that he'd willingly swap it for Mansell's chassis...

Ayrton led away with Nigel tracking him for the first 14 laps before trying an ill-advised move at the final chicane. Senna resisted by braking late and Mansell, on the dirty line, ran straight across the chicane and spun out, then had a go at Ron Dennis about Senna's driving. If anything, Ayrton might have suckered Nigel into it, and Patrese, following Mansell, said: "Nigel decided to go for it where the line was dusty. Ayrton didn't help him but he wasn't unfair. They didn't touch and Nigel went off."

Senna then led until lap 38 when an electrical problem robbed him of gears and put him out of the race, which was won by team-mate Berger.

French GP (Magny Cours) • McLaren-Honda
MP4/7A • Retired, 0 laps, accident damage

Magny Cours was another Williams benefit as Mansell and Patrese shared the front row, Nigel 1.33sec clear of Senna's McLaren on row 2.

On the first lap Ayrton got no further than the Adelaide Hairpin, where Schumacher's Benetton took him out. The race was another Williams 1–2 for Mansell and Patrese, with Martin Brundle's Benetton third.

British GP (Silverstone) • McLaren-Honda MP4/7A
Retired, 52 laps, transmission

This was the scene of a qualifying lap from Mansell that was almost as revered as Ayrton's special lap at Monaco

← Senna at
Silverstone. Had
he just seen
Mansell's pole time?
sutton-images.com

four years earlier. Driving the Williams FW14B like a man possessed, in front of his home crowd, Mansell stopped the clocks in 1m 18.965s. Riccardo Patrese, in the same car, did 1m 20.884s, while Senna qualified the McLaren third on 1m 21.706s.

Mansell scorched off to win the race by 40sec from Patrese, while for 50-odd laps Senna fought hard to overcome Brundle's Benetton. When, on lap 53, Martin was held up lapping F1 debutant Damon Hill's Brabham, Senna saw his chance and dived through, only to retire further round the lap with a universal joint failure.

26 JULY 1992

German GP (Hockenheim)
McLaren-Honda MP4/7A • 2nd

With Canada in mind, the McLaren-Hondas might have been expected to be pole contenders at the high-speed German track, but they weren't even close. Mansell took another pole on 1m 37.960s with Senna third on 1m 39.106s, some 0.6sec quicker than Berger.

Honda had been running higher revs for more power and Senna had an engine failure. He had more trouble in the warm-up when he spun exiting the last corner, writing off the chassis on a high kerb and consigning himself to the spare car for the race.

Off the start Mansell led from Patrese and Senna, but Nigel, believing he had a puncture, pitted early. He rejoined behind Senna and almost collected the McLaren when he outbraked himself into the chicane. He eventually got by and went on to score another win, which gave him a 46-point championship lead over Patrese, who spun off on the penultimate lap trying to wrest second place from Senna.

16 AUGUST 1992

Hungarian GP (Hungaroring)
McLaren-Honda MP4/7A • 1st

Before this race Senna had to suffer two indignities in quick succession. First, he was stopped on the M25 for speeding, his Porsche clocked at 121mph. And, unbelievably, the traffic officer, failing to recognise him, said, "Who do you think you are, Nigel Mansell?" In a story that is probably apocryphal, Senna is said to have replied, "No, officer, I'm considerably quicker than that. I'm Ayrton Senna..."

For once in 1992, Senna, who qualified third at Hungaroring behind the Williams duo, did actually get the

better of Mansell and the Williams FW14B after pole man and early race leader Patrese spun off. Second place for Mansell was good enough to clinch the world title, which Nigel duly did by finishing 40sec behind Ayrton. Senna was now third in the championship, six points behind Patrese and one ahead of Michael Schumacher.

30 AUGUST 1992

Belgian GP (Spa-Francorchamps)
McLaren-Honda MP4/7A • 5th

There was drama in the opening session of free practice when Erik Comas crashed at the very quick Blanchimont. After Comas was rendered unconscious by his Ligier's impact with the tyres, the car came to rest in the middle of the track. Senna, first on the scene, stopped and ran back to assist while medical help arrived. Comas was flown to hospital but was found to be uninjured save for concussion.

Mansell's active Williams was in its element at Spa and Nigel's 1m 50.545s pole was 2.2sec quicker than Senna managed in the McLaren to claim the other front row spot.

With light rain starting just as the grid formed up, it wasn't damp enough for wet-weather rubber and everyone started on slicks, Senna getting the better of Mansell away from the start. On the second lap, Mansell sat it out with Senna around Blanchimont to take the lead but was soon into the pits for wet tyres as Senna continued to brave it out on slicks. He knew he wouldn't beat Williams without a gamble.

Senna drove beautifully on slicks in the wet but the track failed to dry and his gamble proved to be in vain as he was forced to pit for wets after 14 of the 44 laps, rejoining 14th.

As the track dried towards the end of the race, with Mansell leading Patrese, Schumacher and Brundle, Michael's Benetton ran wide at Stavelot. Rejoining behind Brundle, Schumacher noticed the condition of his team-mate's tyres and duly elected to pit and be the first onto slicks. That decision led to Schumacher's first GP win, ahead of Mansell, Patrese and Brundle, with Senna fifth.

13 SEPTEMBER 1992

Italian GP (Monza)
McLaren-Honda MP4/7A • 1st

This became a weekend of off-track drama as the new World Champion revealed that he hadn't been able to come to agreeable terms with Williams for 1993

SENNA UNDERMINES MANSELL'S POSITION

On Sunday morning after the Monza warm-up, Nigel Mansell hosted a press conference to confirm a paddock rumour: he was leaving F1 at the end of the year in order to drive in Indycars with the Newman-Haas team.

Alain Prost was rumoured to have signed a Williams contract for 1993 some seven months earlier, but the Frenchman was still not officially confirmed.

"A deal was agreed with Frank Williams before the Hungarian GP, in front of a witness," Mansell claimed. "But three days after Hungary I was telephoned by a Williams director, who said he had been instructed to tell me that, because Senna would drive for

nothing, I, the new World Champion, had to accept a massive reduction in remuneration from the figure agreed in Hungary – considerably less than I am receiving this year. If not, Senna was ready to sign that night.

"I rejected this offer and said that, if these were the terms, Williams had better go ahead and sign Senna. To say that I have been badly treated is a gross understatement. It was the lack of information, and the sudden changes, that I found disappointing."

The paddock word was that Mansell had been offered $11 million to extend his contract earlier in the year but that negotiations had stumbled over

a contractual detail, believed to be the number of hotel rooms he would have at his disposal. With Prost in the bag and Senna sniffing, Mansell didn't have strong hand.

At McLaren, it is thought that Senna and Berger were told of Honda's imminent withdrawal before team boss Ron Dennis, meaning that Gerhard immediately targeted a lucrative return to Ferrari while Senna chased down Williams – fruitlessly as it turned out. So it was that McLaren announced that its new number two would be 1991 Indycar champion Michael Andretti, whose seat at the Newman-Haas team was passing to Mansell.

← Senna watches Mansell win at Silverstone. With Prost already signed by Williams for '93, Senna's claim that he would drive for Williams 'for nothing' did not help Mansell's negotiating position for '93! When Frank offered the new champion reduced terms, Nigel headed for the USA.

📷 sutton-images.com

and Honda announced that it was suspending its F1 programme at the end of the season.

On the track, Senna put the McLaren-Honda on the front row but Ayrton wasn't able to challenge Mansell in the early stages of the race, although it wasn't as big a walkover as in other races. On the 14th lap Patrese passed Senna to make it a Williams 1–2. Mansell then slowed and let Patrese by: with his championship in the bag Nigel was allowing Riccardo to win his home grand prix in appreciation of his support through the season. But both Williams cars succumbed to hydraulic pump failures after drive belts unseated themselves, allowing Senna through to win, which put him joint second in the championship with Patrese.

27 SEPTEMBER 1992

Portuguese GP (Estoril)
McLaren-Honda MP4/7A • 3rd

Senna endured a dramatic Friday when his McLaren's rear wing collapsed on the main straight, sending the car into a lurid spin on the run down to Turn 1. But he then turned a good lap to qualify third.

Again there was no holding a dominant Mansell, who took his ninth victory of the season – a record at the time. There was a terrifying incident when Patrese's Williams was launched skywards over the back of Berger's McLaren, Gerhard having unexpectedly headed for the pits, but Riccardo was miraculously unhurt. Berger's car was undamaged and he finished second, while Senna took the final spot on the podium after struggling with handling problems and needing multiple tyre stops.

25 OCTOBER 1992

Japanese GP (Suzuka)
McLaren-Honda MP4/7A • Retired, 2 laps, engine

On his last visit to Suzuka, Mansell qualified his Williams exactly a second ahead of Senna's McLaren, with Patrese once again between the pair. Nigel then spoke about the 1993 season and said what everyone was thinking.

"I'm obviously very grateful for the role that developments like active suspension have played in helping me to win the World Championship, but I would just as soon have done it without. It makes me really happy that I'm switching to Indycars, which are not as technically advanced.

"If the Williams is reliable next year and there is not

↑ Senna won at
Monza after both
Williams-Renaults
hit trouble.

sutton-images.com

a comparable driver in the second car, you will probably get Prost winning all 16 races. I would say there is not another engine currently in F1 to compete next year with Renault."

Senna knew that only too well. And when his valve-train warning light came on during the third lap of the Japanese GP, he parked up, climbed out and stood trackside like a man with the weight of the world on his shoulders.

8 NOVEMBER 1992

Australian GP (Adelaide)
McLaren-Honda MP4/7A Retired, 18 laps, accident

Mansell and Senna started their last race together in F1 from the front row, Nigel's dominant FW14B almost half a second quicker than Ayrton's MP4/7A.

Around the Adelaide streets, Senna reckoned he had a better-than-usual chance of being able to give the Williams a race, and, knowing that Mansell was leaving, he was more than usually keen to beat him.

It looked as if it was on the cards too – when the race began Mansell couldn't shake the McLaren from his gearbox. On lap 19, when Nigel lost time behind Nicola Larini's Ferrari, Senna was suddenly on him and well placed to go down the inside at the final corner. But that wasn't what happened next: instead the McLaren cannoned into the back of the Williams and they were both out of the race.

Outwardly it looked as if Senna had simply driven into the back of the Williams, but top drivers don't make mistakes like that without help. And the speed with which Mansell departed the scene told you that there was more to the collision than met the eye.

"I'm glad I'm out of it," said Mansell, somewhat melodramatically, of his career in F1. "He just rammed me at about 40mph more than I was doing. The reason I ran across the track like I did afterwards was that there would have been a big fight and I don't think that is the right way to leave F1."

Senna's version was different. It might not have been quite a brake test, but Mansell had certainly lifted early for the corner in a cack-handed attempt to give Ayrton a moment and spoil his impending outbraking attempt. And the Williams team's reluctance to support Mansell in a visit to the stewards' office – they had the telemetry – told you all you needed to know...

Senna tests a Penske Indycar

Senna's failure to secure a seat at Williams for 1993 irked him to the extent that just before Christmas, on 23 December, he tested impressively in a Penske-Chevrolet PC22 Indycar at Firebird Raceway, Arizona, USA. Fellow Brazilian and F1-turned-Indycar driver Emerson Fittipaldi was instrumental in arranging the test, and was present on the day. Momentarily, it looked as if both Mansell and Senna might be deserting F1!

⬇ Senna tests a Penske Indycar at Firebird Raceway just before Christmas.

📷 sutton-images.com

SHUT-OUT SENNA DROWNS HIS SORROWS

It was in Portugal that Frank Williams confirmed what the paddock had known for most of the season – Alain Prost would be a Williams driver in 1993. Prost had the full backing of Renault, Williams' engine supplier, and his contract had a 'no Senna' clause.

There's no doubt that Frank Williams would rather have had Senna than Prost, but he had to be careful. Renault wanted a French World Champion and, when Senna had been making noises about driving for Williams for nothing, Prost had also been talking to McLaren. If Frank did anything to upset Alain – like telling him he was having Senna, in contravention of their agreement – there was every chance that Frank would lose both the Frenchman and his engines to McLaren. Senna, knowing before Ron Dennis that Honda was leaving, might have seen that coming, but he didn't.

Senna was furious and, post-race, used the press conference to make his feelings about Prost known. Mansell, whose market value had also taken a tumble due to Prost's presence, patted his back in support. The whole spectacle was unedifying.

"I don't accept being vetoed by anyone in the way this has been done," Ayrton stormed. "This is supposed to be the World Drivers' Championship. We had two fantastic championships, this year and last. In 1989 and '90 we had two very bad ones. They were a consequence of unbelievable politics, and bad behaviour by some people. I think that now we are coming back to the same situation.

"If Prost wants to come back, and maybe win another title, he should be sporting. The way he is doing it, he is behaving like a coward. He must be prepared to race anybody, under any conditions, on equal terms. He now wants to win with everything laid out for him.

"It is like going for a 100-metre sprint in running shoes – while everybody else has lead shoes. That is the way he wants to race. It is not racing."

Jo Ramirez remembers what followed:

"We used to have a team dinner in Portugal. Ayrton fancied one of the motorhome girls, Katy... blue eyes, dark hair, a lovely girl. He was very depressed because he'd heard he wasn't going to get the Williams drive. He used to like Haig Dimple whisky... Katy was giving him these whiskies and, because it was her, he was drinking them like water. He was soon completely out of it.

"Gerhard was saying, 'Come on Ayrton, keep going, it's only nine o'clock, we have all evening!' Emerson Fittipaldi was with us, and he and Ayrton were staying at the house of the Brazilian boss of the Nacional bank. He was a lovely retired guy, living in Sintra, who had helped Ayrton from the beginning, and Ayrton was very loyal to him – he even carried Nacional after they stopped paying. But that night Emerson had to carry him back because Ayrton was completely destroyed!"

1993

FINISHING AT McLAREN

Wrong-footed by Honda's unexpected withdrawal at the end of 1992, McLaren boss Ron Dennis tried, but failed, to get a supply of Renault V10s for 1993. He had little option, therefore, but to take the 'customer' Ford HB V8 engine, which was one development step behind the specification of the 'works' units supplied to Benetton.

At Benetton, Martin Brundle was replaced, rather strangely, by Riccardo Patrese as Michael Schumacher's team-mate, Patrese having done a deal with Flavio Briatore early in 1992 on the assumption that the following year's Williams line-up would be Mansell and Prost. At Williams, meanwhile, the Mansell ructions and the 'no Senna' clause in Prost's contract opened up a golden opportunity for test driver Damon Hill.

At McLaren, the £6 million deal for the Ford engine wasn't sealed until late December and so it was a sterling effort to have an active-ride MP4/8 ready for testing at Silverstone on 15 February. The car looked promising too, as Senna, now partnered by Michael Andretti, set the quickest testing time on his return from wintering in Brazil.

Outwardly at least, Senna hadn't committed to the season and began the year on a race-by-race basis. That seemed unlikely and Ron Dennis later confirmed that it was a strategy agreed with Senna in an effort to raise more support from team sponsors to meet Ayrton's $16 million ($1 million per race) financial requirement.

← The first lap of the European GP at Donington was one of those great Senna feats that people still talk about. Fifth at Redgate, the first corner, Ayrton was third by the bottom of the Craner Curves and led at the end of the opening lap.

📷 sutton-images.com

SNEAKY SENNA DUPES F1 NEW BOY ANDRETTI

For anyone doubting the extent to which Senna would go to seek a competitive advantage, there's a lovely tale about Michael Andretti from McLaren's Martin Whitmarsh. Bear in mind that the F1 environment was completely new to Andretti, who wasn't helped by new regulations restricting the number of qualifying laps.

"We had an active-ride car and various other things that we thought were pretty complex," Whitmarsh explains. "So, for the first time ever, I remember saying to Steve Hallam that we ought to have a drivers' manual. At the start of the year, at an early test, we turn up and the day before there's an engineering briefing. At the end of it, Steve pulls out this lovely bound manual and says, 'Look, there are more knobs and various warning messages on the dash display, so here's a book that you can take back to the hotel tonight, read and inwardly digest.'

"Ayrton said, 'No, it's OK, I'm a professional racing driver. Tell me once and I've got it. I don't need to read the book.' So poor Steve is a bit deflated and he puts his book down. Andretti is new to everything in F1, so of course he also says, 'No, it's OK, I'm a professional racing driver and I don't need it either...'

"So the meeting finishes, it's the end of the day and everyone leaves to go back to the hotel – and we're a bit disappointed our drivers don't want our manual. Then, just as everyone has left, Ayrton nips back into the room, picks up a manual, puts it in his bag and disappears! Apart from his great skill as a driver, he never stopped looking for every single edge."

⬇ Discussion with (from left) Steve Hallam, Michael Andretti and Dave Ryan.

📷 sutton-images.com

↑ First lap at
Interlagos, with
Senna on the way to
his second win on
home soil as new
team-mate Michael
Andretti and Gerhard
Berger's Ferrari have
a big accident in the
background.

📷 sutton-images.com

14 MARCH 1993

South African GP (Kyalami)
McLaren-Honda MP4/8 • 2nd

"I'm delighted with what the team has achieved in so little time," Senna said when he managed to put the new McLaren MP4/8 within 0.09sec of Prost's Williams FW15 on the grid at Kyalami. It looked like we might have a season after all.

This was the first time that Ayrton and Alain had shared the front row since the acrimony at Suzuka in 1990 but this time it was clean as Senna led off the line. The McLaren led for the first 23 of 72 laps before Prost came by as Senna started to struggle with difficult handling. A load cell failure in the active suspension had caused the rear ride height to run too high.

Senna then came under pressure from Schumacher but strongly resisted Michael's attempt to relieve him of second place on lap 40. Contact was made, Schumacher spun into retirement and Senna finished runner-up to Prost, the only other driver on the same lap.

28 MARCH 1993

Brazilian GP (Interlagos)
McLaren-Honda MP4/8 • 1st

On Ayrton's home turf at Interlagos, it became pretty clear that when grunt was needed, the McLarens were a little breathless with their older-spec Ford HBs, not that Benetton, with its 'works' Ford engines, was any nearer to the Williams-Renaults.

Uncomfortably for Senna in front of his home fans, Prost took pole on 1m 15.866s with Hill's sister Williams alongside him, while the best that Senna could manage for third was 1m 17.687s.

McLaren's engine agreement was that it would only get the superior pneumatic-valve engine when a further upgraded unit with revised cylinder heads became available to Benetton at the British GP. Senna, meanwhile, was agitating to have the timescale brought forward to the San Marino GP at Imola.

On race day, however, the elements worked in Ayrton's favour. Prost led comfortably on a dry track and

Hill passed Senna on the 11th lap to make it a Williams 1–2. And things looked even less promising when Senna had to serve a stop-go penalty for overtaking Erik Comas's Larrousse under a yellow.

But then came a tropical downpour around the start/finish area. Japanese drivers Aguri Suzuki (Footwork) and Ukyo Katayama (Tyrrell) both spun, as did Christian Fittipaldi (Minardi). Prost had been coming into the pits but didn't properly receive a radio message, which he assumed was telling him to keep going because Hill was already in the pits. Alain did so, aquaplaned out of control, hit Fittipaldi's car and finished his race in the gravel trap.

The Safety Car was duly despatched and, when racing resumed, Hill led from Senna, the cars now back on slicks. Ayrton wasted no time in slicing inside Damon and went on to score his second home victory and McLaren's 100th grand prix win.

⬇ In mixed conditions Ayrton won the European GP at Donington by nearly one and a half minutes...

📷 sutton-images.com

11 APRIL 1993

European GP (Donington)
McLaren-Honda MP4/8 • 1st

The European GP at Donington is perhaps the most discussed of Senna's 41 grand prix victories.

Despite his optimism after the first test in the MP4/8, Senna had come to realise the extent of the task on his hands in 1993. The elements had helped him at his home grand prix but on a dry track at Donington he was again slower in qualifying than the Williams pair, 1.55sec down on Prost. That wasn't so much a gap as a chasm, and he was also behind Schumacher's Ford-powered Benetton for the first time. Little wonder that Ayrton's line with the media was to continue agitating whenever he could for the latest-specification Ford engine.

Again, though, rain on race day made Senna, with his instant feel for grip, the pre-race favourite, provided he could build up a big enough margin in the event of the track drying, in which case he wouldn't be able to hold Prost.

That was the mindset as Senna went to the grid. He knew he might not have long to establish a cushion. Some parts of the circuit were wetter than others and JJ Lehto had already elected to start his Sauber from the pits on slicks.

Senna, however, didn't make the greatest of starts from the left-hand side of the second row and on the run down to the first corner, Redgate, Karl Wendlinger's Sauber passed him on the inside. As Senna tried to go deep into Redgate on the outside, Schumacher edged him wider still, so Ayrton chopped back across to go inside the Benetton. As they accelerated out of Redgate, Senna had one key advantage over Schumacher – traction control – and his McLaren eased ahead.

At that time Benetton, with its works engine deal, didn't have traction control because Ford wasn't confident about the reliability implications of its own system, but McLaren, with its customer deal, had its engines already fitted with its own TAG Electronics traction control. In conditions like those on the first lap at Donington, that was significant.

Down the Craner Curves, Senna swooped round the outside of Wendlinger through the left-hander and had his McLaren on the inside of the Sauber for Old Hairpin to go third. Up ahead, the Williams pair had traction control too, but they didn't have Senna's wet-weather skill or commitment. Hill was surprised to find the McLaren on the inside of him as he was about to turn into the next right-hander, McLeans, and had to give way. Then, coming up the inside for the Melbourne Hairpin, Senna went late on the brakes and, after a twitch from the McLaren, he was past Prost as well – and in the lead as he blasted across the start/finish line at the end of the first lap.

Ayrton was never seen again. The mixed conditions continued, so much so that Prost made no fewer than seven tyre stops en route to a lapped third place – and much media criticism, especially in France. Senna's winning margin over Hill's Williams at the flag was 1m 23s. Although he now sat at the top of the championship table with a 12-point margin over Prost, he knew things couldn't continue in similar vein.

At the post-race press conference Ayrton seemed amused by Alain's discomfort and cheekily asked if he'd like to swap cars. Ayrton didn't eulogise about his Donington drive in the same way that many commentators did: yes, the first lap had been pretty good, he said, but overall his debut win with Lotus in teeming rain at Estoril, without traction control, had been more taxing.

"The only real piece of memorabilia that I've sought from motor racing," says Martin Whitmarsh, "is the steering wheel from the car Senna used in Brazil and at Donington. Brazil was our 100th GP win and then there was that epic Donington race. We were about to give it away, I think to the president of Shell, and I said 'no'. I put it in the cupboard in my office until a few years later, when I negotiated it out of Ron!"

25 APRIL 1993

San Marino GP (Imola) • McLaren-Honda MP4/8
Retired, 42 laps, hydraulics

The top six qualifiers at Imola mirrored the Donington grid, with Williams on the front row, Schumacher a tenth quicker than Senna on row 2, and Wendlinger and Andretti sharing row three.

Once again, Williams had an enormous margin in the dry with Prost's pole time almost 2sec quicker than Senna. In the race morning warm-up, however, the gap was only half a second and when rain fell as start time approached, everyone wondered if it might be Donington all over again.

It wasn't. Hill made the best start this time and Senna shot through into second place ahead of Prost. The

↑ **Ayrton celebrates after his epic Donington drive.**
📷 sutton-images.com

253

additional power of the Renault V10 was more significant at Imola and allowed Williams to run more wing, so Senna could only keep Prost behind him for six laps, by which time Hill was 8sec to the good in front.

Senna stopped for slicks as soon as Prost passed him and gained time by doing so, with the result that the order after the tyre stops was Hill–Senna–Prost, Damon only just hanging on to his lead. He then ran wide at Tosa, delaying Senna, and Prost passed them both. A few laps later Hill spun off on a damp patch at the same place, trying to lap a tail-ender.

Senna chased Prost until a hydraulic failure robbed him of active ride and gears, putting him out after 42 laps. His championship advantage over race winner Prost was now down to just two points.

9 MAY 1993

Spanish GP (Catalunya)
McLaren-Honda MP4/8 • 2nd

Prost and Hill once more occupied the front row of the grid, Alain with a margin of almost 2sec over Senna, who this time got the better of Schumacher on row 2.

The race proved to be a Williams benefit as Hill led the opening 10 laps before Prost went by. Hill didn't give up and reckoned he had been well-placed to score his first win before the engine failed after 41 laps, leaving Senna to finish second, 17sec behind Prost, who now led the championship by two points.

23 MAY 1993

Monaco GP (Monte Carlo)
McLaren-Honda MP4/8 • 1st

As Senna had won the previous four Monaco GPs, many expected him to be fully competitive in Monte Carlo, but he crashed heavily on Thursday on the approach to Ste Devote, escaping with a bruised thumb.

It was an odd shunt, caused by a programming error with McLaren's ride-height control device, which allowed a driver, by means of a button on the steering wheel, to lower the car on the straight for reduced drag. This incident put Senna on the back foot and at the scene of so many amazing previous qualifying laps he could only line up third, a second behind Prost's Williams and 0.36sec adrift of Schumacher's Benetton.

Prost was rolling ever so slightly as the lights changed and, after leading for the first 11 laps, the Williams had to call into the pits for a stop-go penalty. Schumacher took

over the lead and seemed well able to cope with Ayrton, with a 15sec advantage as the race reached the 30-lap mark, but two laps later a hydraulic leak put the Benetton out. Ayrton duly reeled off the remaining laps untroubled to take a comfortable 52sec win. It was one of those nice little quirks that on the day Senna usurped Graham Hill's five Monte Carlo wins with a record sixth, Damon should be second.

19 JUNE 1993

Canadian GP (Montréal)
McLaren-Honda MP4/8 • Retired, 62 laps, alternator

After an engine failure in the opening session, Senna faced the unusual prospect of starting the Canadian GP – where outright power was crucial – from way back in eighth place on the grid, although he was still half a second and four places better off than team-mate Andretti.

Undeterred, Senna picked up four places on the opening lap and was soon past Berger's Ferrari into third position. That became second at the tyre stops and Senna looked able to defend from Schumacher's Benetton until the engine started to cut. After 62 laps Ayrton retired with alternator failure, again losing his championship lead to race winner Prost.

4 JULY 1993

French GP (Magny Cours)
McLaren-Honda MP4/8 • 4th

Damon Hill claimed his first pole position and, for the first time, looked a genuine threat to Prost, leading the race before losing out at the pit stops and then shadowing Alain all the way to the line as Prost took his sixth French GP win. It was a crushingly dominant performance from Williams.

Senna qualified fifth, again almost 2sec down on the Williams pace, and got the car home fourth, 32sec behind the winning Williams. Schumacher's Benetton took the remaining podium place.

11 JULY 1993

British GP (Silverstone)
McLaren-Honda MP4/8 • 5th

True to McLaren's contract, at Silverstone Senna had the Series VII Ford HB V8 for the first time but was lukewarm about it: "It's better than the old one, but not as good as I was told it would be."

If anything, the gap to Williams seemed to be

ANDRETTI UNLUCKY TO BE ACTIVELY REMOVED

When Michael Andretti signed to join McLaren there were a few raised eyebrows. Andretti had shown winning form in the USA and, said Ron Dennis, could clearly overtake. And at a time when Senna was making a bid to join Williams and Prost was also believed to be moving there, it was an interesting move by McLaren.

Nobody had more wide-ranging experience of motor sport than Michael's father, Mario, who transferred from US racing to F1 and became World Champion with Lotus in 1978. If his son, at 29, was going to make the same move, he had to do so sooner rather than later, and an opening with a front-line team like McLaren didn't happen often. But was it a good idea to go up against Senna in the same car? As well as that, those with their eyes open appreciated just how quick McLaren test driver Mika Häkkinen was.

Andretti had a tough baptism, with his commitment to F1 questioned by his unwillingness to base himself in Europe. The seeds of his undoing, Senna's stunning speed apart, was F1's political landscape.

At the time, the FIA was trying to push through bans on high-technology driver aids such as active suspension, semi-automatic gearboxes and traction control, partly on the grounds that it disadvantaged the less affluent teams. But the governing body was meeting with stubborn resistance from the better-funded teams such as Williams and McLaren, who had mastered the technology.

In a bid to prove that it need not all be prohibitively expensive, McLaren's Martin Whitmarsh had suggested selling a McLaren active-ride package to the Footwork Arrows team, which would both make a political point and earn McLaren some money.

"It was one of the luckiest things we ever did!" recalls Whitmarsh. "They were running Derek Warwick and Aguri Suzuki. They were at the tail end of the grid for the first umpteen races, then we got involved in the engineering of them and put active on their car, and at Silverstone they were eighth and tenth. Having become a bit involved in this Arrows exercise, I was standing beside them on the grid and was pleased that we'd pulled them forward, save for the fact that the second McLaren, driven by our Mr Andretti, was 11th...

"Ron decided to walk from Ayrton's car back to our other car and as he went past me he looked at the Arrows in front of our car, mouthed, 'Another bright idea of yours', and walked on. At the time, I told Ron that it highlighted one other thing – that this driver wasn't hacking it. And so at the end of the year we got the luckiest break ever because we had this young test driver, Mika Häkkinen, and put him in for the last three races, at Estoril, Japan and Australia."

For the time being, Andretti had four more races partnering Senna before McLaren dumped him.

← Mika Häkkinen replaced Michael Andretti in Portugal and surprised Senna by outqualifying him.

📷 sutton-images.com

SENNA CAMPAIGNS FOR LAMBORGHINI ENGINE

With four long months having passed since Senna's last win – at Monaco – and a series of poor races in which Schumacher's Benetton appeared the stronger combination, Senna's motivation was questioned for the first time in his career. When someone is paid $1 million per race, it can become a significant bone of contention. An off-the-record press discussion had also gone wrong for Ron Dennis and come back to bite him by upsetting his star driver.

Behind the scenes, however, Senna hadn't given up, as Martin Whitmarsh relates.

"Ayrton had a calmness about him. Obviously he had hot-headed moments in the car but within the team I don't remember many. The worst it got was when we ran a car with a Lamborghini engine mid-season in 1993. At the time Chrysler owned Lamborghini and their engines were in the Larrousse cars. Lamborghini came and showed us their data and it looked like a fantastic engine, with 50–60bhp more than we had and something like 30kg lighter.

"But I didn't believe this data because I could see how slow those cars were. I remember going to Lamborghini, where they ran the engine on the dyno and we saw the needle go round to the power figures they claimed. Then they stopped, drained the oil and put the engine on the scales. Even then I'm shaking my head at Ron and thinking, 'No, they've just done the calibration on that dyno and those scales. Come on guys...'

"In the end we didn't think Chrysler had the commitment and we did a deal with Peugeot for 1994. Contractually, though, we had to test this Lamborghini engine and before we ran it I told our team manager, Dave Ryan, that whatever happened the car must not go any quicker than 'x'. If it did, it would have caused us some big contractual issues. And I added, 'But don't worry, it won't...'

"Well, Dave rang me from the track and said, 'Look, I can't stop this bloomin' car going quicker. It seems quite good, and it's got Ayrton in it...'

"So I told him to stick 100kg of fuel in it and not say anything to anybody – it was a real old mess and I was having to manage that. But Ayrton obviously realised that it was quicker than the Cosworth car and wanted to race it in the last three races of '93, so he was massively pissed off that we wouldn't do that. Ayrton by that stage, of course, was leaving us for '94, and the fact that it had contractual implications for McLaren wouldn't have been on his agenda at all. Screw McLaren, he just wanted the quickest car to beat Prost with.

"So there he was, having his last three races for us, in a strop about the Lamborghini engine, totally demotivated, and we put Mika in – and he promptly outqualifies Ayrton at Estoril in his first race!

"It was a wake-up call and Ayrton did wake up. He passed Mika pretty aggressively on the opening lap in Portugal and then he won the next two races. Without Mika there, I think he would have had a strop on. But with Mika there, given his competitive intensity, he couldn't help himself. It absolutely fired him up.

"For the last two races we had a power braking system on the car that subsequently became illegal. We had been developing an ABS braking system that got banned halfway through the year, but we wriggled a way through the prohibition so that, if we couldn't have full ABS, we could at least have power braking. That helped – but it was more about Ayrton being fully revved up and doing the job."

increasing. Prost took pole with 1m 19.006s and Senna was fourth on 1m 21.986s...

Ayrton made a flier of a start and, with Hill leading, shot inside Prost to take second place. Senna's defence of second for the first six laps reflected his frustration and involved some of the most intimidatory driving he had yet deployed against his bête noire. Chops at Abbey and on the run to the Maggotts/Becketts complex made the scenes at Estoril in 1988 look like child's play.

"It was up to Alain to pass me," Senna said simply.

"I'm not even going to get drawn into talking about it," said Prost.

Cruelly, Hill was robbed of a home win when his engine failed at two-thirds distance, leaving Prost to win again, from Schumacher. Senna should have finished third but ran out of fuel on the last lap for the third consecutive time at Silverstone. Prost now had a 20-point margin over Senna in the championship.

25 JULY 1993

German GP (Hockenheim)
McLaren-Honda MP4/8 • 4th

Williams again took the front row in Germany but Senna's time, within nine tenths of Prost's pole, was closer than may have been anticipated at such a power track. Ayrton blotted his copybook on the first lap, however, when trying to run round the outside of Prost. Alain refused to give way, the McLaren mounted a kerb and spun.

Senna resumed at the tail of the field and fought his way back up to fourth. Prost picked up another win after the luckless Hill had a tyre blow-out just two laps away from his first grand prix win.

15 AUGUST 1993

Hungarian GP (Hungaroring)
McLaren-Honda MP4/8 • Retired, 17 laps, throttle

It was another all-Williams front row as Senna, perplexed by lack of grip, qualified 1.2sec behind Schumacher's Benetton on the second row. Ayrton was less than a second faster than Pierluigi Martini's Minardi and his motivation might have been questioned but for the fact that Andretti was a second and a half slower...

Senna made a good start to run second to Hill early on but got no further than lap 18 before he retired with a throttle problem. Damon finally took a deserved first F1 win.

29 AUGUST 1993

Belgian GP (Spa-Francorchamps)
McLaren-Honda MP4/8 • 4th

Fifth on the grid, almost two and a half seconds from Prost, was Senna's fate at Spa, but the big drama of practice was an almighty accident that Alex Zanardi was fortunate to survive when his Lotus had an active-suspension failure at the bottom of Eau Rouge. When Senna refused to attend the drivers' parade, the unofficial explanation was that he'd been angered by the officials' refusal to consider the safety implications of Zanardi's accident at the earlier drivers' briefing.

Senna ran second to Prost at the end of the opening lap but soon had to cede the place to Hill, who eventually won the race. On lap 14 Ayrton had to relinquish third place to Schumacher, although he tried hard not to by cutting across the Benetton as he exited the pits after his tyre stop. Schumacher was unimpressed: "It was completely unnecessary. I had to go on the grass to get around him, but I didn't lift."

After finishing fourth behind Hill, Schumacher and Prost, a disgruntled Senna said: "After the first few laps I just couldn't keep up."

12 SEPTEMBER 1993

Italian GP (Monza) • McLaren-Honda MP4/8
Retired, 8 laps, accident

Senna got the better of Schumacher in qualifying at Monza to win the 'Ford division' but was still only fourth on the grid, behind Prost, Hill and Jean Alesi's Ferrari.

His race, however, lasted just eight laps. The opening lap was compromised by contact with Hill's Williams at the first chicane, Ayrton finishing it down in 10th place. He then cannoned into the back of Brundle's Ligier at the second chicane on lap 9, putting both cars out.

"It was entirely his fault," Brundle said. "He was adjusting his brake balance going into the second chicane and just completely missed his braking point. He realised he was going to have a big crash, so he used me as a brake.

"He hit me so hard that it sent me forward into the barriers. From being nicely under control under braking I then went and had a big crash. He came running over to see if I was OK. He was really desperate because he thought he'd really hurt me, but as soon as he realised I was OK, he just switched.

"While we're standing there, he's calculating whether he can still win the championship. I said, 'It's not looking too good, is it?' He said, 'Ah, it's OK if Prost has a problem, I might still have a chance.'

Prost, in fact, did have an engine problem that day but the championship table belied Senna's optimism. Prost had 81 points, Hill 58 and Ayrton 53. With just 30 points on the table, it was as good as over.

26 SEPTEMBER 1993

Portuguese GP (Estoril)
McLaren-Honda MP4/8 • Retired, 19 laps, engine

Between Monza and Estoril it was announced that Michael Andretti was returning to race in the US and that Mika Häkkinen would partner Senna in the final three races of the season. Those who'd seen Häkkinen race in Formula Ford, Vauxhall Lotus and F3, before he'd been hamstrung by relatively uncompetitive Lotus F1 cars, knew that this would be interesting. Most of the media were blissfully unaware, however, and so it came as a huge surprise to them when Häkkinen outqualified Senna first time out. As, possibly, it did to Senna. The margin was just 0.05sec, but that wasn't the point.

The effect on Senna could easily be imagined and he spent much time poring over data, trying to establish how Häkkinen had been quicker through the long, final turn on to the front straight. Senna and Ron Dennis were also seen in heated debate in the McLaren motorhome, but that was nothing to do with Häkkinen. Senna was annoyed at some off-the-record remarks from Dennis that had been printed erroneously, and further upset that McLaren wouldn't race a Lamborghini-engined car in the last three races (see page 258). These three races, Ayrton now knew, would very likely be the last in which he would compete against Alain Prost...

A Williams press conference had been called for the Friday afternoon at Estoril and it became obvious why when Prost announced that morning that he wouldn't be staying at Williams for the second year of his contract. The reason was that Frank Williams had finally signed Ayrton Senna.

The timing was unfortunate for Alain. The news totally overshadowed the fact that, on Sunday, he clinched his fourth World Championship, with second place behind Schumacher. Renault had their French World Champion.

The big factor in the way events unfolded was the arrival of Rothmans as title sponsor of Williams for 1994. Rothmans wanted to guarantee the lion's share of TV coverage by having a 'superteam' and, uncomfortable about Senna in a rival car, particularly one sponsored by Marlboro, urged Williams to sign him. Frank didn't really need persuading, having been an ardent Senna admirer since the day he gave Ayrton his first run in an F1 car at Donington

in 1983, back in his F3 days. But there was the 'no Senna' clause in Prost's contract. In the end, Prost was presented with a choice: waive the clause and drive with Senna, or be paid off for the second year of his contract and leave.

Prost was already wearied by political issues throughout 1993 and felt the governing body was singling him out with unwarranted penalties. He announced that he was stopping for good.

"The sport has given me a lot," he said, "but I decided that the game wasn't worth it any more. I have taken too many blows. I will not drive for Williams, nor anyone else. There will not be a comeback." He later did some testing for McLaren but remained true to his word.

Senna, meanwhile, retired from the Portuguese GP after 19 laps with an engine problem, but not before carving aggressively inside a certain Häkkinen to take second place at the end of the back straight on the opening lap. Just to make a point...

24 OCTOBER 1993

Japanese GP (Suzuka)
McLaren-Honda MP4/8 • 1st

With a power braking system and some revised software aimed at curing the MP4/8's high-speed imbalance, Senna very nearly managed to wrest pole position from Prost at Suzuka.

Alain lapped the Williams in 1m 37.154s and Senna got the McLaren round in 1m 37.284s, with Häkkinen commendably close again on 1m 37.326s. Ayrton was adamant that he would have had the pole had he not encountered the Tyrrell of Andrea de Cesaris in the high-speed Esses. "I couldn't be certain he'd seen me," Ayrton said, "so I had to lift momentarily and it cost us pole."

In the race, however, Senna made no mistake and scored a fine win, beating Prost by 11.5sec. His only problem was a near miss while lapping Eddie Irvine, who was having his F1 debut with Jordan and was something of a Suzuka specialist, having spent much of his career racing in Japanese F3000. With the track damp, Irvine, on wets, had been closing on Damon Hill's Williams, on slicks, and they were engaged in a battle. Senna arrived at this point and lapped the Jordan, only to have Irvine briefly repass him and shower Ayrton with dirt as he dropped the odd wheel off the circuit.

"It was very unprofessional," said Senna, incensed. "I think he's a great idiot and wants to learn about how to be a professional driver. I don't think I need to speak to him because it's so obvious."

But Senna did speak to Irvine, which is where things went wrong...

SUZUKA: THE IRVINE AFFAIR

Suzuka had become almost synonymous with Senna and drama: his first world title in '88, acrimony with Prost in '89 and '90, the famous rant of '91. And now, as he went in search of Eddie Irvine after winning the '93 race, Ayrton was about to add a final chapter.

Irvine, long in the body, hadn't had an awfully comfortable afternoon in the Jordan cockpit but had done a good job. Having qualified eighth he'd finished sixth to score a point on his F1 debut. He'd just had a rub-down when Senna arrived to remonstrate about his behaviour when being lapped.

Also in the Jordan room was journalist and Irvine friend/biographer Adam Cooper, who flicked on his recorder when Senna arrived:

Senna: "What the fuck do you think you were doing?"

Irvine: "I was racing."

Senna: "You were racing? Do you know the rule that you're supposed to let the leaders come by when you're a backmarker?"

Irvine: "If you were going fast enough it was no problem."

Senna: "I overtook you! And you went three times off in front of me, at the same place, like a fucking idiot, where there was oil. And you were throwing stones and things in front of me for three laps. When I took you, you realised I was ahead of you. And when I came up behind Hill, because he was on slicks and in difficulties, you should have stayed behind me. You took a very big risk to put me out of the race."

Irvine: "Where did I put you in any danger?"

Senna: "You didn't put me in danger?"

Irvine: "Did I touch you? Did I touch you once?"

Senna: "No, but you were that much from touching me, and I happened to be the fucking leader. [Shouting now] I happened to be the fucking leader!"

Irvine: "A miss is as good as a mile."

Senna: "I tell you something. If you don't behave properly in the next event, you can just rethink what you do. I can guarantee that."

Irvine: "The stewards said, 'No problem. Nothing was wrong'."

Irvine: "Yeah? You wait till Australia, mate. You wait till Australia, and the stewards will talk to you. Then you tell me if they tell you this."

← Senna was annoyed at being held up while Eddie Irvine, a lap behind in his first grand prix, battled with Damon Hill.

sutton-images.com

→ Senna and Irvine
buried the hatchet
at the first test of
'94 in Portugal.

📷 sutton-images.com

Irvine: "Hey, I'm out there to do the best I can for me."

Senna: "This is not correct. You want to do well, I understand, because I've been there. I understand. But it's very unprofessional. If you are a backmarker, because you happen to be lapped..."

Irvine: "But I would have followed you if you'd overtaken Hill!"

Senna: "You should let the leader go by..."

Irvine: "...I understand that fully!..."

Senna: "...and not come and do the things you did. You nearly hit Hill in front of me three times, because I saw, and I could have collected you and hit him as a result, and that's not the way to do that."

Irvine: "But I'm racing! I'm racing! You just happened to..."

Senna: "You're not racing! You're driving like a fucking idiot. You're not a racing driver, you're a fucking idiot."

Irvine: "You talk. You talk. You were in the wrong place at the wrong time."

Senna: "I was in the wrong place at the wrong time?"

Irvine: "Yes. I was battling with Hill."

Senna: "Really? Really? Just tell me one thing. Who is supposed to have the call? You, or the leader of the race who comes through to lap you?"

Irvine: "The leader of the race."

Senna: "So what have you done?"

Irvine: "You, you were too slow, and I had to overtake you to try to get at Hill."

Senna: "Really? How did I lap you if I was too slow?"

Irvine: "Rain. Because on slicks you were quicker than me, on wets you weren't."

Senna: "Really? Really? How did I come and overtake you on wets?"

Irvine: "Huh?"

Senna: "How come I overtook you on wets?"

Irvine: "I can't remember that. I don't actually remember the race."

Senna: "Exactly. Because you are not competent enough to remember. That's how it goes, you know."

Irvine: "Fair enough. Fair enough. That's what you think."

Senna: "You be careful, guy."

Irvine: "I will. I'll watch out for you."

Senna: "You're gonna have problems not with me only, but with lots of other guys and also the FIA."

Irvine: "Yeah?"

Senna: "You bet."

Irvine: "Yeah? Good."

Senna: "Yeah? It's good to know that."

Irvine: "See you out there..."

Senna looked about to turn away to leave, then turned back and punched Irvine in the side of the face before being pulled away by Jordan's Ian Phillips and his own race engineer Giorgio Ascanelli.

The irony was that Irvine had been a great fan of Senna when he started racing Formula Fords in 1985 and had based his helmet design on Senna's.

"I used to think he was the best driver by a long, long way," Irvine said, "but now I think Schumacher is better [Irvine would soon change his mind, see page 277]. Senna's got a serious problem. He thinks he's God's gift."

Australian GP (Adelaide)
McLaren-Honda MP4/8 • 1st

This was an emotionally charged event, the end of an era – Prost's final grand prix and Senna's last race for McLaren. A fabulous qualifying lap meant that Senna started it from his 62nd pole position.

"Before the start of that race," recalls McLaren's

Jo Ramirez, "Ayrton was sitting in the car, in the garage, and he called me over. I thought he wanted me to do his belts. But when I got there he caught hold of my arm and said, 'I really feel very sad to be leaving McLaren.'

"I said, 'You're sad! What about us? We didn't ask you to leave... We wanted you to stay.'

"If we won that race it would make us the most successful grand prix team of all time in terms of wins, with 104, one ahead of Ferrari. I said to Ayrton, 'If you win this race I'll love you forever!'

"He didn't say anything, just crunched my arm. I could see his eyes were wet and I thought, damn, he's getting all emotional and we're just about to start the race...

"But he was an emotional man, even Ron would say that. He was very Latin. Then he went out and drove a simply fantastic race, just like in Japan, and won brilliantly. It was just fantastic. The whole team was ecstatic.

"It was also the last race of the season and we went to the Tina Turner concert at the track. She sang 'Simply the Best' and pulled Ayrton up on stage and said it was for him.

"Then we went to a trattoria in Adelaide. He loved Italian food and he had dinner with the whole team to say goodbye. It was then that I gave him the steering wheel of the car, with a little plaque saying 35 wins with McLaren, 447 points, three World Championships,

↑ **End of an era –
Senna and Prost
share the front row
in Adelaide for
Alain's final grand
prix and Ayrton's
last with McLaren.**

📷 sutton-images.com

→ **Ayrton was
determined to
win that final
confrontation with
Prost. The Adelaide
streets and an
improved MP4/8
allowed him to claim
his 41st and last
victory. Despite the
previous bitterness,
they left smiling.**

📷 sutton-images.com

46 pole positions. And I told him, 'If you can do better than this with another team, go and try! We'll wait for you to come back...'"

18/19 DECEMBER 1993

Elf Master Karting (Paris-Bercy) • Retired

Although they'd stood on the podium together in Adelaide six weeks earlier, the final time Ayrton Senna and Alain Prost faced each other in competition was at the two-day Elf Master Karting extravaganza at the Palais Omnisports in Paris. Organised by former F1 driver Philippe Streiff, wheelchair-bound since his pre-season accident in an AGS at Rio almost five years earlier, the event attracted an excellent turn-out of 14 grand prix drivers.

There was some politics involved, even at this level. The karts – Mike Wilson-built NAP chassis with Italian IAME engines – were decked out in blue with the logos of event sponsor Elf. But Senna, despite having signed with Williams for 1994, remained under contract to McLaren until 31 December, and McLaren's fuel supplier was Shell... The solution was a virgin white kart for Ayrton, decked out with 'Senna' and TAG-Heuer branding.

← Ayrton and Alain met one more time, karting at Bercy, but this event was a relay.
📷 sutton-images.com

The way the event was set up meant that, deliberately one suspects, there was never a proper last head-to-head between Senna and Prost, the competitive part being a relay. To decide the groups, the grand prix drivers were split into Groups A and B and allowed 10 minutes' practice. The fastest in Group A would team up with the fastest in Group B, and then joined by the fastest Elf-backed young driver to form a three-man team. The second quickest men teamed up in the same way, and so on.

The cream of the karting elite – men like Danilo Rossi, Nicola Gianniberti and Mikael Santavirta – were involved in a separate competition, with each and every lap recorded down to the last thousandth of a second and the Speedy (Cables) Trophy awarded for fastest lap. It eventually went to young Frenchman Sébastien Enjolras for a lap in 28.86s, which was almost four tenths quicker than either Senna or Prost would manage. Sadly, Enjolras was killed while testing at Le Mans three and a half years later, a month before his 21st birthday, when his WM Peugeot's rear bodywork became detached.

Fastest of the F1 qualifiers on the opening day was Olivier Panis on 29.46s, with Prost getting down to 29.55s and Senna on 29.56s! Practice had taken

place on Friday and Saturday but Ayrton had only arrived at 7pm on Saturday evening, with girlfriend Adriane Galisteu, and snatched a few practice laps, which included a hefty shunt in the quick right-hander leaving the main arena. Although this was meant to be 'fun', Senna had arranged for a kart to be flown out to Brazil before the event for him to practise on, but he hadn't had the opportunity.

Ayrton's new Williams team-mate, Damon Hill, who had no karting background, could only manage 31.99s and was in trouble with sore ribs from a badly-fitting seat, so bowed out after the Saturday show. Eric van de Poele, Christmas shopping with his wife in Paris, had stopped by the Palais Omnisports to buy a ticket – which properly summed up the unassuming Belgian – and was recruited as Damon's replacement!

On Sunday, Senna got down to 29.39s in qualifying but the arena erupted as Prost did 29.29s. But they were counting without Johnny Herbert, who lapped in 29.25s and milked it for all he was worth.

In the 60-lap relay finale a great battle looked in prospect as Senna homed in on leader Andrea de Cesaris, but then the white kart succumbed to a mechanical problem. The Prost team won the day, sending the French crowd home happy.

SENNA AND FANGIO: A PERSONAL MEMORY

At one of the final grands prix of the 1993 season, memorabilia dealer Peter Ratcliffe approached me and asked if I was going to the Bercy karting event. He'd recently flown to Argentina, where Juan Manuel Fangio, the 82-year-old five-times World Champion, had autographed a number of limited-edition portraits. The great man had signed one specially for Senna, complete with a personal message.

Ratcliffe wondered if I could deliver it to Ayrton.

During a break in proceedings on Saturday evening in Bercy, I went down to the paddock/competitors area and found Senna deep in conversation with the kart and engine guys. It might as well have been 1pm on a Saturday at the Monaco GP. The print was wrapped in brown paper and Ayrton, used to being handed photographs and suchlike on a daily basis, put

it down beside his bag without looking at it.

I knew that Fangio was his favourite driver and so just said, "I can see you're busy, but when you get a moment I think you might like that."

Later that night, in a relaxed, reflective and happy frame of mind with girlfriend Adriane sat beside him, Senna gave the regular F1 press in Bercy a considerable amount of his time. I caught sight of the print, still unopened, in his bag.

The following day, after the Sunday proceedings concluded, I was again down in the competitors' area, chatting and making a few notes. Suddenly I felt a tap on the shoulder. I turned round and was somewhat taken aback to find Senna. Drivers like Ayrton don't normally go seeking out journalists!

"I'm leaving soon," he said, "and just wanted to say how much I appreciate you bringing this for me. Thank you very much. Enjoy your Christmas."

Five months later, the week after Ayrton's Imola accident, *Paris Match* devoted three colour spreads to him. The first was the accident scene, the second was the contents of his briefcase at that final grand prix, and the third was his office in Brazil. There, on the wall, was the print I'd handed him in Paris. Seeing it really brought me up short.

➔ **My copy of the signed Fangio portrait that I delivered to Ayrton at Bercy – I later discovered that he hung it on the wall of his office in Brazil.**
📷 sutton-images.com

RON DENNIS
THE FINAL WORD

T hroughout 1993, Ron Dennis and Senna had their differences. Both, as you will have gathered, were intensely driven, competitive individuals who liked things done their way. Dennis later reflected:

"Even with friends, which is what Ayrton was at that stage more than anything else, not all your emotions are positive. I was upset that his fiscal demands in that last year were quite extreme. We had worked quite closely together to, let's say, encourage the sponsors to raise their game to help meet his demands.

↓ Senna won all three of his world titles in cars overseen by Ron Dennis's team.

📷 sutton-images.com

"That year, and the previous year, Ayrton did take in that his retainer took a lot of the free cash-flow out of the company and we definitely suffered in respect of not having the money to develop the car. Running parallel to that, Williams had lower-paid drivers and could spend on the car, so some of me, maybe unfairly, felt that we'd just spent two years trying to meet Ayrton's demands to the detriment of the team, and then he went and hopped into the car that had all the benefits of that extra investment, for his own ends.

"That was the negative thought process. The positive one was that I fully understood that he raced to win and would always put himself in the best possible position to do so.

"But we actually had a very successful year with the active-ride Ford-powered car and I vividly remember being in Magny Cours, staying in a chateau out in the countryside. We were sat outside talking and within that conversation it was very clear to me that in some ways he regretted leaving.

"He had mixed emotions. I could construct the words and nobody would be able to challenge their authenticity but, most definitely, the message was, 'I don't feel at all comfortable and I'll be back.' As I say, I don't remember the exact words.

"Ayrton saw manufacturer support for a team as a key ingredient and later on, when we had the support of Peugeot for '94, he said: 'If you had shared those negotiations with me, I wouldn't have gone.'

"Putting aside how competitive or not that '94 car turned out to be, the fact was that works factory support for McLaren would have been a key ingredient in him staying.

"I never felt aggression towards him at that point, nor later. It would be easy to talk about his post-McLaren period in a negative way but once he'd chosen to drive for another team, that's for them to talk about, not me..."

When Senna climbed out of the car having won McLaren's Ferrari-eclipsing 104th victory, Dennis met him in parc fermé, put an arm around him and said, "It's not too late..." But it was. Ayrton had given his word and his signature to Frank Williams.

"Not just at that race," Dennis adds, "but at the

two prior to that, he really changed his mind and both the night before and the night after that Adelaide race, we talked about whether we should try and extract him from his contractual obligations at Williams, to stay at McLaren. He had regained a tremendous amount of confidence in our ability to provide him with a winning car. What was going on was a very mechanised assessment of whether or not he'd done the right thing: should he stay or should he go?

"One thing I considered to be a weakness in my approach is my aversion to communicating anything on telephones other than short, brief, factual things. I always felt that a telephone is a very unemotional tool but that is one thing that Frank was very polished at – long telephone conversations. Frank was extremely persuasive about convincing Ayrton to join Williams.

"I think that by the time that post-Adelaide evening had finished, neither of us was particularly lucid and it had lapsed into a bit of emotion, but he was an honourable guy and he had a commitment to Williams. While he definitely reviewed it, I don't think that in the cold light of day there was any set of circumstances

in which he would renege on his word – because his word was more important than anything he had signed, and that was it. The fact that he had done such an exceptional job in the closing races of the season made it hard to get upset."

Dennis says, too, that it wasn't true that Senna went to Williams for a lot less money: "I know a lot about that now. I didn't at the time. That wasn't true, but I cannot elaborate."

↑ **Ron Dennis:**
"It's not too late to
change your mind..."
But it was.

📷 sutton-images.com

"I don't think that in the cold light of day there was any set of circumstances in which he would renege on his word – because his word was more important than anything..."

1994

TRUE TRAGEDY

Ten years after Ayrton Senna drove a Formula 1 car for the first time, a Williams FW08 at Donington in 1983, he finally put his signature to a Williams Formula 1 contract.

Senna had been trying to join Frank's team for more than a year, since his much-publicised 1992 offer – which wasn't wholly serious – to drive for nothing. Williams had been the F1 pacesetters since mid-1991 and would probably have beaten Senna and McLaren-Honda to that year's championship had the FW14 not suffered early-season unreliability.

But, in 1992, with the superb FW14B the only car to benefit from computer-controlled active ride, which optimised the aerodynamics, Williams and Nigel Mansell had cleaned up. Mansell had done his best to play down his car advantage, sometimes to the annoyance of the team, but nobody was fooled.

Alain Prost, sacked by Ferrari at the end of 1991 for being overly critical of the car and team, had had an enforced sabbatical year in 1992 but early on had signed a two-year deal with Williams for 1993. One point Prost had insisted upon in that contract was a 'no Senna' clause, and he had enough bargaining power to enforce it because he had the backing of Williams' engine supplier, Renault, who desperately wanted a French World Champion. Frank had to be careful because, with Honda withdrawing from F1, McLaren was on the hunt for an engine. Ron Dennis

◄ **Senna started his final season with more on his mind than anticipated...**

📷 sutton-images.com

wanted a Renault and, in terms of pinching Frank's engine suppliers, he had 'previous'...

Knowing that he had Prost in the bag, Williams was in the driving seat when it came to negotiations to extend Mansell's contract and, as the provider of the best car on the grid, Frank held all the cards.

Mansell, as the new World Champion, was unimpressed by what Frank had to offer, and defected to the Indycar World Series in the USA for 1993, taking the vacant seat that Michael Andretti freed up with his move to McLaren. That, in turn, opened up a golden opportunity for Williams test driver Damon Hill to partner Prost in Frank's FW15, by far the best car on the grid in '93.

Hill grabbed the opportunity and won three races as Prost cantered to his fourth World Championship title. But the landscape at Williams was changing. Rothmans had been signed as new title sponsor and the cigarette company wanted to guarantee the lion's share of the TV coverage with a 'superteam'.

Rothmans was wary of Senna in a McLaren, backed by rival brand Marlboro. The company urged Williams to sign Ayrton and Frank hardly needed his arm to be twisted. Frank had always been a huge fan of Senna and, in a quiet moment, would probably admit that failing to nail down Ayrton in 1983, after

that first F1 test, was one of his biggest mistakes in his entire career.

It was sad for Alain that in Portugal, the very race at which he clinched his fourth title, he was presented with a fait accompli: either drop the 'no Senna' clause and drive with Ayrton once again, or have the second year of the contract paid out and retire. Alain chose the latter.

In light of the Williams domination of the previous two seasons, nobody expected to see any problems for Senna when he arrived at the team. But there had been pressure from the sport's governing body to do away with much of the technical gizmology – active suspension, traction and launch control, power braking – that was threatening to reduce too far the importance of the driver in the overall performance equation. Senna had been fully behind those principles because he knew that he was the best driver and anything that increased the significance of the driver was beneficial to him. And so, ironically, he joined Williams just as much of the technology behind the team's superiority was outlawed.

Even so, the team had ace designer Adrian Newey working with Patrick Head, as well as plentiful resources and the Renault V10 engine. Senna still went into the 1994 season a strong favourite. But as

→ **Frank Williams was thrilled finally to have Ayrton in his car.**

🖭 sutton-images.com

→ **Senna's Williams race engineer was David Brown, who had previously worked with both Mansell and Prost.**

🖭 sutton-images.com

soon as he drove the new Williams FW16 in pre-season testing, he knew that he had a job on his hands. Worse, when the Benetton B194 appeared, late, he could see that Michael Schumacher was going to be a serious threat.

"Having active suspension banned was a big setback to our 1994 programme," says Newey in Maurice Hamilton's book *Williams*. "I have to admit that in designing the '94 car I underestimated how important it was going to be to get a very broad ride-height map again. I think, having been away from passive cars for longer than anyone else, I disadvantaged us slightly. So when the FW16 first came out it was too ride-height sensitive, which made it very tricky to drive, even for someone of Ayrton's huge talent. It was very difficult to handle over a race distance.

"We were hugely privileged to have Ayrton driving the car. He was a fantastic guy. But we were to have a disastrous start to the '94 season. We took the car to Nogaro in France for a test with Damon. Nogaro is quite bumpy and this was the first time I'd been able to go out and watch the car. It just looked horrific.

"It was clear that we needed some fairly major surgery. I came to the conclusion that the sidepods were too long. If you're tempted to run the front low, which you always want to do with a racing car, it would stall the whole underside aerodynamics of the car and become inconsistent. So we started working on much shorter sidepods, which came later."

27 MARCH 1994

Brazilian GP (Interlagos)
Williams-Renault FW16 • Retired, 55 laps, spin

Interlagos – literally, between lakes – has always been a bumpy circuit and Senna found the FW16 a handful, but it didn't stop him taking his 63rd career pole in his first drive for Williams. He lapped in 1m 15.962s versus Schumacher's front-row time of 1m 16.290s. A slightly bemused Hill was fourth on 1m 17.554s, a second and a half away.

As well as the technology bans, the 1994 season also saw, despite safety fears, the reintroduction of refuelling, adding a strategic element that had been missing for over 10 years.

Senna converted his pole position and led the first 20 laps but he couldn't shake Schumacher, the Benetton within a second of the Williams as they made their first pit stops together, on lap 21. Michael got back out first

and immediately started to pull away. By the time of their second stops, with around 25 laps to go, Schumacher led by 7sec.

After those stops the gap stabilised and Senna even started to make a slight impression before he dropped the Williams, on lap 56, at the final left-hander out on to the main straight. The car spun broadside, its engine dead. He was out and huge swathes of the fervent home crowd started heading for the exits.

17 APRIL 1994

Pacific GP (Aida)
Williams-Renault FW16 • Retired, 0 laps, accident

In what would be F1's one and only visit to the TI Circuit at Aida in Japan, Senna again took pole position (1m 10.218s) to overcome the shortcomings of the FW16 and pip Schumacher's Benetton (1m 10.440s), while this time Hill (1m 10.771s) was closer.

Already, though, there were suspicions being voiced throughout the paddock about how effectively the FIA could police F1's technology ban. Max Mosley was adamant that they could and that there would be draconian penalties for anyone found to be using illegal technology.

The tension increased when an Italian journalist alleged that Ferrari driver Nicola Larini had, absent-mindedly one presumed, talked about "the traction control". And, watching out on circuit, FIA technical director Charlie Whiting had heard a fluttering engine note from the Ferrari.

The FIA later cleared Ferrari, saying that the cause of Whiting's observation had been driver-controlled variable engine maps that weren't influenced in any way by the behaviour of the rear wheels and hence didn't constitute traction control. A sceptical Patrick Head, however, opined that traction control wasn't precisely defined within the regulations and that, had it been Williams under scrutiny, the team would have been on the way home...

Senna, however, was far more concerned with suspicions that Benetton was using the banned technology.

Ayrton's humour wasn't improved when he was collected at the first corner by Mika Häkkinen's McLaren-Peugeot and then T-boned by Larini for good measure. In the Williams pit, team manager Ian Harrison sensed the

← **Williams technical director**
Patrick Head with Senna in Aida.
sutton-images.com

BRAZIL: A PERSONAL RECOLLECTION

On lap 35 of the Brazilian GP, Martin Brundle's McLaren-Peugeot threw a flywheel on the back straight and Martin backed off. Behind him, Eric Bernard in the Ligier was caught by surprise and went left to go round the slowing McLaren. But, behind the Ligier, Eddie Irvine's Jordan was battling with Jos Verstappen's Benetton, which was easing up on his left-hand side. Irvine, looking to get a tow from Bernard's Ligier, which they were about to lap, was unsighted and hadn't seen Brundle slow. When Bernard lifted slightly before trying to negotiate Brundle, Irvine was faced with going into the back of the Frenchman or swerving round him. But, when he swerved, he collected Verstappen, launching the Dutchman into a series of barrel rolls as he crashed out, leaving Brundle with a cracked helmet on the way through.

Although all concerned were happy to accept that it had been a racing incident, the stewards laid blame at Irvine's door, fined him $10,000 and banned him from the forthcoming Pacific GP as Aida (that would be increased to a three-race ban when Jordan lost a subsequent appeal).

As *Autosport*'s F1 editor at the time, I was writing the story on the flight home that evening when Irvine came and plonked himself temporarily on the adjoining seat and started to read over my shoulder.

We got talking and he couldn't actually have cared less about what had just happened to him. All he could talk about was what he'd seen when Schumacher and Senna lapped him earlier in the race. This was the same Irvine who had said, after the contretemps with Senna at Suzuka a few short months earlier, that he'd lost respect for Senna and thought Schumacher was better.

"When they went past me," Irvine said, "that Benetton was like a magic carpet. Michael could put it exactly where he wanted. But the Williams was bouncing all over the road. It was all over the place. How Ayrton was still anywhere near Schumacher I will never, ever know."

It was a sentiment later echoed by Hill, who finished a lapped second in the sister FW16: "I was astounded that he had been able to do that with a car which, if it was anything like mine, simply wasn't handling."

And, of the way Senna was driving, Damon Hill added: "At one stage they were about to lap me. Michael came through and I thought I had better get out of Ayrton's way. But, almost before I'd taken the decision, he dived past me and nearly went off. He was heading towards the grass and just managed to slither through."

I couldn't help but recall Irvine's remarks five weeks later...

⬇ **Despite taking pole, Senna couldn't hold off Schumacher's Benetton in the season-opener at Interlagos.**
📷 sutton-images.com

potential for trouble and set off sharpish for Turn 1 in case anything kicked off when Senna climbed out of his car. Senna, of course, was racing under a suspended ban after the shenanigans with Irvine at Suzuka.

Harrison found Ayrton calmly walking back to the pits and, together, they watched the first few laps from the infield section. Senna was convinced that there were two very different Benettons out there – Schumacher's and Jos Verstappen's. Verstappen was an F1 rookie but rated, and Michael had outqualified him by two full seconds in the opening two races.

Schumacher blew all opposition into the weeds in Aida, lapping everyone bar Gerhard Berger's Ferrari, which finished 75sec adrift. Michael now had 20 points on the board and Ayrton had yet to trouble the scorers. With nobody else apparently able to get remotely near the Benetton and just a four-point margin between first and second places, that was going to take some pegging back, even if Williams could improve the FW16. Imola would be crucial.

← **Ayrton and Nicola Larini tangling in Aida.**
📷 sutton-images.com

1 MAY 1994

San Marino GP (Imola)
Williams-Renault FW16 • 5 laps, fatal accident

One of the blackest events in motor racing history got off to an ominous start on Friday when Brazilian Rubens Barrichello crashed his Jordan violently at the Varianta Bassa chicane on his first flying lap of qualifying.

It looked bad, but Barrichello, an F1 rookie for whom Senna was a boyhood idol, amazingly escaped with relatively minor injuries to his nose and mouth. At that stage, there was room for levity. Gary Anderson, now a respected technical analyst, was Jordan's chief engineer that day. After visiting Rubens, which Senna also did, Anderson said: "He was in good spirits when he came round and said he didn't know what had happened, but that he'd been quick! I told him, 'Yeah, we could see that. You'd previously gone through at 130mph and on that lap you were doing 138mph! You might like to have tried 134mph first...'"

Rubens would miss the race, but he would be back for Monaco. Poor Roland Ratzenberger, however, wouldn't. Eighteen minutes into Saturday's final qualifying session the 31-year-old Austrian's Simtek left the road at the near-200mph Villeneuve kink on the approach to the tight Tosa corner, a damaged front wing following earlier contact with a kerb the suspected cause. The car slammed into the concrete retaining wall. Ratzenberger suffered a broken neck and was pronounced dead at the Maggiore hospital in Bologna an hour later.

The accident affected Senna badly. He had gone to the scene of Martin Donnelly's career-ending accident at Jerez in 1990, stopped to attend Erik Comas at Spa two years later and, having witnessed Ratzenberger's plight on a Williams monitor, commandeered an official car to go to the scene, for which he was later admonished, much to his great disgust, as physio Josef Leberer explains in this book (see page 298).

In his book *Life at the Limit*, F1's chief medical officer, eminent neurosurgeon and close friend of Ayrton, the late Sid Watkins, said: "Senna then went to the medical centre area, where he had been debarred (properly) from entering. But he jumped over the fence at the rear to get to the door of the unit. I took him round to the circuit side of the area and answered his questions with complete honesty. As we talked, Charlie Moody, the team manager of Simtek, arrived. I then had to tell him the bad news that Ratzenberger was beyond medical help. It was tough for me to deal with two such devastated people at the same time, and remain cool and unemotional.

↑ **Roland Ratzenberger in the Simtek at Imola.**
📷 sutton-images.com

← **Rubens Barrichello had a huge crash at Imola in his Jordan during practice. Afterwards Rubens discusses with Ayrton his fortunate escape.**
📷 Getty Images
📷 sutton-images.com

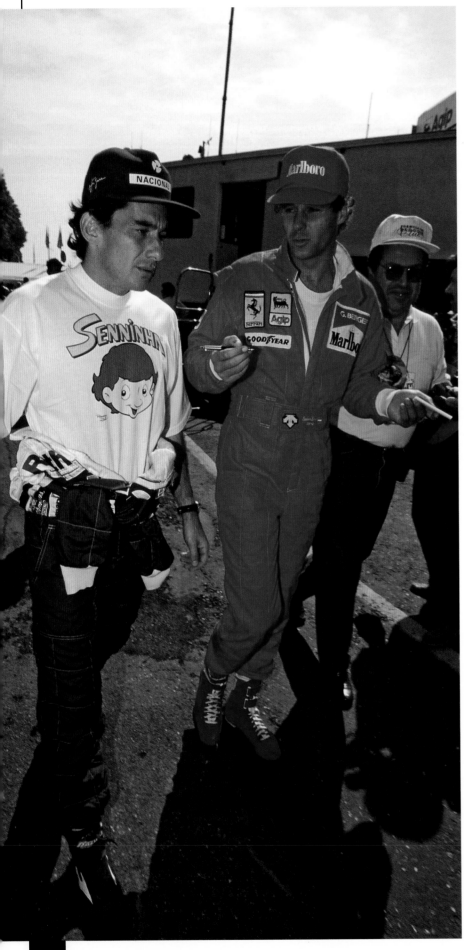

"Ayrton broke down and cried on my shoulder. After all, why shouldn't he? We'd been close friends for many years, we'd fished together, we'd stayed with each other's families – he was a part of my family – we had talked and worried together over many things common to us both in racing and in life."

Watkins didn't think that Senna was in the right frame of mind to race, told him he'd achieved all there was to achieve, and asked him to consider packing it all in. They could then spend more time fishing, he said. Senna told him he had no choice: he had to race.

That evening on the phone to girlfriend Adriane Galisteu, Senna's angst was again all too clear and he broke down once again. But after dinner with Leberer, Willy Dungl and friend Antonio Braga, Senna called Adriane back to say that he was all right and he was going to race.

As well as coping with his upset over Ratzenberger, Senna had also argued with his younger brother Leonardo over his girlfriend, to whom the family felt cool.

On Sunday morning he was pensive. Ironically he'd spoken to his closest friend among the drivers, Gerhard Berger, his McLaren team-mate of three years, and along with Niki Lauda, a consultant to Ferrari at the time, they had determined to re-form the Grand Prix Drivers' Association (GPDA) and have a representative voice on safety matters. Further discussions were to be had at the next race in Monaco.

For the moment, though, Senna had serious concerns about another issue – the introduction of a Safety Car to neutralise a race, with F1 cars circulating slowly behind it whenever there was an accident or debris on the circuit.

Senna believed that running slowly behind what was initially a standard road car caused tyre temperatures and pressures to drop to the point where they were dangerous when racing resumed, due to the cars running lower and bottoming out. But, aware that he already had issues with the organisers over the previous day's events, Ayrton asked Berger to raise the matter in the drivers' briefing on Sunday morning – which Gerhard did.

Berger was unique among Senna's F1 team-mates – the others were Johnny Cecotto, Elio de Angelis, Johnny Dumfries, Satoru Nakajima, Alain Prost and Damon Hill – in having struck up a genuine friendship with him, and Gerhard found Ayrton a warm and very human individual. The other thing Berger realised very early on was that he wasn't going to beat Senna and thereafter, to an extent, prioritised the accumulation of dollars rather than championships.

Berger said his piece in the drivers' briefing. Senna

added a few words. Watkins, meanwhile, had noticed that when a minute's silence in respect to Ratzenberger was observed, Senna again had tears rolling down his cheeks, though he did his best to hide them.

Much has been written about Senna's state of mind and willingness or otherwise to race that day, but there can be no denying that once he climbed into the car for the race morning warm-up, his only focus was to beat Schumacher.

Senna took his third successive pole position for Williams at Imola with a lap in 1m 21.548s to Schumacher's 1m 21.885s. Hill, fourth, was just over half a second slower than Senna in qualifying and was reasonably satisfied with that, but was then absolutely stunned by Ayrton's time in the Sunday morning warm-up.

"It was unbelievable," recalls Damon. "It was almost a second quicker than mine. I thought, 'Whoah, hang on a minute, what's he up to now?' When I'd got to within a few tenths of him I was thinking I was in with a shout. And then he goes, 'Now I'm really pissed off'... and, bang, just does that."

Josef Leberer observed that Senna was the only driver

he has come across who could turn emotion and anger into a great lap time rather than make a mistake. And, yes, there may be a degree of irony in that...

In the second Benetton at Imola was Finnish driver JJ Lehto, who'd fractured his neck in a pre-season testing accident and been replaced by Jos Verstappen while recuperating. In qualifying Lehto was closer to Schumacher, sixth quickest, but was still 0.83sec adrift.

Still concerned about the legality of Schumacher's Benetton, Williams despatched its commercial boss, Richard West, to the roof of the pits with a video camera to record whether or not Schumacher's rear tyres left black lines at the start – as it should without launch control.

The second Benetton certainly didn't leave black lines – but that was because it didn't move at all. Lehto stalled on the grid and was hit hard by Pedro Lamy's Lotus, the young Portuguese driver unsighted from the 11th row. Lamy's right front wheel was torn off and breached the debris fencing, injuring spectators, one seriously, and a policeman. Out came the Safety Car.

This was Senna's worst fear. Not only was the Safety Car out, but it was out right at the start when

← ↑ **Senna voiced his Safety Car fears to Gerhard Berger on race morning.**

📷 sutton-images.com

cars were heavy with fuel and would run at their lowest. That, in conjunction with falling tyre pressures, was potentially problematic.

On lap 5 of the 58, just before the Safety Car pulled off, Senna could be seen pulling alongside and gesticulating for it to speed up. When the Safety Car lights went out, Senna and Schumacher led the field away on lap 6, the first lap at racing speed since the initial start.

Data shows that Senna took Tamburello at 190mph on that lap and footage from Schumacher's Benetton shows that he had a big oversteer moment but caught the car.

"I saw that the car was touching the track at the back quite a lot on the lap before the accident," Schumacher reported. "It was very nervous in that corner, and he nearly lost it. Then, next time through, he did lose it. The car just touched the track with the rear skids, went a bit sideways and then he just lost it."

Adrian Newey elaborated: "Ayrton was hugely determined to win. He was absolutely positive that Schumacher's car was running traction control. So, you had this situation where he was hugely upset by Roland's accident, he knew our car was difficult to drive and he was convinced that Schumacher's team was cheating.

"I don't think we'll ever know what happened. The popular belief was that the car understeered off the road. It didn't; it oversteered off the road. That is clear from the data accumulated afterwards and from the onboard camera on Schumacher's car. You can see the rear of Ayrton's car step out, and then it goes off to the right.

"Looking through what we could find from what was left of the data recorder, Ayrton went from half throttle at the same time as the steering torque reduced, but didn't go to zero. That would be consistent with the rear stepping out: in other words, lift off the throttle and reduce your steering torque. After that he comes off the throttle and gets hard on the brake. The steering torque falls further. I think at that point Ayrton realised he wasn't going to hold it and went into minimising the accident.

"So it doesn't appear to be consistent with a steering column failure. There's no doubt the steering column broke, and there's no doubt it had fatigue marks in it. It was badly designed. But I don't believe that it caused that accident."

Data showed that on that final, fateful lap, Senna had attempted to take Tamburello at 193mph. The Williams failed to negotiate the corner and ploughed into the concrete retaining wall 0.9sec after the loss of control, by which time Senna had gone on the brakes and reduced the impact speed to 135mph.

The car struck at roughly 20 degrees, ripping the right front wheel back into the cockpit area and probably causing the head injury that claimed the life of maybe the greatest racing driver who ever lived.

Sid Watkins didn't have premonitions but, as the cars were released after the five slow laps behind the Safety Car, he'd turned to Mario Casoni, the driver of the medical car, and said: "There's going to be a fucking awful accident any minute."

The red flags to stop the race were out moments later and, somehow, Watkins knew it was Senna.

Ayrton was slumped in the car and, when Watkins arrived, the doctor from the first intervention car was on the scene. For the third time in as many days, Watkins found himself cutting a chin strap to remove a crash helmet. An airway was put into Senna's mouth but he was deeply unconscious. He had a pulse but when Watkins lifted his eyelids he could tell from Senna's pupils that he had suffered an unsurvivable injury.

To everyone watching monitors in the pits, it was obvious that the accident was very serious, but the drivers, in their cars preparing for a restart, didn't know what the situation was.

"The accident scene was being shown on the big television screens," recalls McLaren's Martin Whitmarsh. "I thought, right, we don't want our drivers seeing this, so let's get them to the motorhome with the televisions switched off. So I got Mika [Häkkinen] and Martin [Brundle] out of their cars and told them we were going to the motorhome.

"Mika didn't say much in those days but Martin, on the way, asked how bad it was. I remember saying to him, 'It's big, but I think he'll be OK, I saw him move.' When I look back on it, I wasn't trying to bullshit him. It was just that it was all too big. I couldn't believe what I'd just witnessed... because Ayrton really was God-like. It was almost too big a story, too big a world event, to believe it had just happened in front of me."

One man who did know exactly what had happened was Frenchman Erik Comas, who, after his heavy accident at Spa two years earlier, was eternally grateful to Senna for stopping and running back to help him while he was unconscious. At Imola Comas had pitted at the end of the opening lap for attention to damage sustained at the first corner. He'd been waiting at the end of the pitlane for the race to restart and was mistakenly waved out by a marshal after the red flags. He was forced to pull up right alongside the accident scene when he found the medical helicopter on the track. Comas had no stomach for a restart.

Senna was transferred in the medical helicopter to the same Maggiore hospital that had received Ratzenberger the day before, under the care of the hospital's intensive care anaesthetist, Giovanni Gordini.

The centre of paddock operations at any grand prix is Bernie Ecclestone's big grey 'bus' with its darkened windows, for years simply known as 'the Kremlin'. Inside, in the immediate aftermath of the accident, Ecclestone had been joined by Senna's brother, Leonardo, and FIA press delegate Martin Whitaker. Ecclestone wanted to know what the position was and Whitaker was in touch with Watkins via a walkie-talkie.

In something of a nightmarish misunderstanding caused by the interference that commonly occurs with hand-held radios, Whitaker thought Watkins had said from the accident scene 'he's dead', whereas, in fact, the medical chief had said, 'it's his head'.

Ecclestone had already gone into crisis management mode and saw little point in hiding the truth from Senna's brother who, understandably enough, was immediately distraught. Ecclestone put a call through to Williams for Josef Leberer to come and look after Leonardo and got on with managing the situation.

In terms of brain function Senna was indeed dead as of 2.18pm on that awful Sunday but cardiac death didn't occur until 6.40pm that evening. The misunderstanding quickly became clear but as far as Leonardo was concerned, Ecclestone was callously going ahead with a restart even though his brother was dead.

In fact, hard as it may be to accept when looked back upon now, that's what had always happened. In the sixties and seventies races weren't even halted as drivers burned to death in crashed cars, not that such a thing should be condoned by civilised society. And drivers were rarely pronounced dead at a racing circuit rather than a hospital, especially in countries with legal structures such as Italy's.

It had been 12 years since the previous fatality in a grand prix, when, at the start of the 1982 Canadian GP, Riccardo Paletti ploughed unsighted into the back of Didier Pironi's stalled pole-position Ferrari, an accident very similar to the one that had befallen Lamy and Lehto at Imola.

Logic should tell you that motor racing is dangerous – all entry tickets used to say as much – and that things can, and do, go wrong. But, in Italy at any rate, there was a need to establish blame and it was far from unprecedented. In 1961, German Ferrari driver Wolfgang von Trips was killed at Monza after a collision with Jim Clark in an accident that also resulted in the death of 14

The late Charlie Moody, Simtek's team manager, was devastated by Roland Ratzenberger's accident. He had also been the first man to strap Senna into a Williams, 11 years earlier.
sutton-images.com

spectators. Clark and his Lotus entrant Colin Chapman were initially deemed responsible before being cleared.

In 1970, Chapman was again concerned about manslaughter or culpable homicide charges after Lotus driver and World Champion elect Jochen Rindt died in a qualifying accident when it was suspected that a brake shaft snapped on the 180mph approach to Parabolica. At the following year's Italian GP the Lotus cars were entered under a different name.

Trying to establish the cause of Senna's accident became a cause célèbre and one of the most unpalatable aspects was the besmirching of the names of respectable men, and organisations, of great capability and integrity – men such as Frank Williams, his technical director Patrick Head and designer Adrian Newey. Two years after the tragedy, Italian state prosecutor Maurizio Passarini charged all three with what effectively amounted to culpable homicide, along with Roland Bruynseraede (FIA race director), Giorgio Poggi (Imola circuit director) and Federico Bendinelli (boss of Sagis, the company that ran the track).

The Simtek team was absolved of any blame in the Ratzenberger accident because the front wing was believed to have been damaged on a kerb before Ratzenberger crashed.

⬇ **Bernie Ecclestone tells Damon Hill what he knows.**

📷 sutton-images.com

That didn't prevent Simtek's Charlie Moody, one of the F1 paddock's many good guys, feeling utterly desolate and, on the Saturday evening, going down to Williams to talk to Adrian Newey, with whom he'd previously worked at Leyton House. Ian Harrison, Moody's opposite number at Williams, told journalist Matt James, "I just think he needed someone to talk to. I remember going back to our garage afterwards and thinking, 'Christ, what on earth must this poor bloke be going through?'" Not 24 hours later Harrison would know only too well. But it would have been little help to Moody who, amazingly, was also the man who first strapped Ayrton Senna into a Williams, when he tested at Donington in July 1983.

There were a number of highly emotive issues involved in Senna's accident. Many F1 drivers at the time, as well as Senna's legions of worldwide fans couldn't, and didn't want to, believe that he could have made a mistake at a corner that so many times, in racing parlance, had been described as 'easy flat' – needing no lift of the throttle in other words.

"You will only crash there if you have a technical problem," said Michele Alboreto, while giving evidence for the prosection at the 'Senna trial'. He had personal experience from three years earlier, having written off the ill-starred Footwork-Porsche at the same corner in a 185mph testing shunt when the front wing mount broke. The wing went under the car and Alboreto lost the steering, escaping with two cracked ribs and 15 stitches in his right leg. Racing drivers being what they are, he later joked about it, claiming that as the Italian for stitch was *punti* – the same word as points – he had 15 of them and was therefore second in the championship! If that seems like questionable humour, you need to know the total hopelessness of the Footwork-Porsche in order to properly appreciate it...

Gerhard Berger also had a front wing problem at Tamburello in 1989 that resulted in an appalling-looking crash that caused his Ferrari to burst into flames. In view of subsequent events that accident and its aftermath were deeply ironic.

"I turned into Tamburello and immediately realised something wasn't right," Berger says. "I saw the right front wheel go light and immediately thought I had a left rear suspension failure or a puncture on the left rear. I even looked quickly in the mirror but couldn't see. I didn't realise the front wing was broken. But the car didn't turn. Then I saw the wall coming and remembered that I still had full fuel and had time to think that at this speed, at this angle, with full fuel, it wasn't going to be funny...

"It just shows how much goes through the brain in such a short period, because from the turn-in point to the wall is no more than a couple of seconds. But it was like a slow-motion film. I have to say I had a lot of heavy,

heavy pain and honestly thought that my body was completely burned. Everything was covered in fuel that, at that time, was quite aggressive, and it was difficult to know what was burned and what was just very hot. But considering the size of the accident, the effect on me was quite minimal.

"Next day, Ayrton called me and asked how I was. I said I was OK and he asked me what had happened. I said I didn't know exactly but, one thing is sure, this bloody wall there, one day somebody is going to die in it because it's much too close to the race track. It's so fast there and if you have a technical failure there, you are dead.

"A couple of weeks later, Ayrton and myself walked to the place where I had the accident to see how to move the wall. We both looked over it and said, well, there's this river... The land fell down it and there was nothing really that you could do. We didn't think about putting a chicane there and we walked back thinking well, there's not a lot we can do, it is what it is. Exactly where we looked is the place where he died."

Berger's last memory of his friend is the smile Senna gave him on the grid from the cockpit of his Williams when Gerhard – a Ferrari driver in Italy – received the loudest cheer from the crowd when his name was announced.

One thing that might have saved Senna's life was the rather simple expedient of deploying rows of tyres in front of the wall. During the 2001 Belgian GP Senna's compatriot Luciano Burti survived an impact very similar to Senna's when he went into tyres at high speed after tangling with Eddie Irvine.

At the time, however, there were doubts about tyres because of their propensity to flip cars, something Senna himself had experienced when he went off in Mexico three years earlier. Even if a car didn't flip, it was likely to embed itself in the tyres and suffer the kind of deceleration that would almost certainly be fatal at a corner as quick as Tamburello. Many felt that it was better for an impact to be a glancing blow to a concrete wall, as at American speedways such as Indianapolis, with the energy dissipated as the car carried on down the circuit.

⬆ **Adrian Newey:**
"I don't think we'll ever
know what happened."
📷 sutton-images.com

THE SENNA TRIAL

The Senna trial in Italy began in February 1997, almost three years after the accident, and a verdict wasn't pronounced until the week before Christmas.

The stakes were potentially high for all concerned and, inevitably, the accused, in defending themselves, could hardly avoid raising causal arguments that had implications for their co-accused, thereby increasing tensions in what were emotive, regrettable and ultimately pointless proceedings. The Senna family had legal representation but, it is said, they were more interested in simply trying to establish what had happened than in apportioning blame.

Frank Williams, Patrick Head and Adrian Newey, not to mention the company and team itself, faced irreparable damage to their reputations, while a guilty verdict against the circuit or the governing body quite literally risked the future of motor racing in Italy. If you couldn't operate a racing team in Italy without potentially facing personal and financially ruinous legal charges, who was going to go there in future?

There were widespread cover-up accusations. Had Senna's head injury been caused by part of the suspension penetrating his crash helmet or, in fact, had the helmet come into direct contact with the wall itself? There was an important difference. If it was the latter, then the circuit and organisers might have had a case to answer over inappropriate safety arrangements – even if the drivers themselves had expressed their satisfaction following a prior circuit safety inspection.

Your might expect that forensic examination could have taken place. An autopsy was carried out on Senna on the Tuesday after the accident, before his body was released, flown to Paris by the Italian military and thence onward to Sao Paulo aboard Varig 723, where millions of his grieving countryman were in three days of national mourning and awaiting their hero's burial.

F1 medic Sid Watkins, describing his actions after Ayrton had been helicoptered away from the accident scene, said in his book, "I collected Senna's helmet. His gloves, which I had removed, and my own, were lost. I went to the medical centre to see the staff and to drop off Ayrton's helmet for safe keeping."

← Three years after the accident Frank Williams pays his respects at the Senna memorial at Tamburello.

sutton-images.com

Watkins then had to remain at the track until the end of the restarted race, before heading to the Maggiore hospital. He stated in his book, published in 1996, "I asked about Senna's helmet before I left and was told that the Italian police had confiscated it. They still have it as I write, nearly two years later." From photographs, the helmet had obvious frontal damage, but whether it was damage commensurate with penetration by a jagged suspension component is debatable.

The most controversial aspect of the trial, however, surrounded the steering column, which was pictured broken, with the steering wheel still attached, by the side of Senna's wrecked chassis. The question became: was the broken column cause or effect?

It was complicated by the fact that Senna, who liked to use a large steering wheel and didn't like its positioning in the cockpit, had requested a modification. The column, when examined, had shown evidence of metal fatigue. The modification, it emerged, had been carried out pre-season, was fitted to both FW16s and caused no problems in the opening two grands prix.

Then there was the missing one and a half seconds of in-car footage from Senna's car. In those days the in-car pictures were beamed from competing cars to a helicopter and from there back down to Ecclestone's FOCA's TV control centre, where a director selected three or four to pass on to the host broadcaster to incorporate in their coverage.

At the time of Senna's accident, TV viewers were seeing pictures from Schumacher's Benetton when the Williams, small in the picture, left the road. However over four and a half minutes of footage from Senna's camera had been continuously transmitted

➔ This was typical
of so many banners
in Monte Carlo, two
weeks post-Imola.

📷 sutton-images.com

to the helicopter. When Passarini's investigation requested footage from the car, it ended just 1.4sec before the car hit the wall.

Two principal reasons were given for the cessation. Senna's car, leading, was showing nothing but empty track ahead, and there was also deteriorating picture quality. Many, including Passarini, found the coincidence too much and cast doubt on whether Ecclestone and FOCA was telling the truth, whereupon Bernie threatened to sue for defamation.

Some speculated that the missing footage would have shown that the steering column broke, but, even if it had, this was unlikely given the angle of the camera over Senna's left shoulder. More likely, the footage may have shown whether the helmet itself came into contact with the wall. The answer to that, as far as the circuit and organisers were concerned, might have been considered undesirable.

The pictures that were finally released, following persistence from TV Globo journalist Roberto Cabrini, proved little, even in enhanced form. But that didn't prevent all sorts of further speculation. Some said that Senna appeared to look down just before he left the road, indicating that he was aware of a problem. But it was just as likely that this was the inevitable helmet movement that occurs when driving a racing car over Tamburello's surface ripples at close to 200mph.

Alboreto, backed up by video analysts, believed that the column deflection shown in the video was abnormally high. But a simulation and evidence from David Coulthard, Williams test driver at the time and the man who was drafted into the race team after the accident, contradicted that.

By November 1997, prosecutor

Passarini had dropped charges against Frank Williams himself, the FIA's Bruynseraede and circuit men Bendinelli and Poggi, but pressed for the charges against Head and Newey to be proven.

The week before Christmas, Judge Antonio Costanzo cleared all six but when he finally published his report six months later, the accident was attributed to breakage of the modified steering column. How this conclusion had been reached wasn't clear.

That created two appeals. Prosecutor Passarini believed that those responsible should be held to account. Williams appealed the actual findings. Passarini's 1999 appeal, five years after the accident, was dismissed on the grounds of no further evidence. Williams, meanwhile, succeeded in having Costanzo's steering column verdict overturned.

So, what did happen? Did Senna simply lose it? Did he run over some debris that remained from the startline shunt and suffer a puncture?

During the course of the trial, it was perhaps inevitable that a kind of 'England versus Italy' mentality developed, with Imola and the Italians on one side, and Williams and the English on the other, all deploying myriad witnesses and 'experts'. In fact, Passarini's prosecution was said to lack credibility precisely because all his expert witnesses were Italian.

While Damon Hill and David Coulthard were obviously connected to the Williams team, they are among the most eloquent and honest of individuals with the highest levels of personal integrity. They are also the only men other than Senna who drove a Williams FW16 at Imola both before and on the day of the accident, with the car and circuit in the conditions that Senna encountered. Every racing car is different and even the same car, set up differently, reacts differently. In light of the much-stated belief that Tamburello was 'easy flat', the opinions of both men, sought for this book, are illuminating.

DAVID COULTHARD
WILLIAMS TEST DRIVER

"I'd been the test driver during Mansell and Prost's time, and when Ayrton came along there was much excitement – a legend of the sport coming to Williams on the back of a pretty dominant year for Prost in 1993.

"So there was a lot of expectation, but there was also the transition from active suspension to passive cars, which were quite different. One of the great strengths of the Williams active car was that the aerodynamics allowed it to stay in a key window. The passive car was quite tricky but Senna was obviously able to drag three pole positions out of it.

"At my first test we were both there together and he actually drove the '93 car in passive form. He didn't like the steering wheel being so low, which was a characteristic of Adrian's cars at the time, so during the practice session they literally band-sawed the

top of the chassis away, filled it in and raised the steering wheel for him. That showed just how much Williams was prepared to change to get him into a comfortable position – they'd never done that for Prost or anyone else!

"On my first test day I expected to drive but Ayrton was there. I thought he'd come unexpectedly to test and so I wouldn't be running, but he was there just to listen to what I was saying and make sure that my feedback was in line with his. Once he was satisfied that was the case, he left and went back to Brazil.

"He was really into all the small details and quite different from Mansell, who was quite happy whoever was testing when he wasn't driving. Or that's the impression I got. He had a short but very impressive effect on me. I received a fax on that Sunday from

After Senna's death, Williams test driver David Coulthard, seen here at the British GP, stepped up as Damon Hill's team-mate.

📷 sutton-images.com

Imola, signed by Ayrton, wishing me the very best in the Bank Holiday Monday F3000 race at Silverstone the next day. Which was nice.

"I remember being in the paddock at Silverstone, standing looking at the Avon tyre truck when the Imola race started, then seeing the crash and everybody looking a bit shocked. Then I had to go out and qualify and I got the awful news later.

"Every year we tested at Imola. I remember with the active car at Tamburello, you used to take a breath because if you ran it in its stall mode, where you dropped the rear to reduce drag, a bit like DRS of its time, Tamburello was... take a breath and take the corner.

"Any driver who has raced at Imola knows it's a hell of a corner. It took me seven or eight laps to take it flat with the FW16. Once you'd done it, it was flat, but it took a while to believe that everything was lined up.

"The FW16 was a lot more tricky to drive than the active car, just because of the nature of passive systems – much harsher kickback and feedback in the car. The active car in many ways was like a magic-carpet ride. But, despite its difficulties, the FW16 was a fast car and that's why Senna, the fastest of all, was able to have three pole positions.

"I've seen the data, we went through the court case and it's a fact that the steering column was broken after the accident. But it's also a fact that there was

steering load up until the point of impact. You can't have steering load if there's not a connection."

"I remember Michele Alboreto being there on the side of the prosecution, saying that for him there was no way there was a driver error. Well, either the data was doctored, which is unlikely given that the car was impounded, or it was factually under load until impact, and I have to choose to believe in the data.

"I believe in the team and the system they went through and had that data not been there obviously the outcome of the case would have been different. But obviously it hung over the Williams team, and Frank, Patrick and Adrian, for a long time. I see it as one of those unexplained tragic accidents, as opposed to a car failure."

↑ David Coulthard, test driver for Williams in 1994, confirmed that the early-season FW16 was a tricky car.

📷 sutton-images.com

"He had a short but very impressive effect on me. I received a fax on that Sunday from Imola, signed by Ayrton, wishing me the very best in the Bank Holiday Monday F3000 race at Silverstone the next day."

DAMON HILL
WILLIAMS TEAM-MATE

"The FW16 was very difficult. At the time, before Ayrton's accident, it had a massive rear diffuser on it and was generating a lot of downforce, but it was a bit uncontrollable. We did a lot of work to make it a bit more driveable but nevertheless it was a handful.

"I'd done all my real testing work on the active car, though my very first test for Williams was at Imola in a passive FW14, Adrian's first Williams. The FW16 didn't feel like that and it had some set-up issues. Later on we got to the bottom of how to make it more driveable but at that stage Ayrton and all of us were scratching our heads as to why it was so difficult.

"The idea of Tamburello being 'easy flat' is a myth. It's a corner where you really have to be sure you have committed in the right way. There were bumps there.

⬇ Hill: "Ayrton was an incredibly courageous, extraordinarily powerful, passionate person."

📷 sutton-images.com

Two sets of bumps. I didn't like taking the tighter line on the inside because it was a bit more bumpy. I found a way of taking a slightly wide line that I was more comfortable with. I think Ayrton was taking the tighter line.

"You're not going to find one single cause. When you look at anything that culminates in tragic events it tends to be a combination of factors. You look at a whole lot of factors in play, including the fact that this had been set up as a kind of make-or-break race for Ayrton to turn round the championship, and lots of other things. The whole thing was a cocktail.

"There was poor Roland Ratzenberger. The lower tyre pressures certainly didn't help matters. And there was the Safety Car – that's a really powerful political point because that was a bone of contention. Ayrton was strongly against it and what it was going to do. And unfortunately, I think, he was the victim of all those conditions.

"As well as the car being a handful, we had quite a lot of fuel on board. It was all right if I didn't attack the corner. It's a very fast sweeper, you need to take a line and there was a choice of lines. You don't want to go wide because that makes it slightly narrower on exit but at the same time my view was that if you went too close to the inside kerb you had to deal with the bumps – and you could see that on the onboard camera from Schumacher.

"I went through the data a lot and I went through the onboard footage. I think he was pushing damned hard. I think he had a heavier fuel load than Michael, but didn't realise that, and I think he was approaching it from the view that he was on the same fuel load and needed to stay ahead. And now we know, of course, that he didn't have to. Our strategy wasn't exactly that sophisticated in those days and I think he just had it in his head that there was no way he was going to be beaten by Michael."

"I was staggered when they made these accusations about steering column failure. I just don't hold with that for one very good reason – you can't put opposite-lock on when you have a broken steering column. And he did.

"If a steering column breaks and you're wanting to go left, what happens? Your hands fall further to the left. And they didn't. For me it was a complete red herring.

"In time it will come around. I think a lot of people don't want to believe he made a mistake. He was a racing driver. He pushed himself right to the very

EPILOGUE

Damon Hill, said, "The idea of Tamburello being 'easy flat' is a myth."

sutton-images.com

edge. That was his hallmark. Ayrton was an incredibly courageous, extraordinarily powerful, passionate person. It was just a tragic fact. That was almost his fate, wasn't it? That's my view. He wasn't afraid to push it to the maximum. Even though he had seen what happened to Ratzenberger the day before.

"It was extraordinary watching the *Senna* movie because it was surreal sitting there thinking, 'My God, that's me, I was there!' The whole thing had a spooky kind of nightmarish dream quality to it. But putting it into the context of motorsport, that used to happen on a regular basis. My Dad, Jackie Stewart, they lost guys all the time.

"What happened afterwards was baffling to me. This idea that we've got to find the reason… the reason was that he was racing and he crashed! And it happens. And he knew that. And he wouldn't, in my view, have been looking to blame someone.

"It has been a very unfair blight on Adrian Newey and I'm sure if Ayrton could come back, he'd say, 'Listen, don't you dare touch those guys!' Adrian does everything he possibly can to give drivers a competitive car, but a safe car. I know the guy, love Adrian, and would sit in any of his cars any day of the week. Of course I would."

Noticeably, both Coulthard and Hill were unable to voice the words 'made a mistake' in the foregoing interviews. But their meaning is clear enough… but in need of qualification.

Right from Terry Fullerton's first accounts of Ayrton's karting approach, and his undeterred reaction to a sizeable accident at Jesolo, it's apparent that he was totally committed and abnormally brave throughout his career. While there were those who regarded Senna's death with disbelief, as they did Jim Clark's, because he was simply 'too good', with Ayrton there were others equally convinced that he would never make old bones.

He was a truly extraordinary man. Of that there is no doubt. On the one hand, enough complexity, humility and depth to beguile erudite men such as Professor Watkins and the Bishop of Truro. On the other, utter raw talent and primal, brutal competitiveness. As well as bravery, his refusal to reconcile being beaten is a constant. Those two factors allow his death to be viewed as truly tragic, as in the downfall of a main character who is architect of his own misfortune. But, as Hill says, not in isolation, mitigating 'the mistake' was the combination of factors assailing Senna on the day he died.

Some of those circumstances are unpalatable. The *Senna* movie didn't touch on the developing rivalry with Schumacher. It's a highly uneasy truth that when Senna died he was bringing his other-worldly talents to bear on a task he was determined to accomplish: the defeat of a rival car he was deeply suspicious of. Senna had won 41 grands prix before that black day at Imola. Just over six years later, Michael Schumacher won his 41st grand prix at Monza. Michael, another ruthlessly determined competitor who could neverthess be misunderstood and wrongly maligned, was asked whether it meant anything that he had moved into equal second with Ayrton in the all-time winners list.

Schumacher knew the question was coming and he broke down, completely. For many, that spoke volumes.

JOSEF LEBERER
THE MAN WHO KNEW AYRTON BEST OF ALL?

Josef Leberer, the Austrian physio/trainer/dietician, was mentored by the late Willy Dungl at his famous clinic. Leberer was close to Senna for almost seven years, at first as a professional but then increasingly as a confidant and friend. Outside Ayrton's immediate family, Leberer is possibly the man who knew him best.

"I first met Ayrton in '86 when Dungl launched his new training centre," Leberer says. "The first race I looked after him was in '88 in Rio de Janeiro, which was also the first time I worked with McLaren.

"He was in reasonable shape but not good enough. He wasn't built like Mansell. He was very slight. He was strong in his mind but physically there was improvement to be made and, step by step, he did it.

"The cardio side was important – the weekends were long, the races hot and then you had the warm-up as well on Sunday morning. The core stabilisation and neck were important too. A lot of my work was therapy. There were a lot of forces on the neck, shoulders and arms.

⬇ **Viviane Senna, pictured at Imola in 2004, and the rest of the Senna family urged Leberer to carry on in F1 after Ayrton's accident.**

📷 sutton-images.com

"Ayrton liked to be strapped very tightly into the car. He wanted to be connected, to feel the car and all its reactions through his backside. Sometimes his shoulders were red and badly bruised because he liked to be so tight. There was also a lot of gear shifting then, which made it tougher.

"We had some problems with muscles sometimes. Once, at Imola, I had to come and help him out of the car because he couldn't lift his shoulders and arms high enough. He was so strong in his mind to finish the race but afterwards, when he came down, there was barely any circulation. You saw it again when he won at home in Brazil in '91 and didn't want anyone touching him afterwards – that was in the *Senna* movie. The belts tended to cut into him, so we changed some mounting bolts, put them a little higher and saw some improvement.

"The good relationship between the two of us just grew. First, I really liked to do the job – I also liked Prost – and was working very precisely on the neck and spine. Ayrton was a very intelligent guy and so I explained to him how things were working. He was always quite focused and tense and I taught him that you couldn't be like that all the time. You had to relax and come down.

"You get to know their bodies after so many weeks and months and then he had the trust. He didn't like people touching him generally. And he was very shy. People said he was arrogant but he wasn't arrogant at all. He was just shy and he didn't trust everybody.

"Step by step he relaxed and I taught him that a human being is like an engine – you cannot stress it all the time if you want it to perform to its potential. He realised that and it was important for him. I was always relaxed and more fun. I wasn't saying a lot but when I did it was to the point and I think he liked that. I'm not a psychologist but, if he asked me, I'd give him an opinion on something and slowly he trusted me and I became a friend.

"He didn't trust many people. There was family and then me, more or less. I often travelled with him in his aircraft, then in the mornings I'd be in the helicopter with him or in his car.

"I sometimes went to Brazil in the winter. He liked to spend the winter at home and it was also a good time to do things – work on the basic cardio, the core and anything that might have happened in the season and was being aggravated. There was a guy in Brazil helping him as well. He built up the muscle chain and got better and better throughout his career. It can be counter-productive to build too much muscle, and he didn't.

"Prost was already quite fit. And still is today. I remember him being on the mountain bike when we were at Willy's place and he was very good. But I was very strong as well because I had big legs through going up the mountains. It was very steep and we were always fighting each other. But Senna knew it was important and he worked. When I met them both in '88, Alain was fitter and liked to do sports as well, but Ayrton closed the gap.

"They were good times. We were close and once we made a picture with Fangio. Ayrton introduced me and said this is my trainer, and so on. But I'm not sure what happened to that. It would have been nice to have...

"Once, after he won in Brazil, we were in a bar in Sao Paulo and he said, 'Josef, I would like to introduce you to a friend of mine.' It was Pelé! Someone took pictures then too, but I don't have those either. Stupid, I know...

"I actually have very little. Not a single helmet, suit or anything like that. Why should I take things from a friend? I had no clue at this time how valuable these things would be. But of course I would never have sold them anyway. I have very few pictures. That's why it would have been nice to be in the movie...

"It's funny, actually. A friend of mine is a big F1 fan and was asking me if I had anything. I said I had loads of gloves from Prost and Senna but they're no good any more. He got very excited and said, 'Where do you have them? Where do you have them?'

"I told him the truth – I'd given them to my mother. I'm from a farm and we had a lot of fruit trees. She was using them for gardening and the roses! She said, 'These are fantastic – very soft and good-fitting but protective!' She thought that if they were good enough for Senna and Prost, they were good enough for her. But of course, they didn't last very long doing that, and she just threw them away.

"Working with him, more and more I thought that this guy was something special. Sometimes he'd call me from Brazil, and I'd say, 'What the hell's going on, it's 2am!' He'd say, 'Ah come on, lazy Austrian, we have a good time here in Brazil!' Then he got serious and wanted to talk to me about when we changed colours, by which he meant teams. I felt loyal to McLaren but he said that while we didn't have to talk about friendship, when he changed teams he wanted me to go with him. He said that as long as he was driving he wanted me to look after him. And that's what I did in the end.

"He was often quite reflective. Once we were at a test in Germany in a nice hotel in Heidelberg, in 1992 I think.

Josef Leberer goes to work on Senna's hands during 1988, when a stick shift was still used.

sutton-images.com

We had dinner and he said he really liked the hotel, the food was fantastic and he was just having a good life.

"I said it was interesting that a driver like him was happy. Because normally they're complaining that someone is earning more or someone has a bigger boat. But here was somebody saying he had a fantasic life. He just said it out of nothing.

"I said, 'Even I have a fantastic life!' But you have to be careful. If you're travelling all the time with these millionaires you mustn't get crazy. You have to understand and be a strong character. We have a good life but you have to understand you're not the driver and you mustn't take yourself too seriously. You have your job to do, and you do it. But some people think they make the drivers or that

"He didn't trust many people. There was family and then me, more or less. I often travelled with him in his aircraft, then in the mornings I'd be in the helicopter with him or in his car... I sometimes went to Brazil in the winter."

they're the best, and so on. They wouldn't win without me and so on. Forget it. When he said that he wanted me with him as long as he was driving, that was enough for me. What else do I want when someone like Senna says that?

"They are different. Why did he want to be so strong, so fast, the best? After a while, what's the driving force? That's the interesting thing, isn't it? I often said to him, 'What keeps you going?' If you've earned $10 million, $20 million you have more than enough. So what keeps you going like this? Why are you so different to me?

"I saw other guys too: Michael and the young guys working with Sauber-Mercedes and Häkkinen, Prost, Coulthard, Räikkönen, Massa. Kubica I looked after and Vettel, of course, started with us at BMW. Everyone has a slightly different reason why they're doing it. Some guys just want to be Formula 1 drivers so they can go down to the disco as one, some want to have six boats, some want to give something back to their mother because she was nice. They're all driven by different things. And sometimes they're not sure who they are and almost need guiding.

"It's very interesting and a lot to do with psychology, even if I'm not a psychologist. But when you're working with sportsmen for nearly 30 years you start to know them. It's difficult to explain but you just know the guy. They cannot hide the way they are. And they know it as well. And they get to know you're trying to help and guide them, so they trust you. And can relax. And sometimes, like a father or mother, you have to praise them sometimes, almost reassure them.

"I once asked Ayrton if he was afraid that he'd lose those things, those feelings, that it wouldn't be the same any more? He said he wasn't afraid because he had a fantastic family and was living a fantastic life doing what he loved. He said his life was fulfilled.

"He was a thoughtful guy. I remember in '88 when he'd won his first championship – I was working for the team then, not Ayrton personally. I'd gone back home to Austria and was doing massages at Dungl's clinic. When I got home he'd left a message on the answer machine. He wanted me to come to Paris to be at the FIA prizegiving. It was great! He sent me a business-class ticket from Salzburg to Paris and paid for me at the Hotel de Crillon for four days. Not bad! He said that I'd been important to him and he wanted me to be there.

⇩ Senna liked to be tightly belted, sometimes causing circulation problems. In the background Josef keeps an eye on his man.

📷 sutton-images.com

Der Schmerz und die Trauer sind leichter zu ertragen, wenn man fühlt, viele tragen mit. Herzlichen Dank für ihre Anteilnahme.

The sorrow and grief are easier to carry, when you feel and know, that many suffer with you. Thank you for sharing your sympathie in that tragedy with us.

このたびの事を共に悼んでくださる方々のお蔭で、この心の痛みと悲しみに堪えていけるでしょう。

お悔みに厚くお礼を申しあげます。
ラッツェンベアガー家一同

Familie Ratzenberger

"Some people questioned whether his motivation was the same in that last season after the move to Williams. Of course it was! For me, some of his best performances were in late '93. Japan and Australia were fantastic. He knew it was the end of an era as well, and felt it, was quite emotional about it. People have no clue about the energy he created and what a powerful force he was.

"I remember the first couple of races in '94. In Japan, Aida, he was out at the first corner and stood there looking. The car wasn't as good as he was hoping. Of course he was disappointed but said, OK, now it depends on us and Williams and not the cars as they had been the previous year, when, he said, you could drive with one hand and be on the telephone.

"Now, he said, it was a challenge but he would still win the championship. Definitely. I knew him by then, he had fighting spirit and he was pleased that it would be up to him, Adrian and Patrick – 'We will show the world we can do it and nobody will be able to say it's just because I was sitting in the best car'. He was convinced they could still win it. He always wanted to drive against the best and not avoid anyone. Because he knew he was the best. Schumacher won so many championships but he never wanted that, so it means that the value of his victories wasn't the same. Doesn't it? In my opinion anyway...

"But Ayrton knew they weren't fighting with the same weapons. He said, 'I want to win', and he always said, 'I know I'm better, but I don't have the same possibilities as them because they're cheating.' That's what he said.

"Everybody knew they were doing something but

nobody was doing anything against it. In a way I had a feeling there was support for it to bring another driver into it. Sort of, we need this guy [Schumacher] because the other one is too dominant.

"Ayrton was too strong for them. He had also become more adult and was smarter and not quite so emotional any more. He knew exactly what he wanted and nobody could tell him, 'Do this, this and this.' There were worries about the safety and I remember with Schumacher, Max Mosley said, 'If it's too dangerous for you, why don't you leave?' Michael shut up. But when Senna said something...

"He was a thoughtful guy. I remember in '88 when he'd won his first championship... He wanted me to come to Paris to be at the FIA prizegiving... He sent me a business-class ticket from Salzburg to Paris and paid for me at the Hotel de Crillon for four days. Not bad!"

"The combination of this and the death of Ratzenberger made things hard. It was on my birthday, April 30, and we were supposed to have a birthday party because Willy Dungl had also come over for that race. By this time I was working for Senna and not for Dungl any more, but Willy had been my mentor and was still my friend obviously. He liked Senna and Roland as well. Ayrton knew I was from Salzburg, as was Roland, and said, 'Do you know him? Do you know his family?'

"I had never seen Ayrton so angry as he was earlier that day. He went to a marshal and said he wanted to go out to the accident scene when Roland's crash happened, and did. The FIA said that he wasn't allowed to, it was dangerous, that they were going to punish him... They went to Senna and said this! Can you imagine?

"He was so mad! I'd never seen him like that... 'These guys telling me!' he said. 'We're risking our lives! Every day. And they want to tell me what is dangerous and what is not! I'm trying to make it safer for myself and the other guys'.

"The car at the time was bad and he was also very much against using the Safety Car on the installation lap. The tyre pressures were going and he thought it was just the worst thing they could do. But he didn't really know what to do about it.

"Then there were other things all playing together at the

⬇ **Ayrton makes time for one of his more elderly fans.**

📷 sutton-images.com

same time. There was something going on between the girlfriend and his family but that wasn't the main thing.

"That evening, having dinner, we were asking what sense did it make to race? As a human being he had developed quite a lot. In the beginning I was asking him about the economic situation in Brazil because things were very bad. One time we were there when the inflation was crazy and the money wasn't worth anything any more. I remember all the favelas and I asked him, as a privileged boy, what he felt when he went through them. 'Very difficult,' he said, 'but I'm not powerful enough yet to do anything'.

"Through his family I saw that he was already supporting children but he didn't want to tell anyone. He knew that he earned so much and he just wanted to give something. Other people were doing some media pictures about giving and then letting the sponsor pay for it, but this was a different story already.

"He thought that the media, particularly the English media, was negative about him and it might be slanted the wrong way. Prost had used them against him... 'He thinks he's God' and so on. But I knew what a good human being Ayrton was, how he dealt with his family, what his values were. If you're together so many days over so many years, especially in a pressured environment like F1, it's not easy and you get to know people. They knew that in a few years' time they could be heroes or they could be dead. So he felt that if he was a hero it was time to do something.

"It's not quite the same now. I think now it's more about the technical side, there's more managers around, and so on. In Ayrton's day and before it was more about the guys. I used to tell them: 'You have to take over, you are the master. I was always telling young guys, 'Listen, this is a chance for you.' I know they can't change their characters overnight but they can speed it up. It's a chance for them to speed up their own life development. Learn. Be aware. And he was developing a lot.

"So, it was supposed to be my birthday dinner but nobody was in any kind of celebratory mood. Ayrton was talking about Roland and lots of things, and himself. He was questioning driving but he knew he had to. This was probably the first time on the Saturday night that I didn't do a massage for him. After dinner I went with him to his room. We were alone and he said, 'I have to think a little bit, talk with the family and do a few things'.

"He also said, 'I have to drive. I cannot do anything else. What would people think about me if I didn't drive? I had the feeling, honestly, that he didn't really want to. I would say it was the first time that he wasn't really looking forward to it. For the first time there was a doubt and he was questioning the value, the sense. There were more important things. Somebody had died and I had a feeling he was doubting a little the reason to do it. These feelings were there but he said, 'OK, I have to, it's what people expect of me, it's

↑ **Ayrton and his brother Leonardo.**

sutton-images.com

what my fans are there for, for me to show some strength, and to win.

"On race morning I did his breakfast but he was very quiet, not talking a lot, but that's normal on a Sunday. The closer the race came the less he talked and the more he went into his preparation. There was no real need to talk. I knew what he wanted, when he wanted it, when he was thirsty. Of course, he was thinking and maybe he wasn't as hard with the engineers as usual. Normally he was expecting a lot, checking everything again and again and again. He expected a lot from others but he gave a lot too.

"On the grid he laughed when Gerhard Berger – driving a Ferrari in Italy, of course – was announced and got the loudest cheer. But he was generally quiet. He was quick in the morning warm-up though, a second faster than Damon, who thought he'd gone pretty quickly. He definitely wanted to show something. He was a guy who could transform his frustrations and his emotions into lap times. I never met anybody like him again, as a person or a competitor.

"The day was just horrible and after the accident Bernie Ecclestone asked me to come to his motorhome because Ayrton's brother was in there and we were trying to get in contact with the family. The brother was crying like hell, so I had to look after him. I had no time for mourning.

"As soon as I saw the accident on the screen, saw the way his body was in the car, I just thought, that's it, he's dead, one hundred per cent. For me it was clear.

Then, a bit later, I saw Sid Watkins, he had the helmet, and he just looked at me. I knew already...

"They asked me if I wanted to go on the helicopter to the hospital, so I did that. His brother was there, and Betise [Assumpcao, Ayrton's press agent]. Then Sid came out and said can you tell them, forget it, he's on a life machine and his brain is completely damaged. And so I told them. Of course at this time he was alive and they wanted to know if there was a chance. Because at first it had been reported that he was dead, then it was injured in the head...

"The coffin was on a fire engine and I was behind the first car. Seeing people in wheelchairs, old people, young people, black, white... What this human being meant for that country and for them... you can't begin to explain."

**↑ Josef shares a joke
with Sebastian Vettel.**

📷 sutton-images.com

**↓ Putting another Brazilian,
Felipe Massa, through his paces.**

📷 sutton-images.com

"Sid told me to tell them there was no chance and then asked me if I wanted to see him. I said, 'Yes, of course'. So I put everything on and went in with him. If you can imagine… you know every part of his body, every muscle after six and a half years. It was very difficult.

"Then after I'd seen him I was there with his brother and Gerhard [Berger] arrived. He said he wanted to see him and I said, 'No, it's better you don't.' 'No,' he said, 'I want to see him.'

"I must say, respect to Gerhard. So I went in a second time and I remember when we came out he was hugging me and crying. Two men crying, you know… it wasn't easy.

"Then I went with Ayrton's friend Antonio Braga and his brother to a hotel in Bologna and we stayed there that night. Then, next day, I drove home to Salzburg in a trance. Ayrton's family asked me to come home with the coffin and two days later they sent me a ticket.

"It was very strange on the plane. They had taken the middle seats out of first and business class and put the coffin there with a Brazilian flag and a red rose. His brother was already at home and it was only myself and Betise and three or four other people next to the coffin for 11 or 12 hours. It was a big Varig plane from Paris and there were 200 or so people in the economy section but the family didn't want the coffin in with all the suitcases.

"I don't know if the other passengers knew. I think they definitely knew when we got to Brazil because military jets were following us and there were thousands of people there when the plane landed. If I will remember one thing all my life, it was being behind the coffin for two or three hours.

"For the funeral the coffin was on a fire engine and I was behind the first car. Seeing people in wheelchairs, old people, young people, black, white. Some were crying, others were applauding. Some were kneeling, others were running, filling every place.

"It was incredible. Horrible and incredible. I have never cried so much in my life. It was seeing all these people and their emotions, how close they were – old, young, rich and poor. What this human being meant for that country and for them. It's something you can't begin to explain. There is no sportsman or artist or politician, anybody, who touched these people like that.

"He always said, 'I need time to become powerful, to be able to do something, to give them hope.' We were talking about it quite often and he said that at least every fortnight he was able to give them something they could count on. And he meant it. And they felt that. People aren't stupid. You can't fool people. This incredible power, this incredible strength...

"After the funeral I went home and thought, OK, this is finished for me. It was part of my life and it was over. I thought there was no more sense to do it any more.

But Williams asked me to carry on and Ron Dennis asked me to come back to McLaren. So I finished the season with Williams.

"Ayrton's family also asked what I was going to do. I talked to his mother and father and said that I thought I was going to stop. They said, OK, if you're asking us, it would be nice if you could stay because you were so close to him and a lot of people associate you with him in a positive way. So, if you're asking us, it would be nice if you carried on.

"And I also thought that no matter what I did, working for Dungl or starting my own business, it wouldn't make it better. To overcome it, you have to face it and be there. And so I worked on myself as if I was my patient. If it was a driver you'd tell him to go back immediately. I was interested in other sports and I knew a lot of the Austrian skiers and was working with Thomas Muster at the time, who was world number one tennis player and had a knee injury.

"When I went back I had David Coulthard to work with. I almost felt like I needed to help him. I remember he did something at Monza and Patrick [Head] was so loud with him! My God, the poor guy...

"So I started working with David and we became friends as well. I took him to Austria and we worked very hard because he was very tall but needed to concentrate on the strength training. Then I went back to McLaren and also worked with Mika Häkkinen. I'm still a big fan of McLaren. Ron Dennis was the first one who realised it was important to have someone working on the physical side of the drivers.

"I've been in F1 ever since. I once took a long break: one race, at Silverstone! I was with Sauber, had a knee injury and they had to send someone else. It was the race when Felipe [Massa] was spinning all over the place – a good one to miss!

"It was difficult after Ayrton but there are always challenges, like when Kimi Räikkönen started very young and we had to get him ready. Then there was Vettel and Kubica. Robert is a big shame. There's a racer. We miss him. I feel very, very sorry for him. He had it too..."

When the *Senna* movie was made, the family told the film-makers that Josef Leberer was a good, accurate source of information. They flew him to London and he passed on his knowledge. And so he was perhaps a little disappointed not to actually appear, when so many who had very little contact with Ayrton did feature.

Don't get the wrong impression. Josef is straight-forward, decent and genuine, neither egotistical nor attention-seeking. As he says, he knows he's not the story.

"No problem..." he smiles, a touch ruefully, "It would just have been nice to be able to show the kids what I was doing..."

⬆ **Leberer advising Ayrton's nephew, Bruno.**
📷 sutton-images.com

⬇ **And even some advice for The Boss...**
📷 sutton-images.com

INDEX